melissa's great book of produce

melissa's great

book of produce

Everything You Need to Know about Fresh Fruits and Vegetables

cathy thomas

photography by nick koon

WILEY

John Wiley & Sons, Inc.

For general information about our other products and services, please contact our Customer Care Department within the United States at (800) 762-2974, outside the United States at (317) 572-3993 or fax (317) 572-4002.

Wiley also publishes its books in a variety of electronic formats. Some content that appears in print may not be available in electronic books. For more information about Wiley products, visit our web site at www.wiley.com.

ISBN-13: 978-0-7645-7187-9
ISBN-10: 0-7645-7187-7

Printed in the United States of America

10 9 8 7 6 5 4 3 2 1

acknowledgments

I am enormously grateful to Joe, Sharon, and Melissa Hernandez at Melissa's World Variety Produce for asking me to write this book. To have produce from every corner of the globe at my fingertips made me feel like the luckiest food writer on the planet. Much of the information and culinary insights on these pages comes from the remarkable family of employees at their company.

Special thanks to Robert Schueller, Melissa's director of public relations, and Bill Gerlach, director of research and development, whose knowledge of produce and endless enthusiasm never cease to amaze me. And heartfelt thanks to Ida Rodriguez, Melissa's corporate kitchen executive chef, and her team; they contributed many recipes and tips, as well as produce know-how and jovial support. Thanks also to Debra Cohen, director of special projects, for her tireless fact checking and guidance.

Also, I am extremely grateful to the following:

Photographer Nick Koon, who has a rare gift for making food look irresistible. Working side by side with me as I "styled" the produce, he captured the delectable beauty of every fruit and vegetable.

Editor Anne Ficklen, whose vision, kindness, and devotion to this project made a huge difference. And accolades to designer Joel Avirom, for his imaginative and accessible design.

And finally, some personal acknowledgments. I am grateful to my children and my husband, Phil McCullough, who give me loving support on a daily basis. They tame my anxiety with patience and encouragement. And to my late parents, Loren and Harriett Young, who nurtured my passion for fresh fruits and vegetables. And Sue Young, who helped me establish a culinary career.

—Cathy Thomas

contents

introduction

Don't know a kumquat from a kohlrabi, or a cape gooseberry from a cactus pear? You're not alone. Supermarkets display mind-boggling assortments of fruits and vegetables. They look so alluring lining the produce aisle, their exteriors creating a patchwork of color and texture, sweet tropical scents melding with earthy root vegetables and greens.

Joe and Sharon Hernandez, produce pioneers with combined experience of over half a century, created Melissa's/World Variety Produce Inc. in 1984. Now, Melissa's is the nation's largest distributor of specialty fruits and vegetables, with thousands of items available at any given time.

Almost daily, Joe and Sharon seek out and test new and unusual produce from around the world—tiny pineapples from South Africa; sweet, young coconuts from Thailand; or ruby-red tamarillos from New Zealand. Because of their efforts, a continuous flow of new fruits and vegetables are available in the marketplace.

"What we strive for is flavor," Joe Hernandez says. "It has to taste good; otherwise people won't come back."

Using baby vegetables is just one of the trends they have introduced to chefs around the globe, branding those tender, tiny veggies with the Melissa's label. The Melissa's brand is named after Joe and Sharon's daughter, Melissa, who takes an active role in the company as well.

The Los Angeles–based company has a long history of commitment to consumer education. Product tags include recipes, serving suggestions, and nutritional information. But tags have limited space. And unfamiliar produce can leave buyers with loads of questions. Is it supposed to be halved and seeded or sucked from a straw? Eaten raw or cooked? Should it be firm or soft, bright green or blushed with orange?

This guide's design will help you locate information about specific fruits and vegetables easily. Bold headings will help you quickly locate information about how it looks and tastes, when it is available, and how to use it. Buying and storing tips are also included, along with serving suggestions and recipes.

NATURE'S WHIM

Fruits and vegetables aren't widgets. Unlike machine-manufactured products, they are subject to variations in taste, color, and availability because of weather conditions and soil variables. In this book, the produce information is generalized. Typical appearance, availability, and flavor are described, but nature can play a part in altering one or more of those factors.

In the garlic section, for example, heirloom Rocambole garlic is described as small, pungent, and streaked with purple, available from September to March. But shoppers may find large Rocambole in August with a mild flavor profile similar to common white garlic. Or, if weather conditions sabotage growers, shoppers might not be able to find it at all.

"Fresh produce is a product of nature," Joe Hernandez says. "Weather plays a crucial part. We strive for perfection in appearance and taste, but remember, fresh produce doesn't come from a can."

WHEN CAN I FIND IT: GLOBAL VS. DOMESTIC

Availability refers to availability within the United States. It is broken down two ways. *Global* refers to imported produce grown outside the United States (some produce grown outside the United States is not allowed to be imported). *Domestic* refers to produce grown within the United States.

COMMON USAGE VS. BOTANY

Fruits and vegetables are categorized according to their most common usage. For example, eggplant and tomatoes are fruits, but they are most often thought of (and used) as vegetables. Avocados, winter squash, summer squash, and chile peppers are other examples of fruits that are in the vegetable section.

PRODUCE NUTRITIONAL INFORMATION

The terms *excellent, good,* and *significant* relate to percentages of U.S. RDA (recommended daily allowance). If the fruit or vegetable meets 40% to 99% of U.S. RDA, it is rated *excellent*. If it meets 25% to 39%, it is rated *good*. If it meets 10% to 24%, it is rated *significant*.

fruit

ASIAN PEAR

Common

Korean

Yali

BANANA, BANANA LEAF

Baby (Finger)

Burro

Common (Cavendish)

Manzano

Red

Common Plantain

Hawaiian Plantain

BERRY

Blackberry

Blueberry

Boysenberry

Cape Gooseberry, Ground Cherry

Cranberry (red and white)

Currant (black, red, and white)

Gooseberry

Loganberry

Raspberry (red, gold, and black)

Strawberry

Wild Strawberry, Fraise des Bois (red and white)

BUDDHA'S HAND CITRON

CACTUS PEAR

Green

Red

CHERIMOYA

COCONUT

Common (Brown)

White

Young

DRAGON FRUIT

Magenta

Pink

White

FIG

Black Mission

Brown Turkey

Calimyrna (Smyrna, Royal Mediterranean)

Kadota

GRAPE

Champagne

Common (black, green, and red)

Concord

Globe

Muscat

Muscato (green and red)

GRAPEFRUIT

Cocktail

Melogold

Oro Blanco

Pummelo

Red, Ruby, Pink

GUAVA, FEIJOA

HORNED MELON

JACKFRUIT

JUJUBE

KIWI

Baby

Green

Gold

KUMQUAT

LEMON, LIME, KAFFIR LIME LEAF

Eureka Lemon

Lisbon Lemon

Meyer Lemon

Key Lime

Persian Lime

Kaffir Lime Leaf

LIMEQUAT

LONGAN

LOQUAT

LYCHEE

Green

Red

MANGO

Ataulfo

Haden

Keitt

Kent

Tommy Atkins

MELON

Canary

Cantaloupe

Casaba

Charentais

Crenshaw

Galia

Gaya

Hami

Honeydew (common green, gold, and orange)

Korean

Piel de Sapo, Santa Claus

Persian

Sharlyn

Sprite

ORANGE

Blood

Cara Cara

Navel

Seville (Sour)

Valencia

PAPAYA

Green

Maradol (Mexican)

Strawberry

Yellow-Flesh

PASSION FRUIT

Common

Vanilla

PEACH, NECTARINE

Indian Peach

Saturn Peach

White-Flesh Peach

Yellow-Flesh Peach

Honeydew Nectarine

Mango Nectarine

Saturn Nectarine

White-Flesh Nectarine

Yellow-Flesh Nectarine

PEAR

Bartlett, Red Bartlett

Bosc

Comice

D'Anjou, Red D'Anjou

Forelle

Seckel

PERSIMMON

Cinnamon

Fuyu

Hachiya

PEPINO MELON

PINEAPPLE

Baby Hawaiian

Common (Gold)

Gold

South African Baby

PLUOT, PLUMCOT, APRIUM

POMEGRANATE

QUINCE

RAMBUTAN

SAPOTE

Mamey

White

STAR FRUIT

TAMARILLO

Gold

Red

TAMARINDO

TANGERINE (MANDARIN)

Clementine

Fairchild

Murcott (Honey)

Page

Pixie

Satsuma

UNIQ FRUIT

WATERMELON

Baby (Mini)

Orange

Red

Yellow

YUZU

asian pear, also apple pear

RIGHT AWAY YOU KNOW THEY'RE SPECIAL. In the marketplace, Asian pears line up in prim rows; no higgledy-piggledy piles for them. They're somewhat fragile, because unlike European pears, they're picked when almost ripe. Some, generally thin-skinned Korean pears, are clothed in snazzy mesh jackets to prevent bruising.

There are more than 25 varieties. Most are a modified apple shape, almost spherical, but slightly flattened at stem and blossom end. Only the Yali variety is the more familiar pear shape. Exteriors vary in color and texture—from chartreuse to yellowish-brown to russet, silky smooth to sandpaper rough.

The white flesh is crunchy, like a supercrisp apple or a water chestnut, but much juicier and sometimes subtly gritty. The taste is sweet, with a mild pear flavor. Some have a hint of melon flavor.

Basically, Asian pears are identified in the marketplace in three categories: Yali, Korean, and Brown Asian Pears. Note that the Korean varieties have the thinnest skin; they don't require peeling before cooking.

BUYING AND STORING

Choose fruit that is firm and fragrant. Can be stored at room temperature up to 5 days, or refrigerated up to 3 months.

KOREAN PEARS
Domestic: *none*
Global: *October–March*

YALI PEARS
Domestic: *September–December*
Global: *September–December*

OTHER VARIETIES (INCLUDING BROWN ASIAN PEARS)
Domestic: *June–January*
Global: *February–May*

Yali

PREP

For a glamorous raw presentation, cut unpeeled, uncored fruit into thin, horizontal slices; the core forms a flower-like shape. Because of their crunchiness, these pears can be very thinly sliced and still hold their shape. For other raw uses, they require coring; use an apple corer or a small paring knife. They can be grated, shredded, or cut into wedges. For cooking, they should be cored; all varieties, except Korean pears, require peeling before cooking.

NUTRITIONAL INFO

2 cups are a significant source of vitamin C.

USE

Eat raw, out of hand, or use in salads or slaws; they are great dippers for warm caramel or chocolate fondue. Cooked, they can be used in pies, crisps, and cakes, as well as savory dishes and chutneys. Because of their high water content and crunchy texture, they require longer cooking than European pears.

SERVING SUGGESTIONS

Classy cheese tray: Cut into thin wedges and serve with assorted cheeses.

Crepes or ice cream: Cut peeled and cored fruit into wedges and cook in butter until browned. Off heat, stir in brown sugar and a little pear brandy, to taste. Return to heat and cook until warmed through. Spoon over crepes or ice cream.

Baked skyscrapers: Peel, core with apple corer, and cut into ¼-inch-thick horizontal slices. Stack slices in original order and place in baking dish. Fill cavity with mix of chopped walnuts, brown sugar, juice, and ground cinnamon. Dot with generous pat of butter. Bake in 350-degree oven until tender-crisp, about 45–55 minutes.

Stylish Stuffing: For added crunch, add diced (peeled) Asian pears to your favorite poultry stuffing.

Common

Korean (whole and slices)

MELISSA'S GREAT BOOK OF PRODUCE

COMMON
(brown Asian pears)
More than 25 varieties; Honsui, Shinsui, and Twentieth Century are the most popular. ■ *Yellow-brown to light brown to russet skin. Small, medium, and large varieties.*

KOREAN
(2 most common varieties)
Hwangguem ■ *Yellow, thin skin. Very large and juicy.*
Shinko ■ *Brown, thin skin. Very large and juicy.*

YALI
Green skin. Shaped like European variety (often similar in shape to Bartlett pear).

asian pear turnovers

These scrumptious turnovers are easy to prepare and can be served warm or at room temperature. The raspberry jam complements the subtle sweetness of the pears. If desired, serve them with ice cream or a dollop of crème fraîche or plain yogurt sweetened to taste with powdered sugar.

2 tablespoons butter

2 tablespoons brown sugar

2 tablespoons sugar

½ teaspoon ground cinnamon

¼ teaspoon ground allspice

2 Asian pears, peeled, cored, coarsely chopped

1 sheet frozen puff pastry, defrosted according to package directions

4 tablespoons raspberry jam

YIELD: 4 TURNOVERS

1. Preheat oven to 400 degrees.

2. Melt butter in saucepan on medium-high heat. Add sugars and spices; stir to combine. Add Asian pears, and simmer until tender, about 10 minutes. Set aside to cool.

3. Cut defrosted, cold pastry into quarters. On a lightly floured surface, roll each quarter into 6-inch squares. Place 1 tablespoon jam in center of each square. Place equal amount of Asian pear mixture in center of each square. Moisten edges of pastry with cold water. Fold 1 corner of each square to opposite corner to form triangle. Press to seal, and pinch edges together.

4. Place on baking sheet. Bake in middle of preheated oven for 20–25 minutes, or until puffed and nicely browned.

NUTRITIONAL INFORMATION PER SERVING:
Calories 380; fat calories 162; total fat 18 grams; sat fat 5 grams; cholesterol 15 milligrams; sodium 80 milligrams; total carbohydrates 55 grams; fiber 6 grams; sugars 35 grams; protein 3 grams; vitamin A IUS 4%; vitamin C 8%; calcium 2%; iron 6%.

banana, banana leaf

BABY (FINGER)

BURRO

COMMON (CAVENDISH)

MANZANO

RED

COMMON PLANTAIN

HAWAII PLANTAIN

banana Is it nature's convenient packaging that makes bananas the most popular fruit in North America? The fact that they are so easy to peel and eat is only part of their charm. The smooth texture and floral fragrance team with an alluring balance of sweet and acidic flavors to make them irresistible on all counts.

There are more than 300 banana varieties, and several have become commonplace in supermarkets, such as exotic red bananas with their inviting bronze-tinged maroon skin, petite finger bananas with "digits" about 4 inches in length, and slightly larger manzano bananas, named for their subtle apple-like flavor.

BUYING AND STORING

Bananas are picked "green" (unripened). They develop better flavor when ripened off the plant. About a dozen bananas grow in each bunch. Avoid fruit that has broken skin or moldy stems. Ripen at room temperature, uncovered. Ripe bananas can be stored in the refrigerator for 3–4 days, but the peel will discolor. To freeze, cut into 1-inch slices, and freeze in single layer on baking sheet. When frozen, store in an airtight plastic bag or container. Use in shakes, smoothies, and ice creams, or dip in coating chocolate. Freeze up to 3 months (see Freezing, page 310).

Domestic: *none*
Global: *year-round*

PREP

Remove peel and eat, or cut into slices. When exposed to air, flesh will discolor. To avoid discoloration, brush with lemon (or lime) juice or dip in acidulated water (cold water with a small amount of vinegar or lime or lemon juice).

USE

Eat raw and peeled, out of hand, or use in fruit salads, or shakes, or team with ice cream. Cooked, bananas are delectable in hot and spicy dishes, such as curries or fried rice. Also a delicious addition to cakes, quick breads, and cookies.

NUTRITIONAL INFO

1 cup is an excellent source of vitamin B_6; good source of vitamin C and folate; significant source of riboflavin.

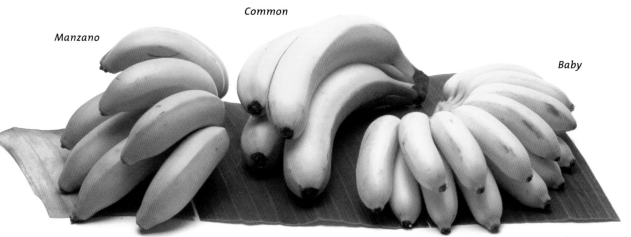

Manzano

Common

Baby

Banana Leaf

BABY
(finger)
Small—only 3–4 inches long— deep yellow with black-brown mottling. Typical bunch is 8–10 bananas. Ripe when gives to gentle pressure and speckled with black. ■ *Creamy white to dark yellow flesh that is very sweet with hints of pineapple and guava.*

BURRO
Deep yellow, chubby, about 6–7 inches long, with an angular peel that has 3–5 lengthwise ridges that look like distinct sides. Ripe when skin is heavily mottled with black. ■ *Creamy white to yellow flesh. Soft on outside, crisper texture in center. Sweet with subtle hints of lemon.*

COMMON
(Cavendish)
About 8 inches long and delicately arched. Ripe when green disappears and yellow from top to bottom. Some prefer further ripening with some black-brown mottling. ■ *Creamy white flesh, sweet with subtle tropical scent. Smooth texture and sweet flesh. Sweeter and softer texture when mottled.*

MANZANO
Thick, 4–5 inches long with deep yellow skin. Ripe when yields to gentle pressure and most skin has black mottling (but color isn't always a good indicator; pressure test is best). ■ *Creamy white flesh that has a firmer texture; it is tannic when underripe. Sweet when ripe, with hints of apple, guava, and strawberry.*

RED
About 6 inches long and gently arched; as they ripen, they turn from maroon mottled with dark green to bronze to bronze-black. Eat when yields to gentle pressure and color is bronze-black. ■ *Flesh varies in color, from pink-tinged ivory to pink. Sweet, firm texture with strong floral aroma.*

SERVING SUGGESTIONS

Double-fancy banana split: Cut banana in half lengthwise; place on baking sheet and sprinkle with brown sugar. Broil 6–8 inches below broiler until caramelized. Place a slice of banana bread in bowl and top with caramelized banana. Top with ice cream, whipped cream, toasted nuts, and chocolate syrup.

Monkey pancakes: Stir sliced bananas and finely chopped pecans into pancake batter. Cook on lightly greased griddle or nonstick skillet. Serve with fresh blueberries and maple syrup.

Banana bombers: Leave banana in peel and cut in half lengthwise, but don't cut all the way through bottom peel. Open like a book and fill with chocolate chips and mini marshmallows. Wrap in aluminum foil, closing it tightly. Grill until piping hot, and chocolate and marshmallows have melted. Cut open lengthwise and set aside until cool enough to eat.

Warm with cream: Slice bananas and place them in a buttered baking dish. Sprinkle with a little brown sugar and place in 450-degree oven 6 minutes. Dot with a little soft butter; sprinkle a little more brown sugar and some ground cinnamon. Serve warm, drizzled with a little cream, or top with plain yogurt.

banana quick bread with coconut and pistachios

This delicious quick bread is dotted with pistachios and sweetened flaked coconut. It's delicious as is, but if you want sweeter bread, a sugar glaze can be drizzled over the top.

2 cups all-purpose flour

¾ teaspoon baking soda

½ teaspoon salt

¼ cup (4 tablespoons) softened butter

1 cup sugar

2 eggs

1 tablespoon apple juice

3 tablespoons plain, low-fat yogurt

1½ cups mashed ripe bananas

½ cup sweetened flaked coconut

1 teaspoon vanilla

¼ cup shelled pistachios

Nonstick spray

YIELD: ABOUT 10 SLICES

1. Adjust oven rack to middle position. Preheat oven to 350 degrees.

2. In large bowl, combine flour, baking soda, and salt; stir with wire whisk to combine. Set aside.

3. In large bowl of electric mixer, beat butter and sugar on medium-high speed until well blended, about 1 minute. Add eggs, 1 at a time, beating on medium speed to combine between additions. Add juice, yogurt, bananas, coconut, and vanilla. Beat on medium speed until blended.

4. Add dry ingredients. Mix on medium speed until just blended. Stir in nuts. Spray 9-by-5-inch loaf pan with nonstick spray. Spoon batter into prepared pan. Bake in preheated oven 55–65 minutes or until toothpick inserted in center comes out clean. Cool on wire rack.

NUTRITIONAL INFORMATION (PER SERVING):
Calories 290; protein 5 grams; carbohydrates 50; fiber 2 grams; fat 9 grams; sodium 180 milligrams.

plantain
Green skin ripens to yellow, yellow skin ripens to black. These long, canoe-shaped bananas are also called cooking bananas. They require cooking except when the skin becomes jet black. But even at its ripest, it has more starch than other bananas. It can be cooked at all stages of ripeness.

BUYING AND STORING

Ripen at room temperature. Plantains ripen more slowly than other bananas. They can take up to 2 weeks to ripen. Look for fruit that is unblemished and without signs of bruising. Ripe plantains can be stored in refrigerator 5–7 days or frozen with skins on for 3 months. Available in some supermarkets with large specialty produce sections and Latin American markets.

Domestic: *none*
Global: *year-round*

PREP

Cut off ends. Cut lengthwise just through top peel. With sturdy knife, cut into 1½-inch crosswise slices. The "greener" the fruit the more stubbornly it peels. Insert thumb into slice in peel and pull away peel bit by bit. Repeat with remaining slices.

USE

Cook like starchy vegetable, such as potato. Boil and mash or add to stews. Can also be deep-fried.

NUTRITIONAL INFORMATION

1 cup is a significant source of vitamins A and C.

SERVING SUGGESTIONS

Cooked, mashed, and flavored: Slice and peel 1 ripe plantain (with black streaks). Place in medium, heavy-bottomed saucepan with ¼ cup water; cook on high for 8 minutes or until all the water is gone and fruit is soft, adding more water if needed. Add 1 tablespoon butter and mash with potato masher. When chunky, add ¼ cup milk or cream. Stir to combine. Add 1½ tablespoons brown sugar; stir to combine.

COMMON PLANTAIN
About 12–15 inches long, thick skin ripens from green to yellow to black. Only ripest, black-skinned plantains can be eaten raw, but they can be cooked at any stage. ■ *Starchy, squash-potato taste. Or, when very, very ripe, a mild banana taste. When green- or yellow-skinned, texture is very firm and difficult to peel.*

HAWAIIAN PLANTAIN
Short and stubby, about 7 inches long and with thick diameters. Same ripening process as plantains. ■ *Same as plantains, but because they are fatter, they make great fried or baked bases for toppings, such as salsa or black bean puree.*

Deep-fried "coins," or "tostones": Cut green- or yellow-skinned plantains in ¾-inch slices and peel. Heat 4 inches of vegetable oil in a deep pot to 350 degrees on medium to medium-high heat. Deep-fry plantain slices in batches until pale golden color. Remove and flatten with mallet or rolling pin. Increase heat to high and raise temperature of oil to 375 degrees. Fry flattened "coins" to golden brown, about 2 minutes. Drain on paper towels. Season with salt and pepper. Accompany with lime wedges or salsa.

Plantain chips: Peel yellow or green fruit and slice thinly, preferably on a mandoline. Heat peanut oil in deep, large skillet to 375 degrees. Fry slices until crisp; do not crowd. Drain on paper towels. Season with salt or garlic salt.

banana leaf Think of corn husks on tamales, or a heat-proof "oven bag" for pot roast. Banana leaves are used to enclose food for cooking. They bind ingredients together and keep them moist, while lending a pleasant scent. They are delicious for wrapping fish or pork, sticky rice mixtures, or sweetened mung-bean paste.

Whole banana leaves are sometimes available in Latin American markets folded in half and bound with twine. Remove rib before wrapping food. Asian markets generally sell them cut into squares, either fresh or frozen. Store fresh banana leaves in the refrigerator for up to 2 weeks.

Burro

Common Plantain

Red

Banana Leaf

berry

BLACKBERRY

BLUEBERRY

BOYSENBERRY

CAPE GOOSEBERRY (GROUND CHERRY)

CRANBERRY (RED AND WHITE)

CURRANT (BLACK, RED, AND WHITE)

GOOSEBERRY

LOGANBERRY

RASPBERRY (RED, GOLD, AND BLACK)

STRAWBERRY

WILD STRAWBERRY, FRAISE DES BOIS (RED AND WHITE)

A BERRY IS A small nugget of perky sweet-tart flesh packed into thin, colorful skin. Some berries, such as blackberries and raspberries are made up of clusters of tiny sacs. Others, such as strawberries and wild strawberries, have skin that is speckled with dry, diminutive yellow seeds. Others, such as blueberries, cranberries, and currants, have smooth, slick skin.

In addition to appearance, tartness is a major distinguishing factor. Many, such as blueberries and strawberries, are sweet enough to eat as is. Others have supertart flavor profiles; these include gooseberries, cranberries, and currants. They can be eaten as is, but most palates prefer added sweetener.

Cape Gooseberry (without capes)

Blueberry

Red Currant

BUYING AND STORING

Choose brightly colored berries without mold, soft spots, or discoloration. If boxed, check to see if berries move freely when container is tilted; if they stick together, they are probably moldy. Refrigerate (unwashed and untrimmed) in single layer on paper towel. Delicate berries, such as raspberries, blackberries, boysenberries, and raspberries, can be stored up to 2–3 days. Refrigerate sturdier berries, such as cranberries, up to 7 days. To freeze, spread unwashed berries on rimmed baking sheet in single layer; freeze, then store frozen berries in an airtight container in freezer. Freezing changes texture of all berries: Except cranberries, they become mushy and are generally best used in cooked dishes. Most do not require defrosting before use.

BLACKBERRY
Domestic: *March–October*
Global: *October–March*

BLUEBERRY
Domestic: *April–October, peak is July*
Global: *year-round*

BOYSENBERRY
Domestic: *May–June*
Global: *none*

CAPE GOOSEBERRY
Domestic: *September–November*
Global: *year-round*

CRANBERRY
Domestic: *October–November*
Global: *none*

CURRANT (BLACK, RED, AND WHITE)
Domestic: *March–July*
Global: *none*

GOOSEBERRY
Domestic: *March–May*
Global: *none*

LOGANBERRY
Domestic: *March–April*
Global: *none*

RASPBERRY (RED, GOLD, AND BLACK)
Domestic: *year-round*
Global: *October–April*

STRAWBERRY
Domestic: *year-round, peak in March–August*
Global: *January–March*

WILD STRAWBERRY, FRAISE DES BOIS (RED AND WHITE)
Domestic: *April–June*
Global: *none*

PREP

Rinse very briefly in cold water; many berries tend to absorb water. Strawberries require hulling; remove leaves and stem with point of paring knife, pointed end of swivel vegetable peeler, or strawberry huller.

USE

Use raw in fruit salads, smoothies, puréed dessert sauces, and compotes; top cereal, puddings, and cakes. Delicious in pie, jam, jelly, and savory-sweet sauces to accompany game. Juice of tart berries, such as cranberries or gooseberries, can be substituted for vinegar in salad dressings.

BLACKBERRY

Cluster of tiny, juicy sacs, purplish-black to midnight-black, about ½–1 inch long. ■ *Succulent; soft tartness with defined sweetness. Tastes best when glossy shine turns slightly dull and fruit is very black.*

BLUEBERRY

Round and small, with a diameter of about ⅜ inch with deep blue skin that often looks "dusted." A new "super" blueberry variety is 2 to 3 times larger. ■ *Crunchy and juicy, with sweet flavor profile.*

BOYSENBERRY

Larger than blackberries, but with similar shape. Skin is reddish-purple. ■ *Plump and juicy, with sweet flavor profile.*

CAPE GOOSEBERRY

(ground cherry)

A thin, papery brown husk makes them resemble a tomatillo. Shaped like a Japanese lantern, the smooth skin turns from pale green to amber as it ripens. Can have tiny edible seeds in center. Capeless gooseberries are the same variety, but capes (the papery husks) are removed for importation. ■ *Gooseberry-like, tart flavor (similar to sour, underripened grape), with texture similar to a cherry.*

CRANBERRY

Small and slightly oblong with smooth, waxy skin that is shiny red. White cranberry is slightly more tart and available only early in season ■ *Seriously tart and mouth-puckering.*

CURRANT

(black, red, and white)

Small, round berries grow in clusters like grapes. Skin is smooth and glossy; black, red, or white varieties. ■ *Intense, perky tartness. Different colors have similar tastes, but black is generally more tart than red. White is mildest and most rare.*

GOOSEBERRY

Small, generally round translucent berries about ½-inch in diameter. Skin varies in color—usually shades of green or amber, but can be pink or purple. ■ *Generally seriously tart.*

LOGANBERRY

Plump, raspberry-colored, with blackberry shape. ■ *Raspberry-like taste, with subtle increase in acidity.*

RASPBERRY

(red, gold, and black)

Cluster of tiny, juice sacs surround narrow, hollow tunnel. Red variety is plump; black and gold varieties can be slightly smaller. All are fragile. ■ *Mild tartness is balanced with pleasant sweet finish. Gold raspberries have subtle apricot taste and are the most rare variety.*

STRAWBERRY

Most often heart-shaped, but vary in size. Vivid red to dark crimson skin, speckled with dry, diminutive seeds. ■ *Flowery fragrance, juicy and sweet taste.*

WILD STRAWBERRY, FRAISE DES BOIS

(red and white)

About the size of a large raspberry and heart-shaped. There are red and white varieties. ■ *Extremely fragrant; tartness is overshadowed by sweetness.*

NUTRITIONAL INFO

(For 1 cup) Blackberries are an excellent source of vitamin C; good source of vitamin K. Blueberries are a good source of vitamin C and vitamin K. Boysenberries are a significant source of vitamin C and folate. Cape gooseberries are a significant source of vitamins C and A. Cranberries are a significant source of vitamin C. Currants are an excellent source of vitamin C; significant source of vitamin K. Gooseberries are an excellent source of vitamin C. Loganberries are a good source of vitamin C and a significant source of folate and vitamin K. Raspberries are an excellent source of vitamin C and a significant source of vitamin K. Strawberries and wild strawberries are an excellent source of vitamin C.

SERVING SUGGESTIONS

Strawberries, uncooked, uncomplicated: Dip whole berries in melted (but not hot) chocolate and place on waxed paper until chocolate hardens. Or serve whole, accompanied by bowls of sour cream and brown sugar for optional dipping.

Raspberry salad dressing: Purée ½ cup fresh raspberries in blender or food processor. Strain through sieve and discard seeds. Whisk purée with ¼ cup raspberry vinegar and ½ cup olive oil (extra-virgin preferred). Season to taste with garlic salt and pepper.

Blueberries and greens: Toss mixed baby lettuces with just enough vinaigrette to lightly coat leaves. Add fresh blueberries and small slivers of red onion; gently toss.

Berry smoothie: In blender combine 3 cups mixed berries, 4 ice cubes, 1 cup milk (either low-fat or soy milk), ⅓ cup plain or fruit yogurt; whirl until smooth.

Raspberry

Strawberry

Blackberry

raspberry coulis

Raspberry coulis is simple to prepare and can add pizzazz to a broad range of desserts. This puréed dessert sauce can accompany ice cream, sorbet, panna cotta, or brownies; it can top fresh sliced fruit, such as pears or peaches, and is also delicious spooned around baked brie. Strawberries can be substituted for raspberries but may require a little more sugar.

2 1/4 cups fresh raspberries

1/4 cup sugar

1 teaspoon fresh lemon juice

OPTIONAL: splash raspberry-flavored liqueur or orange-flavored liqueur

YIELD: ABOUT 1 CUP, ABOUT 6 SERVINGS

COOK'S NOTES: If a thicker sauce is desired, combine 1 teaspoon cornstarch and 2 tablespoons water. Place coulis (without liqueur) in saucepan on medium-high heat. Bring to simmer; stir cornstarch mixture and add to coulis. Bring to boil; boil 1 minute, stirring constantly. Remove from heat; stir in liqueur, if using.

1. Purée berries with sugar, lemon juice and liqueur (if using) in blender or processor; strain through sieve and discard seeds.

2. Pour into nonreactive container and refrigerate, well-sealed, up to 2 days. Stir before using.

NUTRITIONAL INFORMATION (PER SERVING WITHOUT LIQUEUR): Calories 60; fat calories 0; total fat 0 grams; sat fat 0 grams; cholesterol 0 milligrams; sodium 0 milligrams; total carbohydrates 14 grams; fiber 3 grams; sugars 10 grams; protein 1 gram; vitamin A IUs 0%; vitamin C 20%; calcium 2%; iron 2%.

buddha's hand citron,
also fingered citron

GNARLED, YELLOW FINGERS erupt from the fruit's "palm," tapering as they twist into pointed tips. There isn't any soft flesh inside the fragrant Buddha's hand, only zest-covered pith.

In China, this curvaceous citron is a symbol of happiness, longevity, and good fortune. Often, it is given as new year's gifts, used as temple offerings, or placed next to cash registers in shops for luck.

BUYING AND STORING

Choose bright yellow fruit that is firm and fragrant. Avoid those with blemishes or mold. Store at room temperature up to 2 weeks, or refrigerate up to 4 weeks. Can be ordered at supermarkets with large specialty produce sections. Sometimes available at farmers markets.

Domestic: *October–January*

PREP

It looks so intriguing that it may be difficult to take a knife to the digits. Remove zest (colored part of peel) with a zesting device or, for larger pieces, use a vegetable peeler or paring knife.

USE

Zest has lemony fragrance and flavor. Use colored portion of peel in recipes that call for citrus zest. Buddha's hand citron can also be used for decorative purposes or given as "good fortune" gifts.

NUTRITIONAL INFO

¼ cup is an excellent source of vitamin C.

SERVING SUGGESTIONS

Handsome sorbet: Make sorbet using Meyer lemon juice, augmented with shredded zest of Buddha's hand (see Meyer Lemon Sorbet, page 51).

"Good luck, get rich" centerpiece: They look great arranged with other fruit as a centerpiece or incorporated into flower arrangements.

Substitutions: Subtitute an equal amount of finely minced Buddha's hand zest in any recipe calling for either lemon or lime zest.

"Longevity" vodka: Wash Buddha's hand citron well with cold water. Dry thoroughly. Place in wide-mouth jar. Cover with vodka until totally submerged. To hold fruit down, it may be necessary to weight it down with plate or mug. Seal and place in cool, dark location for 4–5 days. Strain into bottle. If giving as a gift, tie a fresh Buddha's hand to neck of bottle. Enjoy in cocktails and pasta sauces that call for vodka.

Buddha's Hand Citron

cactus pear,
also prickly pear, tuna

GREEN	
RED	

CACTUS PEARS are the delectable, elongated, egg-shaped fruit of several varieties of opuntia cactus. About 4–6 inches in length, they are actually berries filled with multiple edible seeds (some varieties have seeds that are very hard, others have seeds that are crispy or soft). Outside, the firm, inedible skin can be a gentle green color or deep red. It's prickly and thick, but fairly easy to peel (see Prep).

Inside, the green-skinned variety has pale yellow-green flesh, while the red-skinned fruit has bright magenta flesh. The taste varies by variety, but most often the flavor is similar to a sweet melon. The flowery aroma and juicy texture is like watermelon.

Red Cactus Pear

Green Cactus Pear

BUYING AND STORING

Look for fruit that gives under gentle pressure but isn't mushy or shriveled. Ripen at room temperature a few days, if firm. Store ripe fruit in crisper drawer of refrigerator up to 1 week.

Domestic: *April–August*
Global: *June–September*

PREP

Seeds are often soft enough to eat, but they sometimes are very hard and need to be strained (and seeds discarded). Wearing gloves to protect hands, cut off both ends of fruit. Using paring knife, make shallow lengthwise cuts about 3 inches apart. Starting at one end, peel off and discard skin. Or cut skin off from top to bottom and discard. Or, to prepare strained purée, cut pear in half lengthwise. Then scoop out pulp with small spoon and force through medium-mesh strainer (discard seeds left in strainer) with back of large wooden spoon into a bowl. Use in drinks or sauces. Purée can be frozen in airtight containers. Thaw before using. To eat raw (if seeds are soft enough to eat), peel and slice.

USE

Eat raw or purée for use in drinks, jam, dessert sauces, and salad dressings. Add chopped to fruit pies or slice to use as colorful garnish.

NUTRITIONAL INFO

1 cup is a good source of vitamin C.

SERVING SUGGESTIONS

Chocolate topper: Spoon strained purée over scoops of chocolate ice cream or chocolate sorbet.

Tropical Shirley Temple: Stir strained purée into tall glass with lemon-lime soda and ice.

Not-so-prickly fruit salad: Gently toss sliced bananas, tangerine sections, and peeled cactus pear wedges (seeded, if seeds are hard). Squeeze on lime juice to taste, as well as orange liqueur, if desired; gently toss.

prickly pear sauce

This sauce is delicious spooned on pancakes, waffles, or French toast. Or it can be ladled over pudding, ice cream, or angel food cake. The recipe calls for 1 tablespoon lime juice and ⅓ cup sugar, but be sure to taste the sauce before serving. You may want to add a little more sugar or lime juice or augment with a little finely minced lime zest (colored part of peel).

3 cups strained cactus pear purée (see Prep), about 14 cactus pears, divided use

⅓ cup sugar

1 tablespoon fresh lime juice

1 tablespoon orange liqueur, such as Grand Marnier

YIELD: ABOUT 2 CUPS

1. In medium saucepan, combine 2 cups strained purée and sugar. Place on medium heat and bring to simmer. Simmer, stirring frequently, until reduced to 1 cup. Cool.

2. Combine cooled mixture with reserved 1 cup of purée, lime juice, and liqueur. Taste and adjust as needed, adding more lime juice or sugar to suit your taste.

NUTRITIONAL INFORMATION (PER TEASPOON): Calories 10; fat calories 0; total fat 0 grams; sat fat 0 grams; cholesterol 0 milligrams; sodium 0 milligrams; total carbohydrates 2 grams; fiber less than 1 gram; sugars 1 gram; protein 0 grams; vitamin A IUs 0%; vitamin C 4%; calcium 0%; iron 0%.

cherimoya,
also custard apple

CHERIMOYAS LOOK a little like lizard-green pine cones. The leathery skin is embossed with scalelike scallops. Inside, the flesh is creamy white and custardy. It's dotted with inedible, slick black seeds.

An alluring sweet blend of pineapple, papaya, vanilla, and banana flavors, cherimoyas were described as "deliciousness itself" by Mark Twain. A member of the custard-apple family, which includes soursops, the cherimoya has more than 500 varieties.

BUYING AND STORING

Because they bruise easily, cherimoyas are often wrapped in protective mesh jackets. Generally sold firm, because once they ripen they deteriorate within 1–2 days. Ripen firm fruit at room temperature, usually about 1 week. Ripe fruit will give, like a peach, to light pressure. Once ripe, refrigerate up to 2 days.

Domestic: *December–June*
Global: *July–November*

PREP

For eating raw with a spoon, cut in half lengthwise and scoop out flesh with teaspoon. To dice, cut into eighths, from top to bottom, then cut off skin and remove seeds. Fibrous center can be removed if still firm (when it's really soft it can be eaten). Or peel with paring knife, cut in quarters and remove seeds and, if necessary, fibrous center. Cut into cubes. Puree, if desired, in blender or food processor.

USE

Best eaten chilled and raw, either out of hand or in compotes, ice creams, drinks, and sorbets. Can be used in jellies, jams, pastries and puddings. Once cut, cherimoya discolors quickly. Place in acidulated water (water mixed with small amount of lemon or lime juice) or squeeze a little orange juice on it, a common way to enjoy cherimoya in Chile.

NUTRITIONAL INFO

$3/4$ cup (without seeds and skin) is an excellent source of vitamin C; a significant source of riboflavin and thiamin; and a good source of vitamin B_6, potassium, and magnesium.

SERVING SUGGESTIONS

Cherimoya smoothie: In a blender, combine 6 ice cubes, $1/2$ cup sweetened condensed milk, 1 cherimoya (peeled, seeded, and diced), and $1/4$ cup milk. Whirl until smooth.

Cherimoya

Tropical dressing: Peel, dice, and seed 1 ripe cherimoya; purée in blender or food processor. Add ¼ cup plain yogurt and ¼ cup mayonnaise. Pulse to combine. Use to dress fruit salad or mixed green salad.

'Moya mousse: Peel, dice, and seed 1 ripe cherimoya; purée in blender or food processor. Add 2 tablespoons orange juice; pulse to combine. Whip 2 cups whipping cream until stiff. Add cherimoya mixture; gently fold fruit into whipped cream. Chill at least 2 hours before serving.

Heat-wave compote: Make sugar syrup. Combine 2 cups water and ½ cup sugar in medium saucepan. Bring to boil on high heat, stirring until sugar dissolves. Set aside to cool. In large bowl, gently toss cooled syrup with 2 cherimoyas (peeled, seeded, and diced), 2 bananas (peeled and sliced), 2 mangoes (peeled, seeded, and diced), 1 tablespoon roughly chopped fresh mint, 1 tablespoon light rum, and fresh lime juice to taste. Chill before serving.

cherimoya crème brûlée

No wonder crème brûlée is such a popular dessert. The custard base, creamy rich and cool, delectably contrasts with the crunchy, butterscotch-like caramel on top. In this recipe, a cherimoya purée adds a tropical tutti-fruitti touch to the custard.

2 cups heavy whipping cream

½ cup sugar

1 vanilla bean, cut in half lengthwise

Pinch salt

4 egg yolks

6 tablespoons puréed cherimoya (see Prep)

½ teaspoon minced orange zest, colored part of peel

FOR TOPPING: 4 teaspoons sugar

YIELD: 4

1. Preheat oven to 325 degrees. In large saucepan, combine cream, ½ cup sugar, vanilla bean and salt. Bring to simmer on medium-high heat. Remove from heat and steep, covered, for 15 minutes.

2. Meanwhile, whisk yolks in separate large bowl.

3. Remove vanilla bean from cream mixture. Add cream mixture to yolks in a very thin steam, whisking constantly. Stir in cherimoya purée and orange zest.

4. Place mixture in 4 (8-ounce) ramekins. Place ramekins in larger pan. Add enough hot water to larger pan to come ¾ of way up sides of ramekins. Cover pan loosely with aluminum foil. Bake in middle of preheated oven for 45–55 minutes, or until set. Remove ramekins from water and cool 30 minutes. Refrigerate at least 6 hours or overnight.

5. Up to 45 minutes before serving, sprinkle 1 teaspoon sugar evenly over the top of each. Caramelize sugar until dark golden brown, either with a culinary torch (small propane torch) or by placing 6–8 inches below broiler element in oven. If using broiler, watch carefully to prevent burning.

NUTRITIONAL INFORMATION (PER SERVING):
Calories 580; fat calories 420; total fat 46 grams; sat fat 28 grams; carbohydrates 38 grams; fiber 1 gram; sugars 32 grams; sodium 125 milligrams; protein 5 grams; vitamin A IUs 40%; vitamin C 4%; calcium 10%; iron 4%.

coconut

White

COMMON (BROWN)

WHITE

YOUNG

THE COMMON BROWN COCONUT—with its oval, dark brown shell covered with bristly, hairlike fibers—is probably the most familiar of the coconuts. Hidden beneath that shell is crisp white flesh, so sweet and nutty that it tastes like candy. Three "eyes" peer out from the smaller end; the circular indentations are entry points for draining the sweet liquid inside. The coconut "water" (or juice) is thin and tasty. But it shouldn't be confused with coconut milk, which is a product made by cooking shredded coconut with water and then squeezing all the juicy goodness out of the flesh.

Before that dark brown shell becomes rock hard, it is more easily penetrable. Coconuts are encased in a thick, fibrous green- or tan-skinned exterior husk. With mature coconuts, the outer husks are generally removed before exportation. But because immature sweet young coconuts (called hut) have soft interior shells and pudding-soft flesh, they are sold with part of that outer husk still intact. Often they are trimmed down to the white husk, shaved into a cylinder with a pyramid point on top and covered with plastic wrap.

White coconuts are more mature sweet young (hut) coconuts but less mature than common brown coconuts. The outer, light-beige shells are hard but not as hard as brown coconuts, and they have long hairlike fibers. Inside, the white flesh is very sweet and has a softer texture than that of brown coconuts.

Common (brown)

Young

BUYING AND STORING

Look for coconuts that feel heavy. For brown coconuts or white coconuts, look for firm "eyes" free of mold. When shaken, they should sound like there is a lot of liquid inside. Some brown coconuts are sold with a "quick crack" feature for easier opening and encased in plastic wrap. They are scored around the fruit's equator, deep enough to make them easier to open but not deep enough to penetrate the shell. Store at room temperature up to 1 month. Once opened, refrigerate wrapped in plastic for 1 week or freeze up to 3 months.

For young coconuts (hut), look for fresh and moist fruit with white husks that are free of mold or brown spots. Store in refrigerator wrapped in plastic up to 1 week.

COMMON BROWN
Domestic: *none*
Global: *year-round*

YOUNG COCONUT (HUT) AND WHITE COCONUT
Domestic: *none*
Global: *year-round*

PREP

Some prefer the "throw-it-on-the-concrete" technique; but for quick-crack brown coconuts (see Buying and Storing), tap around scored equator with hammer, cleaver, or mallet until it snaps open. For white or brown coconuts without quick-crack feature, line floor with newspapers or paper towels and place coconut on top. Cover with kitchen towel and whack with hammer to break into 4–6 pieces. Gently and carefully wedge screwdriver between hard shell and flesh, or heat pieces in 350-degree oven for 15–20 minutes, which makes flesh shrink from shell and easier to remove. Or freeze pieces for 1–2 hours to make them shrink. If desired, remove dark skin with vegetable peeler.

For white coconut, line work area with paper towels or newspaper. Use sharp, sturdy cleaver to cautiously tap around the circumference, about 3 inches from the top until it breaks off. Proceed as with the brown coconut.

For the young coconut (hut), line work area with paper towels or newspaper. Use sharp cleaver to cautiously hack off pointed end. To use as beverage, insert a straw and serve chilled. Provide a spoon to scoop out pudding-like flesh once juice has been consumed.

USE

Eat raw or cooked in sweet or savory dishes, such as puddings, cakes, rice dishes, cookies, pies, or fruit salads. Also coconut flesh is delicious in candy and ice cream. Coconut "water" (juice), especially the very sweet liquid from young coconuts (hut), is delectable used in soups, salad dressings, beverages, curries, and desserts.

NUTRITIONAL INFO

1 cup shredded is a significant source of iron and copper.

SERVING SUGGESTIONS

The "best" cocktail snack—toasted and salted coconut: Use a very sharp knife or mandoline to cautiously cut fresh, shelled brown coconut into ⅛-inch slices. Place in single layer on rimmed baking sheet; do not crowd. Season with coarse salt, such as sea salt or kosher salt. Place in middle of preheated 350-degree oven for 4 minutes. Turn with spatula and bake 3–7 minutes more or until golden brown. Serve warm or at room temperature. Store once cooled in airtight container up to 36 hours.

Youthful containers: Use juice inside young coconuts (hut) as part of liquid for cooking rice, reserving "shells." Serve rice inside shell and advise guests to spoon-up soft coconut along with warm rice. Also, shells can be used as containers for serving coconut milk–based soups (see Sweet Potatoes, page 274).

Frosty coconut snowballs: Shred peeled coconut flesh from brown or white coconut. Place in single layer on rimmed baking sheet. Place in the middle of 350-degree oven until lightly browned, about 4–6 minutes, turning halfway through with spatula. Watch carefully because shredded coconut burns easily. Cool. Use ice cream scoop to make "balls" of vanilla ice cream. Roll in coconut. Serve as is or use to top brownies served in stemmed glasses.

dragon fruit, also pitaya

THE APPEARANCE of dragon fruit is downright surreal. It has eye-popping magenta skin, dotted with bright lime-green spines. The spines of this cactus fruit are supple and plentiful. They curve downward like chartreuse bird wings.

MAGENTA

PINK

WHITE

Inside the fruit, the pulp is spongy soft, the texture similar to a kiwi but grainier. Often it's gray-tinged white, with tiny black specks that are minuscule seeds, but some have purplish-pink flesh with similar black specks. It tastes like a marriage between kiwi and pineapple.

BUYING AND STORING

Look for fruit with "hot pink" skin that is free of soft spots or mold. Ripe fruit will give slightly to gentle pressure. To ripen fruit, leave at room temperature for 1–2 days. Fruit sweetens as it ripens. Refrigerate ripe fruit in crisper drawer up to 3 or 4 days.

Domestic: *August–November*
Global: *none*

PREP

Skin is not edible but is easily removed. Cut fruit in half or in wedges; peel away skin with paring knife. Or cut in half and scoop out flesh with spoon. Discard skin.

USE

Eat raw, out of hand, in salads, or in desserts such as ice cream, sorbet, or quick bread.

NUTRITIONAL INFO

1 cup is a good source of vitamin C.

SERVING SUGGESTIONS

Salad boats: Cut in half lengthwise. With spoon, scoop out flesh. Dice flesh and combine with other tropical fruit, such as diced pineapple or mango. If desired, gently toss with either chopped fresh mint or liqueur. Spoon into dragon fruit shells and serve.

Citrus dragon spurt: Cut peeled flesh into wedges. Place on plate, and squeeze fresh lime juice on top. In Vietnam, a small bowl of coarse salt, combined with ground red chile flakes and ground black pepper, is available for optional sprinkling.

Dragon cakes: Purée dragon fruit, and use in cakes or quick breads. Substitute purée for part of liquid in recipe.

Dragon fool: English fool traditionally uses gooseberries, but dragon fruit can be substituted. Fold chilled puree into chilled whipped cream that has been sweetened with powdered sugar. Spoon into small bowls, and top with diced dragon fruit and sprigs of fresh mint.

White

Magenta

Pink

fig

BLACK MISSION

BROWN TURKEY

CALIMYRNA
(SMYRNA, ROYAL
MEDITERRANEAN)

KADOTA

FRAGILE FIG SKIN surrenders easily to reveal soft-textured flesh filled with a multitude of tiny seeds. A bite produces tiny seed-popping sounds, flesh saturated with honey flavor, and a moist flower-petal aroma. Some varieties have more seeds than others, but all figs are delectable unadorned and eaten out of hand. They're also the perfect sweet-edged foil to salty savories, such as paper-thin prosciutto or slightly tart cheese.

Most likely indigenous to the Mediterranean, figs were brought to the United States by Spanish conquistadors and missionaries—thus the name Mission figs (a variety still grown in California that is often called Black Mission because the deep purple skin turns black when dried).

BUYING AND STORING

Fresh figs are fragile and extremely perishable. Avoid hard fruit; instead, look for ripe fruit that yields to gentle pressure. Store at room temperature and use within 3 days. Or place in single layer on a plate or baking sheet covered with paper towels, then cover with plastic wrap and refrigerate up to 1 week. They can be dried in a dehydrator for longer storage.

BLACK MISSION
Domestic: *July–October*
Global: *none*

BROWN TURKEY
Domestic: *June–September*
Global: *March–May*

CALIMYRNA (SMYRNA, ROYAL MEDITERRANEAN):
Domestic: *July–October*
Global: *None*

KADOTA
Domestic: *July–September*
Global: *None*

PREP

Rinse quickly with cold water and gently pat dry. Cut off any tough stem ends. Skin is edible; peel only when eating raw and the skin is tough (only necessary for some large varieties).

USE

Raw: Eat out of hand or use in salads. Stuff with cheese (cream cheese, soft goat cheese, or blue-veined cheese) and drizzle with balsamic vinegar, or drizzle with liqueur and serve with ice cream or rice pudding.

Cooked: Sauté until caramelized in butter on medium-high heat, or bake in ¼-inch-deep

BLACK MISSION
Small to medium size teardrop shape. Thick, deep-purple (almost black) skin, with pinkish-brown flesh and tiny pale seeds. ■ *Juicy and very sweet.*

BROWN TURKEY
Medium to large size, elongated teardrop shape. Violet to deep-brown thick skin is sometimes green at stem. Red or pinkish-red flesh. Small pale seeds. ■ *Mildly sweet.*

CALIMYRNA
(California version of Turkish Smyrna, sometimes labeled Royal Mediterranean)
Large, rounded teardrop shape. Skin can be greenish-yellow or purple, streaked with green. Flesh is pinkish-red with small white seeds. Most popular fig for drying. ■ *Juicy and sweet with interesting nuttiness.*

KADOTA
(American version of Italian Dattato)
Small to medium size, with rounded shape. Greenish-yellow, delicate skin with light amber or light pink flesh. Very tiny, soft seeds (so small these are often used for preserves). ■ *Very sweet.*

mixture of orange juice, rum, and sugar until plump and piping hot. Or poach them ever so briefly in a mixture of port, water, sugar, star anise, and vanilla. Figs are delicious in muffins and jams or as pizza topping.

Fig leaves also have culinary uses. They can be used to wrap fish or chicken breasts before grilling. Leaves impart a subtle fig flavor and aroma, plus they hold in moisture.

NUTRITIONAL INFO
1 cup is a good source of vitamin B_6 and potassium.

SERVING SUGGESTIONS
Subtle sweet meat: Sauté figs in butter until caramelized; serve with grilled or roasted poultry, pork, or lamb.

Oil sub: Purée peeled, raw figs and use as substitute for oil in baked goods (in a manner similar to substituting applesauce for oil).

Sweet-salty-tart pasta: Place whole figs in baking pan and bake in 375-degree oven for 10 minutes. Meanwhile, cook pasta (such as penne or rotelle) al dente and drain. Chop baked figs into bite-size pieces; toss figs with warm pasta, cooked (chopped) pancetta, chopped fresh basil, and freshly grated Parmesan cheese.

Hot and cold heaven: Place whole figs in baking pan and bake in 375-degree oven for 10 minutes. Sprinkle with sugar to taste. Serve hot, accompanied by vanilla ice cream.

warm figs stuffed with prosciutto and goat cheese

Sweet figs are delectable paired with salty prosciutto and tangy cheese. Serve these irresistible warm figs as a first course or appetizer. Over the last few years, chefs and home cooks have come up with lots of

Brown Turkey

Calimyrna

Kadota

Black Mission

variations on the fig-cheese-prosciutto theme. Some use blue-veined cheeses; others include nuts or serve them on small mixed green salads.

8 fresh figs, trimmed, halved

4 ounces cold goat cheese

9 tablespoons packed light brown sugar

½ teaspoon ground cumin

½ teaspoon salt, kosher preferred

3 ounces thinly sliced prosciutto

6 tablespoons balsamic vinegar

YIELD: 8 APPETIZER SERVINGS

1. Adjust oven rack to about 5 inches below broiler element. Preheat broiler.

2. Use small end of melon baller to remove 1 scoop from each fig half. Use melon baller to scoop cheese into similar semispherical shapes and place in hollowed portion of figs. Place figs cut side up on heavy rimmed baking sheet or on broiler pan.

3. In small bowl, stir 3 tablespoons packed light brown sugar, cumin, and salt. Rub mixture on 1 side of each prosciutto slice. Cut prosciutto into pieces about the same size as fig tops and place, sugar side up, on each fig. Broil until warm and prosciutto is browned, about 3 minutes.

4. In small, heavy-bottomed saucepan, place balsamic vinegar and 6 tablespoons packed light brown sugar. On medium heat, simmer, stirring until sugar dissolves; simmer 1 minute more.

5. Place 2 fig halves on each of 8 small salad plates or appetizer plates. Drizzle with balsamic sauce.

NUTRITIONAL INFORMATION (PER SERVING):
Calories 180; fat calories 54; total fat 6 grams; sat fat 3.5 grams; cholesterol 20 milligrams; sodium 430 milligrams; total carbohydrates 27 grams; fiber 1 gram; sugars 25 grams; protein 6 grams; vitamin A IUs 6%; vitamin C 2%; calcium 8%; iron 6%.

grape

CHAMPAGNE

COMMON (BLACK, GREEN, AND RED)

CONCORD

GLOBE

MUSCAT

MUSCATO (GREEN AND RED)

WHEN IT COMES to grapes, every element has culinary potential. From the seeds used to make oil to the twisted vines used as fuel to flavor grilled foods, from the leaves used for wrapping savory filling to the alluring fermented juices we call wine. It's impossible to imagine life without grapes.

With thousands of varieties, grapes can be classified several ways. First, some have seeds, while others are seedless. However, trace seeds, known as vestigial seeds, are commonly present even in seedless varieties. Second, they can be classified according to use, either as wine grapes (such as Cabernet) or table grapes (such as Flame). Third, they can be categorized by color: green (pale yellow-green to light green), red (light to dark red), or black (light red to very dark purple).

BUYING AND STORING

Look for firm grapes that are plump and fragrant. They should be fairly firm but not rock hard. Grapes are picked ripe; they do not ripen once removed from vine. If grapes are detached from their stems, look at the area that once surrounded stem; it should be free of discoloration, mold, or soft spots. Avoid shriveled fruit. Store unwashed grapes in perforated plastic bag in crisper drawer up to 10 days.

CHAMPAGNE
Domestic: *June–September*
Global: *none*

COMMON BLACK
Domestic: *August–January*
Global: *December–June*

COMMON GREEN, COMMON RED
Domestic: *May–December*
Global: *December–June*

CONCORD
Domestic: *August–September*
Global: *none*

GLOBE
Domestic: *August–January*
Global: *January–June*

MUSCAT (RED AND GREEN)
Domestic: *none*
Global: *March–May*

MUSCATO (GREEN AND RED)
Domestic: *June–October*
Global: *none*

Champagne

Common Red

Common Black

Common Green

CHAMPAGNE
(Corinth)
Tiny, pea-sized seedless grapes, deep purple to reddish-purple, densely clustered on stem. ▪
Sweet, mild flavor with crisp texture. Some consider the smaller part of their stems edible.

COMMON BLACK SEEDLESS
(Autumn Royale, Beauty, Kyoho, Maroo, Ribier)
Generally plumper than green grapes; color ranges from purple to almost black. Occasionally, they have seeds. ▪ *Very juicy and sweet with moderate acidity.*

COMMON GREEN SEEDLESS
(Thompson Seedless, Perlette, Sugraone, Calmeria)
Pale yellow-green to light green. Firmly attached to stem. ▪
Tangy sweetness with low acidity. Delicate musky overtones.

COMMON RED SEEDLESS
(Flame, Ruby, Christmas Rose, Emperor, Crimson, Rouge)
Medium-sized, often with exterior bloom (a dusty film produced by cells on or near surface form a natural waterproofing and prevent delicate skin from cracking). ▪
Juicy, crisp, and crunchy, with low acidity. Delicious sweet-tart flavor profile.

CONCORD
Deep blue to purple to almost black grapes with a dusty bloom (see Common Red). These round grapes are encased in rather thick skin that slips off in the mouth. Both seeded and seedless varieties. This is the grape taste associated with commercially produced grape juice and jelly. ▪ *Medium-sweetness with slightly tart finish. Pulp is distinctively musky.*

GLOBE
Large, oval red grapes, usually with seeds. ▪ *Similar flavor and texture to Common Red grapes.*

MUSCAT
(green and red)
Medium oval grapes that are typically red, but there is also a green variety. ▪ *Deliciously juicy with intense sweetness and fragrance. Popular grape for dessert wines.*

MUSCATO
(green and red)
Green Muscato is a cross between Thompson Seedless and Muscat. Medium-sized oval grapes with green and gold skin. Seedless. Red Muscato is a cross between the Italia, Tokay, and Muscat grape varieties. Medium-sized, oval grapes with dark-red skin. Seedless. ▪ *Green Muscato is much sweeter than common green grapes. Red Muscato is much sweeter than common red grapes.*

PREP

Rinse well in cold running water before use. Drain or shake off excess water. To serve at table, cut into small bunches with scissors. If cooking grapes with seeds, cut in half and pluck out seeds with tip of a small pointed knife.

USE

Generally eaten raw, out of hand, or in salads, but they can be cooked. They are delicious cooked in creamy sauces, as in Chicken Veronique, or rice dishes (to which they are added in the last few minutes of cooking). Tasty in jams or salsas. Very sweet grapes, such as Muscato, are delicious in granitas or sorbets. To use as garnish, grapes can be "frosted": Lightly paint clusters of grapes with egg whites beaten with a little cold water. Dust lightly with sugar and dry on rack.

NUTRITIONAL INFO

1 cup is a good source of vitamins C and K.

SERVING SUGGESTIONS

Frozen snack: Freeze individual grapes in single layer on rimmed baking sheet. Once frozen, store in freezer bag or airtight container.

Salad with grapes: Cut grapes in halves (removing seeds if necessary), and toss with tuna or chicken salad (especially nice with a little curry powder added to dressing). Grape halves are also a great addition to classic Waldorf salad. Or add to green salad such as arugula mixed with slivers of Belgian endive. Toss with vinaigrette, crumbled blue cheese, and toasted walnuts.

Roasted grapes: Cut 1/2 pound red seedless or black seedless grapes into small clusters. Place on rimmed baking sheet and drizzle with 1 tablespoon extra-virgin olive oil. Season with coarse salt and roast in middle of preheated 500-degree oven about 15 minutes, or until soft inside and slightly crisp outside. Use to accompany roast game, pork, or poultry.

Cheese-coated grapes: Combine equal parts blue cheese and cream cheese in food processor fitted with metal blade; process until blended. If desired, a little finely diced candied ginger can be added. Roll seedless grapes in mixture to coat (use palms of hands, pressing mixture around grape). Roll in chopped, toasted pecans, and chill in single layer on rimmed baking sheet. Serve cold.

Muscat

Red Muscato

Concord

Green
Muscato

grapefruit

COCKTAIL

MELOGOLD

ORO BLANCO

PUMMELO, POMELO, POMMELO

RED, RUBY, PINK

WAKE-UP ACIDITY balances with subtle sweetness, as membranes release copious juice and give a gentle crunch. No tastebud snoozes when grapefruit or pummelo is on the menu. Flavor and juiciness differ among pummelo and the different grapefruit varieties, but that signature perky edge and fragrance are consistent.

Many botanists contend that the grapefruit is a natural hybrid of orange and pummelo, but they disagree about whether it was a sweet or sour orange that played a role.

grapefruit The name is derived from how the grapefruit grows on the tree, clustered like bunches of grapes. Skin colors range from pink to bright lemon-yellow, with flesh from reddish-pink to all shades of yellow, as well as orange.

BUYING AND STORING

Generally harvested before reaching maturity, they often have green-tinged skin. Look for fruit that is heavy for its size and that feels springy when pressed. Store at room temperature 5–7 days, or refrigerate 2 weeks. Juice can be frozen.

COCKTAIL
Domestic: *January–March*
Global: *None*

MELOGOLD
Domestic: *October–April*
Global: *None*

ORO BLANCO
Domestic: *November–March*
Global: *None*

RUBY, PINK, OR RED
Domestic: *Year-round*
Global: *None*

PREP

Cut in half and scoop out segments with spoon; or loosen segments from rind with grapefruit knife (a serrated knife that is gently curved at the blade end) or grapefruit spoon (a spoon that is serrated at the tip). Grapefruit can also be cut into segments. Cut off, deep enough to expose fruit, top and bottom ends of fruit. Set cut side down on cutting board. Cut peel off in strips from top to bottom, deep enough to remove all pith. Hold fruit over bowl and remove each segment by cutting toward center on either side of each segment membrane. Let each segment fall into bowl. When all segments have been removed, squeeze membrane to extract remaining juice.

COCKTAIL

Cross between pummelo and mandarin. Orange-yellow, fairly thin skin with orange-yellow flesh, about 4–5 inches in diameter. Some with seeds, some without seeds. ■ *Very sweet and juicy. Low acidity.*

MELOGOLD

Green-tinged yellow skin and white flesh. It can be more than 6 inches in diameter and weigh several pounds. Skin is thick and easily peeled. Hollow central core. Few seeds. ■ *Tastes similar to pummelo: sweet and juicy with low acidity.*

ORO BLANCO

Light yellow to lemon-yellow with fairly thick skin often tinged with green; light yellow flesh with few seeds. ■ *Pleasing acidity balanced with sweetness.*

RUBY, PINK, OR RED

Pink-blushed, fairly thin skin with deep red or pink flesh and few seeds. About 3½–4 inches in diameter. ■ *Sweet-tart flavor, but more acidic than pummelo or Oro Blanco. Often, the redder the color, the sweeter the taste.*

USE

Eat raw, cut in half, and scooped with spoon. Or sprinkle the cut fruit with raw sugar and broil until caramelized. Use in fruit salads, vinaigrettes, and sorbets. Can be substituted for oranges in many recipes.

NUTRITIONAL INFO

1 cup is a significant source of vitamin A and potassium; excellent source of vitamin C. Amounts of vitamin A vary according to flesh color; red and pink varieties contain higher amounts.

Oroblanco

Ruby

SERVING SUGGESTIONS

Simple sorbet: Serve sweet-tart grapefruit sorbet between courses as a refreshing palate "cleanser." Substitute grapefruit juice for lemon juice (see Meyer Lemon Sorbet, page 5)

Sauce makes fish taste sweet: Make grapefruit beurre blanc sauce to top grilled fish. Peel and segment 2 grapefruit, reserving juice. In heavy-bottomed, medium saucepan place 2 minced shallots, 1/3 cup dry white wine, 1/2 cup grapefruit juice, and 2 tablespoons white-wine vinegar; boil on medium-high heat until reduced to about 2 tablespoons. Remove from heat and stir in 1/2 cup butter (1 stick), 1 tablespoon at a time, whisking to incorporate butter. If mixture becomes too cool to incorporate butter, return briefly to heat. Chop half of grapefruit segments and stir into sauce. Season with salt and pepper; spoon over grilled fish. Garnish with grapefruit segments.

Melogold

Shrimp, avocado, and grapefruit salad: Toss 3–4 cups bite-sized lettuce with 3/4 cup cold, cooked shrimp, 1 avocado (cut in wedges), and 1 grapefruit (cut in segments). Combine 1/4 cup grapefruit juice and 3 tablespoons vegetable oil; whisk with salt and pepper to taste. Pour over salad and gently toss. Taste and adjust seasoning. Top with crumbled bacon, if desired.

Caramelized crowns: Cut grapefruit in half through "equator." Place cut side up on heavy rimmed baking sheet or broiler pan. Adjust oven rack to 6–8 inches below broiler element and preheat broiler. Sprinkle grapefruit with raw sugar. Broil until lightly browned, about 2–4 minutes.

pummelo, also pammelo, pomelo, pommelo

Picture citrus fruit that's as big as a volleyball. Pummelo are wildly popular in many Asian cuisines. Their taste can vary from tangy-tart to spicy-sweet.

Their soft rinds are 1–2 inches thick and vary in color: yellow, brownish yellow, lime green, or pink. The flesh inside also varies in color, from light yellow to deep pink. It's generally drier than grapefruit, so it can be peeled and sectioned by hand. Its drier texture helps sections hold their shape better in salads.

BUYING AND STORING

Avoid fruit that has blemishes or is soft. Skin should be shiny and shouldn't appear dried out. When pressed, fruit should feel springy. Can be stored 2–4 days at room temperature or 5–7 days in refrigerator. Juice can be frozen.

Domestic: *November–March*
Global: *None*

PREP

Remove peel by hand and divide into segments, as you would an orange. Remove membrane from each segment. Generally segments are torn into smaller pieces.

USE

Use in fruit salads or green salads. Thick peel can be candied. Can be substituted for grapefruit (see grapefruit serving suggestions).

NUTRITIONAL INFO

Good source of vitamin C and potassium.

southeast asian pummelo salad

This salad showcases the alluring sweet-sour-salty-spicy flavors that are typical of Southeast Asian cuisine. If serving as part of a buffet, line a large platter with romaine lettuce, then spoon salad on top. Garnish platter with sprigs of cilantro or mint and, if desired, place a few unpeeled rambutan off to the side for additional color (see Rambutan page 101).

1 teaspoon Asian chili paste

3 tablespoons fresh lime juice

2 teaspoons sugar

1 tablespoon fish sauce

2 tablespoons vegetable oil or canola oil

1 tablespoon chopped fresh mint

½ pound cooked shrimp, lobster, or crab

1 medium carrot, peeled, grated

1 large pummelo, peeled, membranes removed, torn into bite-size pieces

3 tablespoons chopped roasted peanuts

GARNISH: sprigs of fresh cilantro

YIELD: 4–6 SERVINGS

1. In large bowl, combine chili paste, lime juice, sugar, and fish sauce; stir to blend. Whisk in oil and mint.

2. If necessary, cut seafood into bite-size pieces. Add to dressing and marinate 10 minutes. Add carrot, pummelo and peanuts. Toss. Taste and adjust seasoning as needed. Garnish with sprigs of cilantro. Serve.

NUTRITIONAL INFORMATION (PER SERVING):
Calories 140; fat calories 63; total fat 7 grams; sat fat 0.5 grams; cholesterol 75 milligrams; sodium 320 milligrams; total carbohydrates 10 grams; fiber 3 grams; sugars 6 grams; protein 10 grams; vitamin A IUs 30%; vitamin C 45%; calcium 2%; iron 8%.

guava, feijoa

NATIVE TO BRAZIL, some guavas are rounded, some are pear-shaped, and others are elongated ovals. But it's the flesh inside the sturdy skin that is so beguiling. Cut a guava in half, and scoop the gritty goodness with a teaspoon. The floral aroma melds with sweet-sour flavors of pineapple, banana, and crab apple. Flesh color differs from one variety to the next: gray-white, yellow, pink, and red. Some are seed-filled; others aren't.

Feijoa, often called pineapple guava, isn't really a guava (although sometimes it's labeled "guava"). These elongated ovoid, dark green, slightly bumpy fruit are from an entirely different genus, but both are members of the myrtle family. The feijoa's interior has a semisoft texture and a sweet-tart taste, blending pineapple, citrus, and purple grapes.

BUYING AND STORING

Guavas and feijoas are harvested when fairly firm; they should give slightly to gentle pressure, like a ripe avocado. Ripen at room temperature, if needed. Store ripe fruit at room temperature for up to 1 week or refrigerate up to 2 weeks.

GUAVA
Domestic: *September–March*
Global: *year-round*

FEIJOA
Domestic: *April–June and October–January*
Global: *April–June*

Feijoa

Guava

PREP

Peel with paring knife, or cut in half (through the "equator"), scoop out pulp with spoon and discard shell.

USE

Guavas and feijoas are interchangeable in recipes. They can be substituted for strawberries or kiwi in recipes as well. Eat raw or use in pies, preserves, syrups, sorbets, sauces, or juices.

NUTRITIONAL INFO

1 cup is an excellent source of vitamin C; significant source of vitamins A and B_6, potassium, and niacin.

SERVING SUGGESTIONS

Saucy guavas: Peel and cut 2 guavas or feijoas into small cubes. Place in heavy, medium-sized saucepan. Add $1/2$ cup dry red wine, $1/4$ cup honey, and $1/2$ cup water. Bring to boil on high heat; reduce to low and simmer about 45 minutes. Season with salt to taste. Serve over rice, quinoa, or couscous.

Guava daiquiri: In a blender, combine 4 ripe peeled guavas or feijoas, 1 tablespoon sugar, 1 tablespoon lime juice, 1–2 ounces light rum, and 8 ice cubes. Whirl until smooth. Serve in 2 martini glasses.

Tropical quick bread: Prepare your favorite banana bread recipe, but omit bananas and substitute an equal amount of peeled, mashed, very ripe guavas or feijoas.

Garnish perfection: Arrange peeled and sliced guavas or feijoas on top of sweet-sour savory dishes, such as takeout Asian entrees like Pineapple Chicken or homemade Pineapple Ginger Beef (page 92).

horned melon

THOSE SPIKY POINTS may threaten fearful fingers, but there's nothing scary about horned melon's jelly-like interior. That ominous shell, golden yellow to bright orange, is cuttable but firm. Inside, squishy, lime-green flesh clings to edible, soft, cucumber-style seeds.

It's a member of the same large botanical family as cucumber and zucchini. The flavor is subtly sweet and slightly tart, with a hint of cucumber.

BUYING AND STORING

The more orange the shell, the riper the fruit. It is generally sold ripe and can be stored at room temperature 2–3 weeks. Look for fruit with undamaged shell and firm spikes.

Domestic: *July–April*
Global: *February–June*

PREP

For a garnish, cut in half lengthwise, then cut lengthwise again to make canoe-like wedges; or cut in half lengthwise, place cut side down and cut into ¼-inch-thick slices. To use shell as container, cut in half lengthwise and scoop out flesh and seeds with bowl of spoon; use same technique when using pulp in recipes.

USE

Use raw in salad dressings, sauces, salads, and beverages, or use as a garnish. Use shell as colorful container.

NUTRITIONAL INFO

1 cup is a good source of vitamin C.

SERVING SUGGESTIONS

Spiky boats: Use as container for fruit salad, rice dishes, or sorbet (see Prep).

Green margarita: Purée seeds and flesh in blender; strain. Use in cocktails, such as frozen margaritas. For a nonalcoholic drink, combine strained juice with sugar to taste and a squeeze of fresh lemon or lime juice. Stir until sugar dissolves. Add water and ice.

Ice cream topper: Combine pulp of 2 horned melons with pulp of 3 passion fruit; add 2 tablespoons sugar and stir until sugar dissolves. Spoon over ice cream, custard, or angel food cake.

Salad dressing: Add fresh pulp along with seeds to favorite vinaigrette dressing. Seeds add pleasing texture. For example, whisk together 1 cup extra-virgin olive oil and ⅓ cup fresh lemon juice. Whisk in 3 tablespoons horned melon pulp with seeds, plus salt and pepper to taste.

Horned Melon

jackfruit

OBLONG AND densely dotted with conical spines, jackfruit can weigh up to 80 pounds. It's considered the world's largest fruit, growing relatively low to the ground on the trunk of the jackfruit tree.

The prickly skin is bright green, but it turns yellow-brown when ripe. Inside, the flesh is bright yellow and juicy, and tastes subtly sweet. The taste is banana-like to some, while others taste a combination of mango and melon. The scent of fresh jackfruit is offensive to some. To their noses, it can smell faintly of spoiled onions. In the U.S., jackfruit is most often sold canned or dried.

It should be noted that durian is another very large tropical fruit that is covered with conical spikes. Durian spikes are sharper, and because it is hazardous to carry, it's often packaged in a mesh bag. Only sold frozen in the United States, it has a very pronounced aroma reminiscent to some of a combination of sweaty gym socks and ripe Camembert cheese. The taste is unique and difficult to pin down—perhaps a blend of grapefruit, banana, and cheese.

BUYING AND STORING

Choose jackfruit that gives to gentle pressure, without bruises or soft spots. Store at room temperature up to 7 days. Once cut, refrigerate well sealed up to 2 days.

Domestic: *none*
Global: *May–July*

PREP

Using sturdy knife cautiously cut in half through equator (if fruit is green, use rubber gloves when cutting, because fruit will exude a sticky latexlike substance). Inside, fruit is divided into bulblike chambers; only those covered with white tissue are edible. Divide into chambers, cut away tissue and remove seeds.

USE

Eaten before it ripens (light green flesh), it's starchy and requires cooking. Used like a vegetable at this stage, it can be boiled, fried, or roasted. When ripe (yellow flesh), it is consumed raw. Used like a fruit, it can be eaten out of hand or included in fruit salads with other tropical fruit.

NUTRITIONAL INFO

1 cup is a significant source of vitamins A and C.

SERVING SUGGESTIONS

Jackfruit lassi: In a blender, combine 4 ice cubes, 1½ cups plain yogurt, ¼ cup sugar, and ⅔ cup jackfruit (peeled, seeded, and diced). Whirl until smooth. Pour into 2 glasses.

Jackfruit martini sundae: Purée jackfruit (peeled, seeded, and diced) with splash of orange or banana liqueur. Spoon about 2 tablespoons into each chilled martini glass. Tilt glass to cover sides with puréed jackfruit. Add scoop of vanilla ice cream. Top each with small amount of finely diced jackfruit and drizzle with a smidgen of orange or banana liqueur. Garnish with sprig of fresh mint.

Rice pudding: Top rice pudding (or custard) with (peeled, seeded, and diced) jackfruit. Add a dollop of whipped cream and chopped pistachios.

Jackfruit salad with shrimp: To make dressing, combine 2 tablespoons brown sugar, 3 tablespoons fresh lime juice, squeeze of Asian hot sauce (to taste), 1 shallot (minced), and 3 tablespoons minced cilantro. Stir until sugar dissolves. Add 3 cups (peeled, seeded, and diced) jackfruit and 1 tablespoon (chopped) fresh mint. Gently toss, cover, and chill. Place small handfuls of mixed greens on 4 salad plates. Top with jackfruit mixture. Garnish with grilled shrimp.

Jackfruit

jujube, also chinese date

HIGHLY PRIZED in Asia, jujubes vary in size and color. Most often they look like tiny elongated apples with yellow-green skin, dappled with rust-colored splotches, about 1 to 1½ inches long. Some varieties have blood-red skin.

It would be difficult to take a secret bite. Its smooth, shiny surface makes a loud crackling sound when ruptured. Inside, the crunchy, greenish-white flesh is spongy, neither as dense as an apple nor as juicy. The taste is unique, slightly astringent and not very sweet. At the heart is a small, inedible pit.

They have limited availability fresh, but are sold dried in Asian markets, often labeled "Chinese dates" or "red dates." When dried, they are sugared, and are about the size of a small olive.

Jujube

BUYING AND STORING

Look for firm fruit without soft spots, cracks, or bruises. Avoid those with shriveled skin. Refrigerate in bowl up to 2 weeks.

Domestic: *July–October*
Global: *none*

PREP

Eat raw out of hand, avoiding inedible pit. Both skin and flesh are edible. If cooking (except when stewing whole), remove pit. Cut in half from top to bottom. Twist in opposite directions and pull apart. Pit will probably be attached to one side; cut that side in half from top to bottom. Pit will probably still be attached to one quarter. Use a paring knife to cut around pit.

USE

Eat raw or cooked. Use raw in salads and relishes. Can be sautéed or stewed.

NUTRITIONAL INFO

1 cup is an excellent source of vitamin C.

SERVING SUGGESTIONS

Fruit salad bonanza: Line salad plates with peeled orange slices. Toss pitted, thin jujube wedges (not peeled) with enough vinaigrette to lightly coat fruit (½ vegetable oil whisked into 3 tablespoons cider vinegar, 2 tablespoons minced fresh mint, and garlic salt to taste). Mount jujube mixture in center of oranges. Garnish with fresh mint sprigs and candied nuts.

Slow-cooked breakfast: Just before bedtime, put jujubes and the following ingredients in slow-cooker. By morning your house will be scented with cinnamon and warm, stewed jujubes. Pour ½ cup apple juice in slow-cooker. In small bowl, stir 1½ tablespoons sugar and 1 teaspoon Chinese five-spice powder. Stir into apple juice, reserving ½ teaspoon. Add 12 whole jujubes. Cover and cook on low setting for 6–8 hours. Serve warm, topped with yogurt and sprinkled with reserved sugar mixture. Watch out for pits.

Sugared, sautéed, and served with cheese: Remove pits from 8 jujubes, and cut each into 8 wedges (do not peel). In large, deep skillet, melt 4 tablespoons butter on medium-high heat. Add jujube wedges and sprinkle with 3 tablespoons sugar. When one side is nicely caramelized, toss and brown opposite side. Remove with slotted spoon, and place on 4 dessert plates next to small wedges of creamy blue cheese (such as Gorgonzola). Serve as dessert.

kiwi, also kiwifruit, chinese gooseberry

BABY

GREEN

GOLD

BENEATH THE deceptive, fuzzy brown skin, a delicate, sweet-tart treasure awaits. Kiwi's interior is filled with alluring colors: either bright lime green or brilliant gold flesh is speckled with a ring of tiny edible black seeds that surround a soft, yellowish-white core. The oblong-shaped fruit is juicy and tender, a pleasing blend of strawberry, pineapple, and sweet ripe melon. And although the flesh is soft, it is firm enough to hold up to slicing.

Native to China, kiwis were called Chinese gooseberries by Westerners until New Zealand developed their commercial production and renamed them after their fuzzy national bird.

Standard green or gold kiwis are about 2 to 3 inches long, while the baby variety are only about an inch long and have green flesh. Gold kiwi have smoother skin and a milder, more honeyed flavor profile than green kiwi. Babies are fuzzless and eaten whole, unpeeled. They are eaten slightly firmer than larger kiwi.

BUYING AND STORING

Look for fruit with unbroken skin that gives slightly to gentle pressure and has a fragrant scent; avoid mushy and soft kiwi. If necessary, ripen at room temperature 2–3 days, until fruit gives to gentle pressure. Ripening time can be shortened by placing in loosely sealed paper bag with an apple, banana, or pear at room temperature. Refrigerate ripe kiwi (unwashed and unpeeled) in crisper drawer 3–5 days.

BABY KIWI
Domestic: *September–October*
Global: *January–February*

GREEN KIWI
Domestic: *October–March*
Global: *March–October*

GOLD KIWI
Domestic: *none*
Global: *June–November*

PREP

Wash with cold water. Kiwi skin is almost paper thin (except on very large fruit) and can be eaten. But when fuzzy, the skin can be unappealing to some. To peel, cut off ends, then use paring knife or vegetable peeler to remove skin, or cut in half lengthwise and scoop out flesh with spoon. Baby kiwi are generally eaten whole, like grapes.

USE

Kiwi is generally eaten raw. Use puréed kiwi to make sorbet or icy cocktails, such as margaritas. Use as garnish on tarts, cakes, and sundaes, or crème brûlée or chicken salad. Include in fruit salsa, fruit salads, or eat, as is, as a snack. Kiwi contains an enzyme that prevents gelatin from setting (so forget the idea of molded kiwi gelatin). That enzyme has beneficial effects when it comes to tenderizing meat. To increase meat tenderness, cut kiwi in half lengthwise and rub over uncooked meat; discard kiwi and let meat stand 20–30 minutes before cooking.

NUTRITIONAL INFO

1 cup is an excellent source of vitamins C and K; significant source of folate and potassium.

SERVING SUGGESTIONS

Kiwi sauce: Make simple syrup by combining 2 cups water and 1½ cups sugar in saucepan. Bring to boil and lower heat to medium. Simmer 2 minutes. Cool. Purée 4 ripe, peeled kiwi (not baby kiwi) with 4 tablespoons sugar and

3 tablespoons simple syrup in blender or food processor fitted with metal blade. Leftover syrup can be refrigerated, well-sealed, for 3 months. Spoon over ice cream, yogurt, or angel food cake. Or place 1 to 2 tablespoons in a martini glass. Tilt glass to cover all sides with kiwi sauce. Scoop warm rice pudding into glass and serve immediately, garnished with a fresh sprig of mint.

Kiwi bruschetta: Top thin, toasted slice of rustic bread with thinly sliced tomato and fresh mozzarella and sliced and peeled kiwi. If desired, drizzle with a little balsamic vinegar.

Good morning sunshine: Peel and slice kiwi on your breakfast cereal.

Chocolate fondue dippers: Along with strawberries, orange segments, and chunks of pound cake, serve thick slices of peeled kiwi to dip into warm chocolate fondue.

Gold Kiwi

Green Kiwi

Baby Kiwi

kumquat

THESE BEAUTIFUL ORBS look like tiny round or oval oranges, about 1 to 2 inches long. The entire kumquat is edible: sweet rind, tart interior, and small seeds. If eating whole, first roll fruit gently between palms to release fragrant oils.

Thought of as a symbol of prosperity in China, it's a frequent gift during the Asian New Year season. The name kumquat translates from Cantonese as "golden orange." Indeed, the color is spectacular, but the flavor and fragrance are irresistible, too.

BUYING AND STORING

Look for fruit that is shiny with good color. Avoid those with blemishes or soft spots. Store in cool location up to 7 days, or refrigerate unwashed, wrapped in plastic, in crisper drawer up to 2 weeks.

Domestic: *November–July*
Global: *none*

PREP

Wash and dry just before using. Do not peel. Can be eaten raw, either whole, sliced, halved, or chopped. Larger seeds can be plucked out using knife tip and discarded, if preferred; ignore smaller white seeds.

USE

Eat raw whole, or slice and add to a green or fruit salad, or use as garnish. Poach, sauté, bake, boil, or simmer. Candy them in simple syrup or juice mixtures; team with fish, pork, or game; use in marmalade or relish.

NUTRITIONAL INFO

1 tablespoon is a good source of vitamin C.

Kumquat

SERVING SUGGESTIONS

Candied kumquat topping: Cut about 24 kumquats into crosswise, 1/8-inch slices and remove large seeds (see Prep). Place in large saucepan; add 2 cups apricot nectar and 1/2 cup sugar. Bring to boil on high heat; reduce heat and simmer, covered, 5 minutes. Remove fruit with slotted spoon and set aside. Boil mixture uncovered for 15 minutes or until thick. Remove from heat and cautiously add 2 tablespoons orange juice or orange liqueur and kumquats. Stir and spoon over angel food cake, pudding, or pound cake. Or cool and serve over ice cream or chocolate sorbet.

Chocolate dipped: Wash and thoroughly dry whole kumquats. Place coating chocolate (often sold in produce section next to strawberries) in saucepan. Heat chocolate just enough to melt; it shouldn't be hot, just warm. Dip 1 side of kumquat in chocolate and place on waxed paper to harden chocolate.

Kumquats with pears: Cut 15 kumquats into 1/8-inch-thick slices and remove large seeds. Place in large saucepan; add 1/2 cup sugar and 3/4 cup apricot nectar. Bring to boil on high heat; reduce heat to medium and simmer 3–5 minutes. Remove from heat and add 1/8 teaspoon minced lime zest (colored part of peel). Slice 3 fresh, ripe, peeled, and cored pears; place in 6 heat-proof bowls. Top with kumquats and poaching liquid. Garnish with fresh mint sprigs. Accompany with cookies, if desired.

fillet of salmon with squash and kumquats

Kumquats make a delicious sweet-tart accompaniment to salmon. These tasty foil-wrapped packets bake just long enough to perfectly steam the fish and crookneck squash. If you prefer, other fish can be used in this recipe, such as halibut, red snapper or cod. Or if chicken sounds more appealing, substitute chicken tenders.

1 (1 1/2-pound) center-cut salmon fillet, pin bones and skin removed, cut crosswise into 4 equal pieces

Salt and freshly black ground pepper to taste

Aluminum foil

1/4 cup extra-virgin olive oil, divided use

1 large onion, chopped

1 large clove garlic, minced

6 kumquats: 2 cut into 1/8-inch slices, large seeds removed, 4 finely chopped by hand, divided use

2 to 3 yellow crookneck squash, trimmed, cut in 1/2-inch slices

1 1/2 tablespoons sliced fresh chives or thinly sliced green onion

GARNISH: chopped Italian parsley

YIELD: 4 SERVINGS

1. Adjust oven rack to middle position. Preheat oven to 425 degrees.

2. Each salmon piece will probably be thinner at 1 end. Fold thin portion under to create a similar thickness all the way across (this won't be necessary if flap has been trimmed at market). Season with salt and pepper.

3. Tear 4 squares of aluminum foil, about 18 by 18 inches. Place 1 piece salmon in center of each.

4. In medium, heavy-bottomed skillet, heat 1 tablespoon oil on medium-high heat. Add onion and cook, stirring frequently, until nicely browned. Add garlic, half of sliced kumquats and squash; cook 2–3 minutes, stirring frequently. Season with salt and pepper. Spoon over salmon, dividing among 4 servings. Seal packets, scrunching sides together, and place on baking sheet with sides. Bake 10–12 minutes.

5. Meanwhile, prepare relish. In small bowl, combine remaining oil, finely chopped kumquats, and chives. Stir to blend. Season to taste with salt and pepper. When packets have finished baking, open and slide contents of each packet onto dinner plate. Spoon relish on top of each serving and top with parsley. Garnish with remaining kumquat slices.

NUTRITIONAL INFORMATION (PER SERVING):
Calories 490; fat calories 252; total fat 28 grams; sat fat 4 grams; cholesterol 120 milligrams; sodium 690 milligrams; total carbohydrates 12 grams; fiber 4 grams; sugars 4 grams; protein 45 grams; vitamin A IUs 8%; vitamin C 40%; calcium 8%; iron 15%.

lemon, lime, kaffir leaf

EUREKA LEMON

LISBON LEMON

MEYER LEMON

KEY LIME, MEXICAN LIME

PERSIAN LIME

LEMONS AND LIMES are culinary love gifts. Their tangy juice and fleshy pulp can turn dreary into delectable, bringing flavor balance to everything from apple pie to simple vinaigrette. Added to water, the juice of lemons or limes can prevent cut fruit or vegetables (such as potatoes or apples) from discoloration. And, when they're combined with sugar, their just-right acidity is the foundation of many irresistible desserts.

Even their skin offers a prize. The zest, the outside colored portion of the peel, is filled with flavorful oils. Removed to avoid the bitter white pith below (see Zester, page 309), lemon or lime zest is an essential ingredient in many ice creams, pies, and sauces.

lemon

Lemons fall into two categories: super-sour and semisweet. Eureka and Lisbon are the two most common varieties of very tart lemons. Their bright yellow, medium-thick skins are pebbly rough, and their flesh and juice is highly acidic. Meyer lemons have a sweet, tangerine-like scent and low acidity. Often they are juicier than Eureka or Lisbon lemons. They are a hybrid (between a tart lemon and a sweet orange) brought from China to the United States in 1908 by Frank Meyer. Their rinds are smooth and fairly thin, sometimes with a subtle orange blush. Because of their sweeter flavor, pastry chefs generally use less sugar when baking with Meyer lemons.

BUYING AND STORING

Look for fruit that has brightly colored skin with no tinge of green and that feel heavy for their size. Refrigerate in plastic bag for 2–3 weeks or at room temperature for up to 1 week.

EUREKA AND LISBON
Domestic: *year round*
Global: *none*

MEYER
Domestic: *October–May*
Global: *none*

PREP

If using zest, remove it before cutting lemon (see Zesters, page 309). When juicing, for best results, first bring lemons to room temperature or heat for 10 seconds in microwave. Or, roll on counter, pressing down with palm, to help break up segments. Lemons can be cut into lovely garnishes (see Strippers, page 309).

USE

Use minced zest, juice, or both in sauces, soups, and salad dressings, and desserts, beverages, and entrées. Whole lemons can be preserved in salt and olive oil, then used in Moroccan dishes. Lemon peel can be candied and used to garnish both sweet and savory dishes.

Meyer Lemon

Persian Lime

Eureka Lemon

Kaffir Leaf

Key Lime

NUTRITIONAL INFO

1 cup without peel is an excellent source of vitamin C; lemon juice loses its vitamin power soon after squeezing.

SERVING SUGGESTIONS

On the rocks: Combine lemon juice with another juice to make a tangy drink. Use half lemon juice and half pineapple, orange, strawberry, or pomegranate juice.

Gremolata glamour: Make a gremolata garnish by combining minced fresh parsley, minced lemon zest, and minced garlic. Sprinkle on osso buco, roast chicken, or pork chops.

Lemon Curd: This creamy mixture can be spread on pound cake, cookies, cake, or tart shells. In top of double boiler, whisk ½ cup Meyer lemon juice, 2 teaspoons minced lemon zest, ½ cup sugar, and 2 large eggs. Place over simmering water; whisk until thickened and smooth (or 175 degrees), stirring constantly. Strain and cover with plastic wrap; refrigerate up to 1 week.

Simple but splendid greens: Meyer lemon juice adds the perfect acidity to salad. Place mixed greens in large bowl. Toss with enough extra-virgin olive oil to lightly coat leaves. Sqeeze half Meyer lemon on top and toss; taste and add more juice, as needed. Season with freshly ground black pepper and garlic salt.

lime
The thin, shiny green rind of Persian limes encases pale, yellowish-green, seedless flesh. Sometimes these limes are referred to as "common limes." Left to ripen on the tree, these, as well as most lime varieties, become yellow. The high-acid juice is plentiful, and although it seems just as sour as the juice of a Eureka lemon, it is more aromatic, with subtle peppery overtones.

Key limes, sometimes called Mexican limes, have smooth, thin rinds that are greenish yellow. They're smaller than Persian limes, and rounder. They are intensely aromatic and very juicy. Sometimes they're called "bartender's limes," because they are so delicious in gin and tonics or margaritas.

BUYING AND STORING

Avoid limes that are hard or shriveled or that appear dry. Look for fruit that is heavy for its size. Store Persian limes in refrigerator in plastic bag up to 2 weeks. Store Key limes at room temperature until ripe, then refrigerate up to 2 weeks.

Domestic: *October–March*
Global: *year round*

Persian Lime

Key Lime

Kaffir Leaf

PREP

Same as lemons.

USE

Use minced zest, juice, or both in sauces, soups, and salad dressings and in desserts, cocktails, and entrées. Use to "cook" seafood in ceviche. Squeeze on papaya or honeydew melon to perk up flavor.

NUTRITIONAL INFO

1 cup is a good source of vitamin C.

SERVING SUGGESTIONS

Better butter: Stir lime juice into softened butter. Add a little finely minced serrano chile if you want it spicy. Roll into cylinder in waxed paper and refrigerate. Cut small coins of lime butter and place on top of broiled fish, poultry, or cooked vegetables.

Tropical topper: Make a tangy topping for ice cream or rice pudding by stirring 2 tablespoons lime juice, 1 teaspoon minced lime zest, 2 tablespoons sugar, and a good splash of rum until sugar dissolves. Add 2 diced ripe mangoes and toss.

Southeast Asian soup: Perk up chicken soup by adding a generous amount of lime juice, a little sugar, and a smidgen of Asian hot sauce. Garnish with chopped cilantro.

kaffir lime leaf

Although the kaffir lime tree bears small, bumpy limes, it's the uniquely shaped leaves that are most used for cooking, especially in Thai cuisine. The leaves look like two leaves joined end to end and have an alluring, flowery citrus aroma. When cooked in broths or sauces, the leaf permeates the dish with its perfume. Kaffir leaves are sold fresh or dried in Asian markets and super-markets with large Asian specialty sections.

Domestic: *year round*
Global: *none*

meyer lemon sorbet

This tangy sorbet can be served between courses as a "palate cleanser" or as dessert. The Meyer lemon juice gives it a subtle orange scent. If you don't have Meyer lemons, substitute $2/3$ cup freshly squeezed lemon juice and $1/3$ cup freshly squeezed tangerine or orange juice.

1$1/2$ cups chilled simple syrup (see Cook's Notes)

1 cup fresh Meyer lemon juice

1 tablespoon finely minced Meyer lemon zest, colored part of peel

OPTIONAL GARNISH: sprigs of fresh mint

YIELD: 2$1/2$ CUPS, ABOUT 4 SERVINGS

COOK'S NOTES: To prepare simple syrup, combine 1$1/2$ cups water and 1$1/2$ cups sugar in medium saucepan. Bring to boil on high heat; reduce to medium-low and simmer 3–4 minutes or until sugar is completely dissolved. Cool. Leftover syrup can be stored airtight in refrigerator at least 3 months.

1. Combine 1½ cups syrup with juice and zest; pour into bowl of ice cream machine. Freeze according to manufacturer's instructions. If desired, garnish each serving with mint sprig.

NUTRITIONAL INFORMATION (PER SERVING):
Calories 210; fat calories 0; total fat 0 grams; sat fat 0 grams; cholesterol 0 milligrams; sodium 0 milligrams; total carbohydrates 55 grams; fiber 0 grams; sugars 51 grams; protein 0 grams; vitamin A IUs 0%; vitamin C 50%; calcium 0%; iron 0%.

key lime and pistachio parfaits

Alternate layers of tangy Key lime filling and crunchy, sweet graham cracker crumbs. These showy parfaits can be prepared as much as 5 hours ahead and chilled.

⅓ cup shelled pistachios

3 tablespoons butter

2½ tablespoons sugar

½ cup graham cracker crumbs

1 (14-ounce) can sweetened condensed milk

1½ tablespoons minced Key lime zest, colored portion of peel (see Cook's Notes)

½ cup fresh Key lime juice

¾ cup chilled heavy whipping cream

YIELD: 6 SERVINGS

COOK'S NOTES: Remove zest from limes before squeezing juice.

1. Roughly chop pistachios and place on baking sheet. Place in 350-degree oven for 2–4 minutes, or until lightly toasted. Watch carefully because nuts burn easily. Set aside.

2. Melt butter in small skillet on medium-high heat. Add sugar and graham cracker crumbs. Cook, stirring constantly, until crumbs brown nicely, about 3–4 minutes. Remove mixture from skillet and place on plate or in bowl. Cool.

3. In large bowl, stir together sweetened condensed milk, zest, and juice until well-combined; mixture will thicken. Set aside.

4. In large bowl of electric mixer, beat whipping cream until stiff. Fold whipped cream into lime mixture.

5. Place 6 wine glasses on counter. Standard white-wine glasses work well; avoid glasses with small mouths, such as Champagne flutes. Add nuts to graham cracker mixture and toss. Place about ¼ cup of lime mixture in each glass. Top each with a generous tablespoon of crumb mixture, sprinkling it so that it covers evenly. Top each with another ¼ cup of lime mixture; to create even tops, quickly shake glasses side to side a couple of times. Top with remaining crumbs and refrigerate at least 2 hours.

NUTRITIONAL INFORMATION (PER SERVING):
Calories 460; fat calories 234; total fat 26 grams; sat fat 15 grams; cholesterol 80 milligrams; sodium 140 milligrams; total carbohydrates 51 grams; fiber 1 gram; sugars 45 grams; protein 8 grams; vitamin A IUs 15%; vitamin C 15%; calcium 20%; iron 4%.

limequat

LIMEQUATS have an oval shape that is similar to most kumquats. Slightly larger than a big red grape, they have thin, yellow-green skin and bittersweet flesh. Developed in 1909, the limequat is a cross between a Key lime and a kumquat. The entire fruit may be eaten; the skin has a slightly sweet edge, while the flesh inside has a Key lime flavor and is dotted with tiny edible seeds.

Limequat

BUYING AND STORING

Look for firm fruit with a rich citrus scent. Avoid those with soft spots or discoloration. Store at room temperature up to 1 week, or refrigerate in crisper drawer up to 3 weeks.

Domestic: *July–November*
Global: *none*

PREP

Wash thoroughly. Use whole, sliced, or quartered. Seeds are edible, but they can be removed by cutting fruit in half, quarters, or slices; pluck out seeds using pointed tip of paring knife.

USE

Can be eaten out of hand, but limequats are most often used either as garnish or in marmalade. Add zest to baked goods, seafood salads, or relishes (see Zesting, page xx).

NUTRITIONAL INFO

1 cup is a good source of vitamin C.

SERVING SUGGESTIONS

Fancy gin and tonic cocktail: Add a squeeze of limequat to a gin and tonic. For garnish, skewer 2 limequat halves on cocktail pick and add to drink.

Limequat cubes: Use limequat ice cubes in cocktails, sodas, or iced teas. Place a thin limequat slice in each pocket of ice cube tray; fill with water and freeze.

Cranberry-limequat relish: Using food processor fitted with metal blade, pulse 12 ounces fresh cranberries until coarsely chopped; place in bowl. Add 12 halved, seeded limequats (see Prep) to processor; pulse until finely chopped; add to cranberries. Add 1 cup sugar and 1/3 cup minced crystallized ginger; stir until sugar dissolves. Refrigerate at least 5 hours and up to 1 week, covered.

Candied dandies: Place 1 cup water and 1 cup sugar in large saucepan; bring to boil on high heat; reduce heat and simmer 2 minutes. Add 3 cups halved and seeded limequats; simmer about 10 minutes or until tender. Using slotted spoon, transfer limequats to heat-proof bowl. Reduce syrup to 1/2 cup, boiling about 6 minutes. Pour over limequats and cool. Spoon over ice cream, cheesecake, or pudding.

Key lime pie glamour: Trim ends off limequats and discard. Cut into thin, crosswise slices. Garnish top of Key lime pie or lemon tart.

longan

NO WONDER it's dubbed "dragon's eye" in China. Whether it is spherical or ovoid, longan's translucent, grayish-white flesh has a peeled-grape, eyeball-like appearance. In the center lies a smooth, jet-black seed.

Use a thumbnail to crack open its easy-to-peel brown shell. The peeled fruit inside is small enough to fit easily in grown-up mouths. Munch around the inedible seed, relishing the flesh for its mild, lychee-like flavor that's sweeter than rambutan or lychee. It has a tropical flavor, and it's juicy, with both musky and floral aromas.

BUYING AND STORING
Look for fruit without cracks that feel heavy for their size. To store, leave in shells. Wrap in paper towels to absorb excess moisture, then enclose in perforated plastic bag; refrigerate 2–3 weeks (although some flavor loss will occur with long storage). Longan can also be frozen in airtight containers up to 3 months. For best texture, eat frozen longans partially thawed. When totally thawed, texture can be squishy.

Domestic: *October–May*
Global: *none*

PREP

Use either a small knife or thumbnail to open shell; fruit will pop out easily. If eating out of hand, pop into mouth and eat around seed. To remove seed, use scissor-style cherry pitter (see Pitters, page 309) or cut in half with small knife and cut out seed.

USE

Eat raw out of hand, or use in fruit salads or sweet-and-sour dishes, rice dishes, or stir-fries. Can be dried or preserved in simple syrup (see page 51).

NUTRITIONAL INFO

3 longans are a significant source of vitamin C.

SERVING SUGGESTIONS

Ice cream topper: Poach longans in simple syrup (2 cups water simmered with 1½ cups sugar until sugar dissolves). Add peeled and pitted longans; gently simmer 3 to 5 minutes. Remove from heat. Cool. Spoon over ice cream, yogurt, or pudding.

Fruit salad supreme: Combine peeled and pitted longans with fresh berries and mint.

Sweet-and-sour dishes: Add peeled and pitted longans to sweet-and-sour chicken or pork. Use as garnish on Pineapple Ginger Beef (see page 92).

Substitutions: Use as a substitute in recipes calling for lychees.

Longan

loquat, also mayapple, japanese plum, japanese medlar

WITH EDIBLE ORANGE SKIN and juicy flesh, loquats look like teardrop-shaped apricots. The core is filled with large and shiny mahogany-colored seeds that are inedible but easy to remove. The heavenly taste is a sweet-sour blend of apricot, cherry, and tart plum flavors; their aroma is a blend of apricot, banana, and damp grapes.

Native to China, loquats have been cultivated in Japan for thousands of years. They are also grown in Europe, Central America, Israel, India, and the United States (mostly in California, Florida, and Hawaii).

Loquat

BUYING AND STORING

Loquats bruise easily and are highly perishable. Choose smooth-skinned, tender-ripe fruit; don't worry if there are small brown spots on the skin. They are sold fresh in some supermarkets with large specialty produce sections and at some farmers markets in California and Florida. At Asian markets, they are available canned and dried.

If ripe, store in refrigerator in single layer up to 1 week. Cooked loquats can be frozen up to 3 months.

Domestic: *April–June*
Global: *November–December*

PREP

To eat out of hand, loquats can be peeled or eaten with skin on. To peel, use a small paring knife to cut away the thin layer of skin. To remove seeds, cut in half horizontally (around the "equator"); open and pop seeds out. To cook, peel and remove seeds as noted.

USE

Eat raw out of hand, or poach peeled and quartered fruit. Loquats are delicious in jams or purées and used as a coulis sauce to accompany desserts (see Raspberry Coulis, page 16).

NUTRITIONAL INFO

1 cup is an excellent source of vitamin A; good source of potassium.

SERVING SUGGESTIONS

Tropical compote: Poach ¾ cup peeled and quartered loquats in simmering mixture of 1 cup water, ½ cup sugar, and 2 tablespoons lemon juice until tender, about 5 minutes. Cool; stir in fresh berries and, if desired, lychees. Serve as is or top with a dollop of vanilla yogurt, or serve with ice cream.

Mango tango salsa: Add more tropical zing to mango salsa by adding diced loquats. Combine 2 cups (peeled) diced mango, 1 cup (peeled) diced loquats, ¼ cup diced red onion, ½–1 teaspoon minced jalapeño (fresh or pickled), 1 tablespoon lime juice, and 1 tablespoon minced fresh mint or cilantro; toss. Add salt and pepper to taste, and serve over grilled fish, pork, or chicken.

Rainbow fruit salad: Combine raw peeled and sliced loquats with sliced strawberries, peeled and sliced kiwi, and peeled lychees.

Cucumber-loquat salad: Combine 1 hothouse cucumber (peeled, cut in half lengthwise, seeded, and sliced), 1 cup (peeled, seeded, and sliced) loquats, 3 (trimmed and sliced) green onions (include part of dark green stalk), 2 tablespoons orange juice, 1 teaspoon rice vinegar, and 1 tablespoon extra-virgin olive oil. Toss and season with salt and pepper. Serve as an accompaniment to spicy grilled meat or fish.

lychee, also litchi, litchi nut, lichee

GREEN
RED

ITS SPINY BUMPS make the shell look impenetrable, but all it takes is a hungry push of a thumbnail to reach the fragrant, white-gray orb inside. Peel away just enough to expose one juicy end, then squeeze into open mouth. About the size and shape of a peeled grape, the lychee has an alluring fragrance that is rose-like, and a taste that is a blend of supersweet cherry and banana. Hidden inside, there's an inedible, glossy brown seed.

Lychees have been one of China's most prized fruits for more than 2,000 years. Because of its delectable flavor profile, it steals the show whether eaten raw on its own, included in fruit salad, or incorporated in cooked dishes.

BUYING AND STORING

The freshest lychees have vibrant rust-red shells about 1–2 inches long. Some prefer the sweetness of those mottled with brown patches; this color change occurs several days after harvesting. They are best if they feel heavy for their size. Avoid any with splits or wrinkles. Refrigerate in plastic bags 7–10 days; freeze up to 3 months. Long-term freezing (over 4 hours) changes the lychee's texture and reduces its fragrance, but it is still delicious.
Domestic: *May–June*
Global: *May–September*

PREP

Press near one end to break shell, then peel to expose one end; pinch remaining shell to pop lychee from shell. If small or medium-sized, use scissor-style cherry pitter to remove seed (see Pitters, page 309). Or cut in half with small knife and cut out seed.

USE

Eat raw out of hand or in fruit salads. Or add to creamy chicken or rice dishes near the end of cooking.

NUTRITIONAL INFO

Good source of vitamin C and potassium.

SERVING SUGGESTIONS

Sorbet peeled from the shell: Freeze lychees in shell for 3–4 hours. Let sit at room temperature about 10 minutes and serve. Freezing a short period creates a sorbet-like consistency that's irresistible.

Fruit salad: Add pitted lychee to favorite fruit salad recipe. Blackberries, strawberries, and lychees are a great combination.

Lychee-sake martini: Spear seeded lychee with toothpick or cocktail pick and use as garnish for a sake martini. Fill cocktail shaker with cracked ice. Add 1½ ounces vodka and ½ ounce sake; cover and shake vigorously, then strain into martini glass; garnish with lychees (peel and pit over glass, allowing any juice to fall in).

Tropical fruit tart: Fill baked, cooled pastry shell with vanilla custard or pudding. Top with concentric rings of lychees, strawberries, and kiwi slices. To glaze, brush with a little melted apricot jelly; if too thick, stir in small amount of water or dry white wine.

lychee and crystallized ginger salsa

This salsa has an addictive taste that combines sweet, sour, and spicy flavors. Serve it spooned over grilled fish or chicken or as a dip with tortilla chips. Rambutan or longan can be substituted for lychee.

1 pound fresh lychees, peeled, halved, and seeded

½ yellow bell pepper, cored, seeded, and finely diced

½ red bell pepper, cored, seeded, and finely diced

1 fresh jalapeño chile, seeded and minced (see Cook's Notes)

3 green onions, trimmed, finely chopped, including ½ of dark green stalks

3 tablespoons fresh lime juice

1 tablespoon finely chopped crystallized ginger (see Cook's Notes)

1 tablespoon sugar

Salt to taste

YIELD: ABOUT 2 CUPS

COOK'S NOTES: Use caution when working with fresh chiles. Wash hands and work surface thoroughly upon completion; do NOT touch face or eyes. Crystallized ginger (or candied ginger) has been cooked in sugar syrup and coated with coarse sugar. Look for it in small cellophane packets in the produce section or the Asian specialty section of the supermarket.

1. Chop lychees. Combine all ingredients in medium mixing bowl. Gently toss to combine. Taste and add more salt if necessary. Can be made 24 hours ahead and stored in airtight container in refrigerator.

NUTRITIONAL INFORMATION (PER 2 TABLESPOONS): Calories 25; fat calories 0; total fat 0 grams; sat fat 0 grams; cholesterol 0 milligrams; sodium 75 milligrams; total carbohydrates 7 grams; fiber less than 1 gram; sugars 5 grams; protein 0 grams; vitamin A IUs 2%; vitamin C 50%; calcium 0%; iron 0%.

Lychee

mango

ATAULFO
HADEN
KEITT
KENT
TOMMY ATKINS

THE SOFT FLESH of a ripe mango is an alluring blend of pineapple and tree-ripened peach, but it's sweeter and more exotic. The scent is enticing, too; a blend of pine forest and tropical jungle. No wonder it is the most widely consumed fruit in the world.

There are hundreds of varieties that range in size, shape, and color. Commercially grown varieties include oval, almost-round, and kidney-shaped mangos. Skin color varies; it can be green, yellow, or red. They can weigh as little as 6 ounces or as much as 26 ounces.

Green, unripened mangos are sold in Asian markets. In Southeast Asian cuisines, they are used shredded into salads dressed with tangy dressing.

BUYING AND STORING

Look for ripe fruit that yields to light pressure, but don't squeeze the Kent variety, as it is very soft. Avoid those with loose or shriveled skin. If necessary, ripen at room temperature for 1–3 days. Or place 2 or more mangoes in loosely sealed paper bag. When ripe, refrigerate in plastic bag up to 3 days.

ATAULFO, HADEN, KENT, TOMMY ATKINS
Domestic: *none*
Global: *year-round*

KEITT
Domestic: *July–October*
Global: *year-round*

PREP

Mangoes should always be peeled (some people have an allergic reaction when they eat the skin). The easiest way to peel it is to first dice it. Hold mango on work surface with stem end pointing up. Notice that it is elliptical when viewed from the top. Using

sharp knife, make a vertical slice along one of the long sides, about 3/8 inch from stem. If you hit the seed, move knife over a little and try again. Make a second slice on other side, about 3/8 inch from stem. The long seed is in the center slice left behind. Place a double layer of clean kitchen towel in your hand. Place one of the seed-free "halves" cut side up in towel-lined hand. Using small, sharp knife, make parallel diagonal slices across mango about 3/4 inch apart, taking care not to slice through peel. Make second set of slices in opposite direction. Push up the center of the slice on skin side to expose small mango

chunks. Run knife just above mango skin to slice away chunks. Repeat with other "half." Peel center slice that contains seed. Cut 2 long strips from either side of mango seed and dice.

USE

Eat raw or cooked (seed and skin should not be eaten). Eat raw, out of hand, or use in sorbet, cocktails, smoothies, and fruit salads. To cook, include in sweet or savory rice dishes and pork dishes.

NUTRITIONAL INFO

1 cup provides an excellent source of vitamin C, a good source of vitamin A, and a significant source of vitamin B_6.

Tommy Atkins

Ataulfo

ATAULFO
(baby, Mexican, mini, and Champagne)
Small, kidney-shaped with greenish-yellow to deep golden skin. About 6–12 ounces. ■ *Very sweet and rich in flavor. Not fibrous.*

HADEN
Large, oval, with yellow or green skin with red blush. About 16–24 ounces. ■ *Sweet and mildly flavored. Moderately fibrous.*

KEITT
Very large oval (with noselike protuberance at tip) with red and yellow patches. About 20–26 ounces. ■ *Firm, sweet flesh. Minimal fiber.*

KENT
Very large oval with greenish-yellow skin and red shoulders. About 20–26 ounces. ■ *Very rich and very sweet. Soft, butterlike texture is not fibrous.*

TOMMY ATKINS
Medium-sized, oval. Skin is yellowish-orange with deep red blush. About 12–24 ounces. ■ *Sweet and juicy. Can be more fibrous than other varieties.*

SERVING SUGGESTIONS

Easy "sorbet": Partially freeze 2 cups peeled and diced mango (about 3 hours in freezer). Place mango in blender or food processor with 8 ounces cold nonfat vanilla yogurt, ¼ teaspoon fresh lime juice and, if desired, a pinch of sugar. Pulse until coarsely puréed. Serve garnished with fresh mint.

Mango salsa: Combine 2 cups finely diced mango with 1 tablespoon chopped cilantro, ½ minced jalapeño (seeded), juice of 1 lime, and salt to taste. Gently toss with ¼ cup finely diced red onion and, if desired, a splash of orange juice. Add a little minced fresh ginger, if desired. Use with grilled poultry, pork, or seafood, or toss with cooked rice, couscous, or other grains. Refrigerate and use within 24 hours.

Prosciutto wraps: Make appetizers by wrapping mango wedges with prosciutto. Secure with toothpicks and place on serving dish. Sprinkle with squeeze of fresh lime juice and, if desired, a little finely chopped cilantro.

Cobblers, crumbles, and rice desserts: Include diced mango in traditional baked dishes; mango teamed with blackberries is a delectable combination. Or combine with cooked glutinous rice, coconut milk, and sugar to make a Thai sweet-rice dessert.

mango roast pork loin

Roast pork and fresh mango make a luscious combination. In this dish, a pork loin cooks under a blanket of mango chutney, while a shallow mixture of pineapple and juice scented with curry powder simmers around the base. It's served with diced fresh mango that has been tossed with fresh ginger and cilantro.

2 tablespoons butter

2 tablespoon vegetable oil or canola oil

1 tablespoon curry powder

4 cups diced fresh pineapple

1 cup pineapple juice

1 cup chicken broth

1 (3½-pound) boneless pork loin

Salt and pepper to taste

⅔ cup prepared mango chutney

OPTIONAL: Curry-Pineapple Rice (see Cook's Notes)

MANGO GARNISH: 2 fresh mangoes, peeled and diced (or sliced) and tossed with 1 tablespoon minced fresh ginger and 1 tablespoon minced cilantro

OPTIONAL: Additional mango chutney

YIELD: 8 SERVINGS

COOK'S NOTES: To prepare rice, place 1 cup juice-broth mixture (see Step 3) and 3 cups water in large saucepan. Add pinch of salt. Bring to boil. Add 2 cups long-grain rice, cover, and reduce heat to low. Simmer, covered, 18 minutes. If any liquid remains, cook a few more minutes. Remove lid and fluff with fork. If desired, stir in some pineapple wedges that cooked with pork.

1. Preheat oven to 350 degrees. Place butter, oil, and curry powder in large, deep skillet. Cook over medium heat 3 minutes, stirring frequently. Add pineapple and stir to coat. Add pineapple juice and broth and bring to boil on high heat. Boil 8 minutes.

2. Meanwhile, trim pork of excess fat, leaving a thin layer on top. Place fat side up in shallow roasting pan. Using slotted spoon, scoop up pineapple from skillet and place around meat. Pour ⅓ cup juice-broth mixture over top of meat. Place roasting pan in middle of preheated oven. Roast 1 hour, uncovered.

3. Reduce juice-broth mixture by half in volume by boiling on high heat 8–10 minutes. As pork roasts, if pan looks dry, spoon a little of this reduced juice-broth mixture over roast to baste. (If preparing rice, reserve 1 cup of juice-broth mixture; set aside. See Cook's Notes).

4. Remove roast from oven, and season with salt and pepper. Spread chutney over top of roast, as well as sides and ends. Return to oven and roast 30 minutes more (roast should have internal temperature of 150 to 160 degrees). Add more juice-broth mixture to pan if it looks dry. Prepare Curry-Pineapple Rice (see Cook's Notes), if desired. Let rest 10 minutes before slicing. (If using, place rice on serving platter.) Arrange pork slices, overlapping them to form a pattern. Place mango garnish around pork. Serve immediately.

NUTRITIONAL INFORMATION (PER SERVING WITHOUT RICE): Calories 400; fat calories 126; total fat 14 grams; sat fat 4.5 grams; cholesterol 105 milligrams; sodium 480 milligrams; total carbohydrates 31 grams; fiber 2 grams; sugars 12 grams; protein 38 grams; vitamin A IUs 25%; vitamin C 60%; calcium 4%; iron 10%.

melon

CANARY

CANTALOUPE

CASABA

CHARENTAIS

CRENSHAW

GALIA

GAYA

HAMI

HONEYDEW (COMMON GREEN, GOLD, AND ORANGE)

KOREAN

PIEL DE SAPO, SANTA CLAUS

PERSIAN

SHARLYN

SPRITE

THERE ARE hundreds of melon varieties. Although many are now available year-round, peak production occurs from May through September. Some have netted, thinner skin; others have smooth, thicker skin. And some are in between, with skin that is almost smooth with very shallow netting.

CANARY, CASABA, CRENSHAW, GALIA, PERSIAN
Domestic: *May–September*
Global: *November–December*

CANTALOUPE, COMMON GREEN HONEYDEW
Domestic: *year-round*
Global: *year-round*

CHARENTAIS
Domestic: *May–September*
Global: *January–May*

Crenshaw

BUYING AND STORING

Choose those that feel heavy for their size and are free of bruises or cracks. Many varieties are fragrant when ripe and blossom end will give slightly to gentle pressure. If unripe, ripen at room temperature (uncut) up to 4 days. Once cut, refrigerate in airtight container 2–3 days.

GAYA
Domestic: *none*
Global: *May–July*

GOLD HONEYDEW, ORANGE HONEYDEW
Domestic: *May–July*
Global: *none*

HAMI
Domestic: *May–July*
Global: *none*

KOREAN
Domestic: *May–September*
Global: *October–April*

PIEL DE SAPO, SANTA CLAUS
Domestic: *May–September*
Global: *March–April*

SHARLYN
Domestic: *May–September*
Global: *none*

SPRITE
Domestic: *June–September*
Global: *May–June*

Korean

Santa Claus

Sharlyn

CANARY
Looks like bright yellow honeydew, oval to oblong, with smooth skin that can have shallow, lengthwise furrows. Cream-colored flesh. ■ *Crisp, firm texture, and delicate sweet flavor that is closer to cantaloupe taste than a honeydew flavor. Juicy.*

CANTALOUPE
Round with netted skin. When ripe, light gold color between webbing. Bright orange flesh. ■ *Very juicy and flowery fragrance. Sweet.*

CASABA
Large, rounded oval, pointed at one end. Lengthwise furrows that gather at ends. Skin is golden yellow (some with green streaks). Honeydew-green flesh. ■ *Delicately sweet, reminiscent of mild cucumber.*

CHARENTAIS
Small, spherical, with smooth greenish-tan skin with length-wise green streaks. Deep orange flesh. ■ *Juicy with complex sweet flavor and flowery aroma.*

CRENSHAW
Large and almost spherical with deep, lengthwise ridges and wrinkles. Dark green skin turns yellow when ripe. Bright salmon-orange flesh. ■ *Dense but tender flesh, highly aromatic. Sweet and pleasingly spicy.*

GALIA
Spherical, medium, netted like cantaloupe but with a dull-green skin between webbing. Smaller seed cavity than cantaloupe. Honeydew-green flesh. ■ *Firm, dense texture with very pleasing sweetness like honeydew, only more so.*

GAYA
Very small, rounded ovals. Smooth white skin dotted with apple-green streaks and blotches. White flesh. ■ *Sweet flavor, a gentle mix of banana and cantaloupe. Sweet aroma. Firm texture.*

HAMI
Large and oblong, skin is yellow with lengthwise green streaks (almost the size of two side-by-side cantaloupes). Orange flesh. ■ *Juicy sweet. Very close to cantaloupe flavor but crunchier.*

HONEYDEW
(common green, gold, orange) Round to oval shape, larger than cantaloupe; skin is smooth. Turns from pale green to white to creamy yellow as it matures, except the gold variety, which has light gold skin. Common green and gold varieties have same light green flesh; orange variety has orange flesh. ■ *So sweet it is considered one of the sweetest melons. Known for soft, swishy texture.*

KOREAN
Small, bright yellow skin with deep ridges unlike any other melon variety. White flesh. ■ *Apple-like crispness with very sweet flavor profile.*

PIEL DE SAPO, SANTA CLAUS
Round to oval with dark-green skin or yellow-green skin. Light green flesh similar to common green honeydew. ■ *Mildly sweet, crunchy.*

PERSIAN
Medium-sized, round to oval, with delicate netting set against grayish-green skin. Pink-orange flesh. ■ *Sweet flesh with firm texture. Buttery texture.*

SHARLYN
Medium-sized, oblong, with delicate netting over tan to yellow skin. Pale green flesh. ■ *Flowery fragrant. Dense but tender flesh. Sweet and pleasingly spicy.*

SPRITE
Small, oval to round. Skin turns from cream to white with yellow mottling when ripe. White flesh. ■ *Almost apple-like crispness with very sweet flavor profile.*

PREP

Wash well with cold water. Cut in half through equator. Scoop out seeds and strings with bowl of spoon. Cut in half or quarter. Cut into spheres with melon baller. If cutting into cubes or wedges, cut off rind.

USE

Eaten raw. Include in salads, cold soups, and smoothies. Skewer cubes to use as a garnish for beverages or add to fruit salsa. Use halved as containers for fruit salad, cold soup, or salsa.

NUTRITIONAL INFO

1 cup provides an excellent source of vitamin C and a significant source of potassium.

SERVING SUGGESTIONS

Sweet-salty appetizers: Wrap small wedges of ripe melon with paper-thin slices of prosciutto. Serve as a first course with knife and fork or secure with toothpick to make portable.

Spicy-sweet soup: In food processor, whirl cubes of ripe cantaloupe with enough Gewürztraminer to make a thick soup. Add fresh lemon juice to taste and a smidgen of curry powder. Serve cold and garnish with sprig of fresh mint.

First or last: Halve chilled small melons and remove seeds. Cut thin slice off bottom to stabilize. Fill half full with chilled wine, such as Gewürztraminer, and place each in a shallow bowl. Serve as first course or dessert.

Spicy salad: Arrange melon cubes on serving platter. Sprinkle with chopped cilantro and modest amount of minced serrano chile (seeded). Sprinkle with rice vinegar and chill 30 minutes. Add salt to taste and serve.

Rice salad with melon chunks: Toss cold cooked rice with melon chunks, toasted almonds, and chopped mint. Make dressing by combining either mayonnaise or plain yogurt with mango chutney. Toss with just enough dressing to lightly coat salad. Season to taste with salt and pepper.

Common Green Honeydew

Casaba

Persian

Orange Honeydew

orange

BLOOD (MORO, TAROCCO, SANQUINELLO)

CARA CARA

NAVEL

SEVILLE (SOUR)

VALENCIA

STRIP AWAY THE STUBBORN PEEL; the fragrant prize inside is worth the effort. With their juice-packed segments tidily arranged like spokes of a wheel, oranges are irresistible. Still considered exotic in the early 1900s, they are now one of the biggest commercial fruit crops in the world.

Oranges are generally classified as either sweet or sour. Along with flavor, color and shape vary greatly. Some are round, others oval. Some have orange flesh, while other varieties are purplish-red or coral-pink.

A recent U. S. Department of Agriculture study showed that a compound found in orange and tangerine peel lowers cholesterol more effectively than some prescription drugs.

Navel

Cara Cara

Blood Orange

BLOOD

Orange skin with deep purplish-red blush. Flesh is (or is streaked with) deep crimson. Often more mature fruit has more blood-red color. Small to medium, generally easy to peel. Often seedless. ■ *Sweet-sour flavor profile with a hint of raspberry. Lower in acid than many varieties.*

CARA CARA

Exterior resembles navel variety. Flesh is deep salmon-pink. Skin is sometimes difficult to peel. Size varies from small to large; generally seedless. ■ *Juicy and sweeter than navel, with subtle hint of grapefruit and tangerine.*

NAVEL

Most popular eating orange worldwide. Thick bright-orange skin is easy to peel. Segments separate easily. Generally large and seedless. ■ *Delectably sweet and juicy.*

SEVILLE (sour)

Skin is yellowish-orange to orange, highly scented, and thick. Pulp is slightly dry. May contain a few seeds. ■ *Tart, this high-acid fruit is used for marmalade.*

VALENCIA

Skin is deep orange, thin and smooth. Medium to large in size. More difficult to peel than navel. Typically seedless. ■ *Very juicy, sweet. Great for juicing. When harvested in summer, may be green areas on skin, but this doesn't affect flavor of flesh.*

BUYING AND STORING

Look for fruit that feels heavy for its size, without soft spots. Oranges can be stored at cool room temperature for about 1 week, or refrigerated up to 3 weeks. Juice and zest can be frozen.

BLOOD (MORO)
Domestic: *December–May*
Global: *year-round*

CARA CARA
Domestic: *December–April*
Global: *year-round*

NAVEL
Domestic: *October–May*
Global: *year-round*

SEVILLE (SOUR)
Domestic: *January–February*
Global: *year-round*

VALENCIA
Domestic: *June–September*
Global: *year-round*

PREP

Wash thoroughly. If using zest, remove it before peeling or cutting orange. If using a more difficult-to-peel variety, slice away skin and pith (see Cutting Citrus into Segments, page 310).

USE

Eat out of hand, use for juice, or include in salads, desserts, sauces, and marmalade or relishes. Also makes beautiful garnishes. Peel can be candied or dried.

NUTRITIONAL INFO

1 cup is an excellent source of vitamin C and a good source of thiamin.

SERVING SUGGESTIONS

Red-hued cocktails: Use blood orange juice to produce stunning colors. Make mimosas (juice and sparkling wine, such as Champagne) or red birds (rum, juice, and Galliano).

Moroccan carrots à la orange: Combine grated carrots with an oil and lemon- or orange-juice vinaigrette seasoned with a little honey and a pinch of ground cumin and cinnamon (see Simple Vinaigrette, page 310). Peel and slice oranges. Place orange slices in single layer on platter and top each with generous spoonful of salad. Garnish with finely chopped red onion and mint leaves.

Orange gremolata: Sprinkle this delectable mixture over cooked fish, roasted or grilled vegetables, or rice. Combine minced or grated zest (colored part of peel) of 1 orange, 2 tablespoons minced fresh Italian parsley or cilantro, 1 tablespoon minced fresh mint leaves, and 1 large shallot (minced).

Sunshine roast chicken: Place whole fryer in roasting pan. Cut orange in half and squeeze over top, then place "used" halves inside cavity along with either 2 or 3 sprigs fresh rosemary or thyme. Season with salt and pepper. Roast in 425-degree oven for 15 minutes; reduce heat to 350 and roast 1 hour.

rosemary-scented orange and grapefruit compote

Cara Cara oranges and Cocktail grapefruit make a very flavorful team, but feel free to substitute other citrus fruits. This convenient dish can be prepared several hours in advance and refrigerated. Accompany with cookies, if desired.

1 cup sugar

½ cup water

3 tablespoons light corn syrup

3 sprigs fresh rosemary

5 oranges, Cara Cara preferred

5 grapefruit, Cocktail preferred

GARNISH: fresh rosemary sprigs

YIELD: 8 SERVINGS

1. Combine sugar, water, corn syrup, and rosemary in medium saucepan. Bring to boil on medium-high heat. Boil 5 minutes. Remove from heat and cool completely. Discard rosemary.

2. Peel and section oranges and grapefruit over bowl to catch juice (see Cutting Citrus into Segments, page 309).

3. Pour cool syrup over fruit. Cover and chill until ready to serve. At serving time, spoon into individual bowls and, if desired, garnish each with small rosemary sprig.

NUTRITIONAL INFORMATION (PER SERVING): Calories 230; fat calories 0; total fat grams; sat fat 0 grams; cholesterol 0 milligrams; sodium 10 milligrams; total carbohydrates 58 grams; fiber 4 grams; sugars 49 grams; protein 2 grams; vitamin A IUs 40%; vitamin C 160%; calcium 8%; iron 0%.

papaya

GREEN

MARADOL (MEXICAN)

STRAWBERRY

YELLOW-FLESH

PAPAYA'S JUICY-SWEET FLESH has subtle flavor and slightly musky aroma. Low in acidity, it's often served with a squeeze of lime or lemon juice, perhaps augmented with salt or pepper. Taste and color vary according to variety. Under the thin skin, soft flesh can be salmon-pink, canary yellow, or bright orange.

With the exception of green papayas (not unripe papayas but a specific variety), a hollow pocket holds multiple shiny black seeds. The contrast between flesh and seeds is stunning, the round black seeds glimmering like beads of caviar resting in a brightly glazed bowl. The seeds are edible, with an appealing peppery flavor, but most often they are discarded.

Green

Yellow-Flesh

Green

Yellow-Flesh

BUYING AND STORING

Except for the green papaya, which remains firm, look for fruit that gives very slightly to pressure, less than a ripe avocado, for instance. To ripen all but green papaya, use brown bag approach (see Brown-Bag Ripening, page 309). Refrigerate unwrapped when ripe 3 to 5 days.

GREEN
Domestic: *none*
Global: *year-round*

MARADOL
Domestic: *none*
Global: *year-round*

STRAWBERRY AND YELLOW-FLESH
Domestic: *year round*
Global: *year-round*

PREP

Cut in half lengthwise. Scoop out seeds (if desired, use seeds as peppery garnish or in salad dressing). If desired, peel papaya with vegetable peeler or paring knife. Cut into strips or dice, as needed. Or leave halves unpeeled and serve with spoon to scoop out flesh, or use as container for ice cream or salad. Green papayas (variety, not unripe fruit) are generally peeled and shredded.

USE

With the exception of green papayas, fruit can be used in sweet or savory dishes, raw or cooked. It is delicious in ice cream, sorbet, fruit salad, smoothies, and salsa. Papaya contains an enzyme that tenderizes meat, so it can be added to marinades. That enzyme also prevents gelatin from setting.

Green papaya is generally shredded and tossed with tangy dressing.

NUTRITIONAL INFO

1 cup is a good source of vitamins A and C and a significant source of potassium.

SERVING SUGGESTIONS

Papaya butter: In electric mixer, combine ½ cup honey, 1 cup (2 sticks) unsalted butter, and ½ cup chopped ripe (peeled and seeded) papaya. Beat until well blended. Place on parchment paper and roll into cylinder. Chill until firm. To use, cut into ½-inch-thick disks. Use as a topper for French toast or bagels.

Southeast Asian green papaya salad: Shred peeled green papaya. For dressing, combine 4–5 tablespoons fresh lime juice, 3 tablespoons sugar, 3 tablespoons fish sauce, and ½ minced serrano chile. Toss and top with minced cilantro and chopped peanuts.

Poached Maradol: Make simple syrup: Combine 2 cups water and 1 ½ cups sugar. Boil until sugar dissolves. Reduce heat to medium. Add wedges of peeled Maradol papaya, ¼ cup fresh lime juice, and 2 cinnamon sticks. Simmer 3–4 minutes. Chill. Remove cinnamon sticks. Serve plain or drizzled with crema Mexicana or sour cream.

Breakfast papaya: Cut papayas in half lengthwise and scoop out seeds. Fill cavities with warm cereal and milk or cream.

Maradol

*Strawberry
Papaya*

papaya mint dressing

This tangy dressing can be used with green salads or fruit salad. If using papaya in a fruit salad, add it last and reserve some seeds, if desired, for a peppery taste; rinse seeds, drain, and use as garnish. A little dressing is delicious drizzled over grilled fish, too.

1 ripe papaya, yellow or strawberry, peeled, seeded, chopped

³/4 cup canned papaya nectar

2 tablespoons rice vinegar

1 tablespoon sugar

¹/3 cup vegetable oil

¹/2 cup finely chopped fresh mint leaves

YIELD: ABOUT 3¹/2 CUPS

1. In blender, combine papaya, nectar, vinegar, and sugar. Process until smooth. Add oil and process until blended.

2. Pour into container. Add mint and stir. Chill at least 1 hour but not more than 1 day. Use to dress fruit salad or mixed greens, or drizzle a little over grilled fish.

NUTRITIONAL INFORMATION (PER TABLESPOON): Calories 15; fat calories 13.5; total fat 1.5 grams; sat fat 0 grams; cholesterol 0 milligrams; sodium 0 milligrams; total carbohydrates 1 gram; fiber 0 gram; sugars 1 gram; protein 0 grams; vitamin A IUs 2%; vitamin C 6%; calcium 0%; iron 0%.

passion fruit

COMMON

VANILLA

IT WASN'T THE HEAVENLY TROPICAL TASTE that prompted the name, although it's easy to be passionate about its distinct sweet-tart flavor and aroma. In Brazil, early European missionaries saw symbols of Christ's crucifixion in its flowers (crown of thorns, hammers, and nails) and named the fruit after the Passion.

Common passion fruit can be round or shaped like blunt-ended eggs. The skin is purple-tinged brown and is wrinkled when ripe. Inside that inedible rind, there are myriad edible, crisp seeds. Each seed is surrounded with almost transparent chartreuse pulp. The yellow-green pulp is jelly-like and turns an eye-popping egg-yolk color on the outside edge. The taste dazzles, like a combination of banana, guava, lime, and honey—but more intense.

Vanilla passion fruit (sometimes dubbed banana passion fruit) is a variety that looks a little like a pointed-at-the-ends baby banana. The skin wrinkles and turns from green to yellow as it ripens. Inside, the edible seeds are larger and darker than those in the common variety. And the flesh that surrounds them is mossy green. Taste is similar to its common cousin, but its flavor is less tangy and has a hint of vanilla. And it yields twice as much pulp. Generally, this variety is harder to find; it debuted in United States in 2003.

BUYING AND STORING

When buying either variety, look for fruit with shriveled skin (a sign of ripeness). Ripe vanilla variety will be yellow. If skin is smooth, ripen at room temperature and turn occasionally. Store ripe fruit in a plastic bag in vegetable drawer of refrigerator up to 1 week.

COMMON PASSION FRUIT
Domestic: *July–February*
Global: *March–June*

VANILLA PASSION FRUIT
Domestic: *none*
Global: *March–June*

PREP

For common variety, cut in half through equator. For vanilla variety, cut in half lengthwise. Scoop out seeds, pulp, and juice with bowl of spoon. Discard shells or use as inedible containers. Enjoy its crunchy texture; seeds have consistency similar to pomegranate seeds. Or strain through medium-meshed sieve, pushing with spoon to remove seeds; use pulp and discard seeds.

USE

Use raw seeds, pulp, and juice in salad dressings, cake filling, or as topping for ice cream, pound cake, or pudding. Use strained pulp and juice in sorbet or frosting.

NUTRITIONAL INFO

1 cup is an excellent source of vitamins C and A and a significant source of riboflavin, potassium, niacin, magnesium, and copper.

SERVING SUGGESTIONS

Fancy fruit salad: Serve fruit salad without dressing. Place cut-in-half passion fruit on side. Diners squeeze or spoon passion fruit over salad as vibrant dressing. For small salad, serve ½ passion fruit per person.

Vinaigrette for grilled fish, chicken, or vegetables: Whisk 2 tablespoons lime juice and ¼ cup extra-virgin olive oil; add 4 tablespoons unstrained passion fruit and whisk to combine. Add salt and pepper to taste; whisk to combine. Spoon over grilled entrée of choice. Garnish with cilantro or thinly sliced chives, if desired.

Champagne with passion: Pour champagne into fluted glass. Add strained passion fruit to taste; stir and enjoy.

Catchy coulis: Serve strained pulp on desserts, either on the side or spooned on top. Delicious with cheesecake, chocolate mousse, or tapioca pudding.

Common Passion Fruit

Vanilla Passion Fruit

pavlova

Only a dessert as light as a cottonball cloud could be named for a famous ballerina. Pavlova certainly fits that bill, especially when garnished with passion fruit. Billows of crisp baked meringue topped with whipped cream and fresh fruit create this delicacy, which is the national dessert of Australia and New Zealand and named for the Russian prima ballerina, Anna Pavlova.

Butter and flour for preparing baking sheet

4 large egg whites, room temperature (see Cook's Notes)

½ teaspoon salt

1 cup superfine sugar (see Cook's Notes)

2 teaspoons cornstarch

2 teaspoons distilled white vinegar

2 cups heavy whipping cream

2 tablespoons powdered sugar (see Cook's Notes)

Optional: 1 teaspoon liqueur, such as Grand Marnier

3 kiwi (peeled and sliced)

pulp and seeds from 3–4 ripe (wrinkled) passion fruit

OPTIONAL GARNISH: mint leaves

YIELD: 8 SERVINGS

COOK'S NOTES: To bring cold eggs to room temperature, place in warm water to cover for 5 minutes; remove and dry eggs. To create superfine sugar, place about 1½ cups sugar in food processor (perfectly clean and dry) fitted with metal blade; process 30 seconds. Measure 1 cup. If assembling Pavlova more than 30 minutes before serving, increase amount of powdered sugar in whipped cream to ¼ cup. This will help to stabilize the whipped cream.

1. Butter and flour baking sheet; invert and shake off excess flour. Using 7-inch plate or bowl as guideline, trace a circle with your finger or with point of knife. Adjust oven rack to middle position. Preheat oven to 300 degrees.

2. Place egg whites in large bowl of electric mixer. Beat on medium speed until foamy. Add salt and increase speed to medium-high. Beat until soft peaks form. Add 1 tablespoon superfine sugar and beat for 1 minute on medium-high speed. Repeat procedure, adding 1 tablespoon of sugar and beating for 1 minute, until all sugar has been incorporated.

3. In small bowl, stir cornstarch and vinegar until blended. Fold cornstarch mixture into egg white mixture. Spread to form circle in traced area of prepared baking sheet. Make well (about 6 inches wide and 1 inch deep) using bowl of large spoon or flexible metal frosting spatula. Straighten up outside edges. Place in middle of preheated 300-degree oven; immediately turn oven to 250 degrees. Bake until outside of meringue is firm and pale tan in color, about 1 hour 15 minutes. Place sheet on cooling rack for 15 minutes. Using large spatula, transfer Pavlova to serving plate. (Don't worry if there are cracks in the meringue. The whipped cream will cover them up.) It may stand, uncovered, at room temperature up to 8 hours.

4. Using large bowl of electric mixer, whip chilled whipping cream until soft peaks form. Add powdered sugar (and liqueur if desired) and beat until stiff. Fill well in meringue with whipped cream and spread cream over top and sides. Place kiwi slices on top in circle around perimeter, overlapping slightly. Passion fruit pulp may be served 2 ways: Either make a ½-inch-deep well in center of whipped cream and spoon in passion fruit and garnish with mint leaves. Or cut Pavlova into wedges and place on individual dessert plates, then spoon passion fruit on top and garnish with mint. Serve.

NUTRITIONAL INFORMATION (PER SERVING):
Calories 350; fat calories 198; total fat 22 grams; sat fat 14 grams; cholesterol 80 milligrams; sodium 200 milligrams; total carbohydrates 36 grams; fiber 2 grams; sugars 31 grams; protein 3 grams; vitamin A IUs 20%; vitamin C 40%; calcium 4%; iron 2%.

peach, nectarine

INDIAN PEACH

SATURN PEACH

WHITE-FLESH PEACH

YELLOW-FLESH PEACH

HONEYDEW NECTARINE

MANGO NECTARINE

SATURN NECTARINE

WHITE-FLESH NECTARINE

YELLOW-FLESH NECTARINE

FEW FRUITS CAN COMPETE with the melting texture and intoxicating fragrance of a truly ripe peach or nectarine. Nectarines are subspecies of peaches, and although their juicy-sweet flavor profiles are very similar, nectarines can be slightly firmer and have skin that is fuzz-free smooth. Crossbreeding over the past several years has produced nectarines with more tender, peachlike flesh. Peaches generally have fuzzier skin, but to meet customer demand, they are often mechanically "brushed" after harvest to remove much of the fuzz.

Classified by how easily the flesh separates from the stone, peaches and nectarines are either freestone (flesh separates easily from pit) or clingstone (flesh separates only with the aid of a knife blade). Most clingstone peaches are sold to canneries.

INDIAN PEACH
(Indian red)
Freestone or clingstone, blood-red skin with velvety fuzz. Flesh is white with red marbleized streaks. ■ *Delicately sweet, juicy flesh.*

SATURN PEACH
Freestone, one-third the size of an average peach. Lifesaver-like shape flattened at top and bottom with dip in center at pit. Skin is most often light yellow with red blush. White-fleshed varieties are rare. ■ *Very juicy, fairly firm, with smooth texture and delicious sweetness.*

WHITE-FLESH PEACH
Usually freestone. Tender red skin and creamy white flesh. Often almost fuzzless skin. ■ *Often the sweetest peach and very juicy. Best for eating out of hand or raw in salads or relishes rather than cooking.*

YELLOW-FLESH PEACH
(common)
Often freestone. Generally fuzzy skin that is yellow with red blush. ■ *Succulent and sweet.*

HONEYDEW NECTARINE
Freestone, shape and size of apricot. Light green, meaty flesh. ■ *Sweetness similar to honeydew melon.*

MANGO NECTARINE
Freestone. Bright yellow skin and yellow flesh. ■ *Tastes subtly like mango with slightly fibrous texture.*

SATURN NECTARINE
(flat nectarine)
Freestone, one-third the size of an average nectarine. Lifesaver-like shape flattened at top and bottom with dip in center at pit. Skin is most often light yellow with red blush. White-fleshed varieties are rare. ■ *Very sweet and juicy.*

WHITE-FLESH NECTARINE
Freestone with striking red markings on skin with creamy-white flesh. ■ *Very juicy and sweet.*

YELLOW-FLESH NECTARINE
Freestone with striking red markings on skin and orange-yellow flesh. ■ *Richly flavored, sweet and juicy.*

BUYING AND STORING

Avoid fruit with any tinges of green, bruises, or shriveling.

For peaches, look for fruit that is plump and gives to gentle pressure at the shoulders but without any soft spots or mushiness. Red blush isn't necessarily a sign of ripeness. Peaches should be fragrant, with a rich peachy smell. They do not continue to ripen after harvest; Brown-bag ripening (page 309) will improve texture but not sweetness. Refrigerate ripe fruit loose in crisper drawer up to 5 days (but note that refrigeration is not recommended because it changes the taste).

For nectarines, look for fruit that is plump and fairly firm but not rock hard. Ripe nectarines will give to gentle pressure when pressed at suture (lengthwise seam) and have a sweet

White-Flesh Peach

fragrance. A red blush isn't necessarily a sign of ripeness. (See Brown-Bag Ripening, page 309). Refrigerate ripe fruit loose in crisper drawer up to 5 days.

PEACHES (WHITE AND YELLOW FLESHED)
Domestic: *May–October*
Global: *November–May*

PEACHES (SATURN)
Domestic: *June–August*
Global: *none*

PEACHES (INDIAN)
Domestic: *August–September*
Global: *none*

NECTARINES (WHITE AND YELLOW FLESHED)
Domestic: *May–October*
Global: *December–May*

NECTARINES (SATURN AND HONEYDEW)
Domestic: *July–August*
Global: *none*

NECTARINES (MANGO)
Domestic: *June–August*
Global: *none*

PREP

Peaches can be peeled with paring knife or dropped into boiling water for about 1 minute, then refreshed with cold water and the skin slipped off. But if they are freestones, they should be pitted before peeling.

For freestones, cut fruit in half from top to bottom, along suture (seam). Twist halves in opposite directions and lift out pit (then peel peach). For clingstones, peel peach and cut into quarters or eighths, cutting toward pit; lift off sections, cutting next to pit if stubborn flesh won't pull away.

Nectarines have very thin skin and do not need to be peeled.

Use right away, or to prevent discoloration, rub with lemon or dip in acidulated water (cold water mixed with a little lemon or lime juice).

Saturn Peach

Yellow-Flesh Peach

USE

Eat raw or cooked. Slice, then top cereal, pudding, ice cream, or pancakes. Add to fruit salad, shortcake filing, salsa, or cold soups; or to blended drinks, cocktails, or dessert sauces. Can be pickled. To cook: broil, bake, grill, or sauté. Use for jam, jelly, pies, and coffeecakes.

SERVING SUGGESTIONS

Red wine peaches or nectarines for dessert: In glass or ceramic bowl, whisk 1 cup sugar into 2½ cups fruity red wine, such as Zinfandel or Merlot; stir with whisk until sugar dissolves. Add 4 sliced large nectarines or peaches (peel peaches). Cover and chill. Serve in 4 wine or martini glasses; accompany with biscotti or sugar cookies.

Grill: Cut peaches or nectarines in half and remove pits. Brush with vegetable oil and grill on medium-hot fire about 2–3 minutes per side.

Peach sangria: In large glass or ceramic pitcher, combine 3 cups rosé wine, 3 peeled and sliced peaches, and ¼ cup sugar. Stir until sugar dissolves. Add ½ cup peach schnapps, ice, and 2½ cups sparkling water; stir and serve in 4–6 tall glasses.

Nectarine sundaes: Cut nectarines in half and remove pits. Place in roasting pan cut-side up. Place ½ teaspoon butter in recess of each nectarine half and sprinkle with ½ teaspoon dark brown sugar. Roast in 450-degree oven until piping hot. In each shallow bowl place one half nectarine. Top each with a scoop of ice cream and chocolate sauce. If desired, top with whipped cream and toasted almonds. Serve immediately.

peach or nectarine buckle

This old-fashioned buckle can be served as a breakfast coffee cake or a dessert accompanied with ice cream or whipped cream. It looks beautiful glazed with melted jam that has been augmented with liqueur or peach juice. But for an easier approach, the glaze can be omitted.

Butter for greasing pan, plus flour for dusting pan (or use nonstick vegetable spray)

5½ cups peeled and sliced (ripe) fresh peaches (or unpeeled nectarines)

1 cup plus 2 tablespoons sugar, divided use

⅓ cup butter

1 teaspoon baking powder

¼ teaspoon salt

2 large eggs

1 cup plus 2 tablespoons all-purpose flour, divided use

1 teaspoon ground cinnamon, divided use

OPTIONAL GLAZE:

⅓ cup peach or apricot jam

1 tablespoon orange liqueur or peach juice

OPTIONAL GARNISH: fresh mint sprigs

YIELD: 8 SERVINGS

COOK'S NOTES: If using food processor to make batter, be careful not to overmix ingredients. Process just enough to blend.

1. Grease 11½-by-9-inch gratin pan (oval baking dish) or any shallow 2½-quart baking pan with butter; dust with flour and invert to remove excess flour. Or spray generously with nonstick spray; set aside. Fifteen minutes before baking, preheat oven to 350 degrees.

2. Place peaches or nectarines in non-aluminum bowl. Add ½ cup sugar and lightly toss. Let stand 1 hour. Drain and reserve syrup.

3. Using electric mixer or food processor fitted with metal blade (see Cook's Notes), cream butter until fluffy. Add ½ cup sugar, baking powder, and salt; beat until combined. Add eggs and beat until blended. Add 1 cup flour and beat until just blended. Spread over bottom of prepared pan. Top with peaches or nectarines.

4. Combine reserved peach syrup with 2 tablespoons flour and ½ teaspoon ground cinnamon; stir to blend. Pour over fruit. In separate bowl, combine 2 tablespoons sugar and ½ teaspoon cinnamon; sprinkle over top.

5. Bake in middle of preheated 350-degree oven for 50–55 minutes, or until cake is cooked through and is deep golden brown. (This dish can be made a day before serving if desired. Cool and cover (unglazed) buckle with plastic wrap. To serve warm, reheat just until warm in microwave oven. Brush with glaze, if desired).

6. To prepare glaze, melt jam in heavy-bottomed saucepan on medium heat, stirring frequently. When melted, stir in orange liqueur or peach juice. Strain. Using pastry brush, brush on top of warm buckle.

NUTRITIONAL INFORMATION (PER SERVING)

Calories 340; fat calories 81; total fat 9 grams; sat fat 5 grams; cholesterol 75 milligrams; sodium 160 milligrams; total carbohydrates 62 grams; fiber less than 1 gram; sugars 37 grams; protein 5 grams; vitamin A IUs 15%; vitamin C 15%; calcium 6%; iron 8%.

White-Flesh Nectarine

Yellow-Flesh Nectarine

pear

BARTLETT, RED BARTLETT

BOSC

COMICE

D'ANJOU, RED D'ANJOU

FORELLE

SECKEL

SWEET WITH PROVOCATIVE JUICES, a perfect pear is buttery, with melt-in-your-mouth texture and irresistible aroma. But in most markets, pears are sold rock-hard and almost scentless. That's because when left on the tree to ripen, pears become grainy mush. But letting them lounge at home in a loosely closed brown bag can bring unripened pears to perfection (see Brown-Bag Ripening, page 309).

So first impressions may be based on eye appeal: voluptuous contours and paint-box colors. Long arched necks, gentle teardrop curves, or charmingly rounded. Red, yellow, brown, or green, freckled skins or blushed; large, small, and in between. There are hundreds of varieties.

BUYING AND STORING

To allow time to ripen, it's best to buy several days before serving. Once ripened in paper bag, refrigerate 3–7 days. Or, for slower ripening, store firm pears at room temperature out of direct sunlight. They are ripe when they give to gentle pressure at the neck. Look for unblemished fruit without bruises. Handle gently; even hard fruit can bruise.

Bosc

Bartlett

DOMESTIC:
Bartlett and Red Bartlett: *June–March*
Bosc: *June–March*
Comice: *September–March*
D'Anjou and Red D'Anjou: *September–July*
Forrelle: *September–March*
Seckel: *September–February*

GLOBAL: *All varieties December–April*

Seckel

Forelle

Red D'Anjou

D'Anjou

Comice

BARTLETT, RED BARTLETT

"Pear-shaped" rounded bell at bottom with definitive shoulders and smaller neck. Bartletts turn from green to yellow when ripe. Red Bartletts don't change color. ■ *Same flavor and texture for both: aromatic, sweet, and juicy with smooth texture. Great for canning, baking, or eating raw. When using Red Bartletts in salads, leave peel intact for appealing color contrast.*

BOSC

Long tapering neck with curved stem and earthy brown skin that is often russeted (mottled). Firm flesh with slight sandlike texture. ■ *Sweet and aromatic. Attractive shape and stay-together texture make them perfect for poaching or baking whole.*

COMICE

Rounded with very short neck. Greenish-yellow skin, sometimes tinged with brown or pink. ■ *Rich, buttery-sweet flavor makes them great for eating raw (alone or with cheese). Soft, juicy texture.*

D'ANJOU, RED D'ANJOU, sometimes labeled ANJOU, RED ANJOU

Short, tapering neck without distinct shoulders (almost egg-shaped). Yellowish-green skin. Red D'Anjou (no surprise) are red. ■ *Fine textured and sweet, they can be stored unripened in cold storage for long periods. Best used for baking or roasting before reaching maximum ripeness.*

FORELLE

Small, only about 2½-inches long, it is called a "snacking pear." Skin turns from green to bright yellow as it ripens, with attractive red "freckling" and rosy blush. ■ *Mild, sweet flavor and slightly crisp texture. Small size makes them convenient for children's lunchboxes.*

SECKEL

Small but slightly larger than Forelles, slightly rounded with olive green and maroon skin. ■ *Sweet, slightly spicy flavor and juicy-but-crisp texture. Small size makes them ideal for poaching or pickling whole.*

USE

Once cut, pears discolor quickly. To prevent browning, dip in acidulated water (cold water with a little lemon or lime juice). Can be eaten with or without skin, raw or cooked. Pears can be baked, poached, roasted, or sautéed. Generally, peel before cooking. If poaching, choose pears that are naturally firm, such as Bosc or Seckel. If baking, use ripe Bartlett, Comice, or D'Anjou.

Pears are delicious in baked goods, or chutneys, or served with cheese. They pair well with meats and game, as well as chocolate, mint, or ginger. Generally, they can be substituted for apples in recipes.

NUTRITIONAL INFORMATION

1 cup sliced is a significant source of vitamin C.

SERVING SUGGESTIONS

Caramelized fruit and cheese: Peel and halve 2 pears lengthwise; core. Sprinkle with 2 tablespoons sugar to coat. Sauté in 2 tablespoons butter on medium-high heat, browning both sides. Remove pears and deglaze pan with 2 tablespoons Champagne vinegar or white wine, scraping up any brown bits. Pour over pears. Serve warm with blue-veined cheese, such as Gorgonzola or Stilton.

Roast: Peel, halve 2 pears lengthwise; core. Cut into 1/3-inch-thick lengthwise slices. Toss with 2 tablespoons melted butter and 2 tablespoons sugar. Spread onto baking sheet with sides. Roast in 500-degree oven for 10 minutes; turn and roast 5 minutes more. Garnish mixed green salad, or use to accompany poultry, game, or pork.

Wine-kissed poaching: In large saucepan or Dutch oven, combine 3 cups dry red wine, 2/3 cup sugar, and 1/2 cup tangerine or orange juice; stir and bring to boil on high heat . Reduce to medium and add 4 whole pears (peeled and cored). Cut parchment paper same size as pan and place over pears. Cover and gently simmer, turning occasionally, until pears are tender when pierced with knife, about 20 minutes. Remove pears and boil liquid until reduced to about 1 cup. Cool pears in syrup. Serve with ice cream, gingerbread, or rich soft cheese, such as brie or Saint André.

Cranberry-pear relish: In medium saucepan, combine 1 (16-ounce) can whole cranberry sauce and 1/2 cup raspberry spreadable fruit or jam; cook until melted, about 3 minutes. Stir in 3/4 cup chunky salsa and 2 pears (peeled, cored, and diced). Cook 2 to 4 minutes. Taste and adjust seasoning, adding a pinch of dried pepper flakes if desired for spicier version. Serve with beef, poultry, or pork (ham is especially delicious).

pear pizzas with caramelized onions

To turn these delicious pizzas into appetizers, cut them into small wedges. The sweetness of the pears and caramelized onions is balanced nicely with the salty, tangy cheeses. Use low-moisture mozzarella in this recipe, the type somtimes referred to as "regular."

1 1/2 tablespoons butter

1 large sweet onion, peeled, thinly sliced

½ teaspoon sugar

4 (6-inch) store-bought baked pizza crusts, such as Boboli

8 ounces cream cheese, room temperature

1 cup shredded mozzarella cheese

2 medium-ripe pears, peeled, cored, and sliced

1 cup crumbled blue cheese, such as Gorgonzola

YIELD: 4 PIZZAS, OR 16 APPETIZER SERVINGS

1. Preheat oven to 450 degrees.

2. Melt butter in large skillet on medium-low heat. Add onion and cook, stirring frequently, 5 minutes. Add sugar and cook, stirring occasionally, until golden brown and softened, about 15 minutes.

3. Place pizza crusts on large baking sheet. Spread with cream cheese and top with mozzarella, pear, and blue cheese. Bake about 10 minutes or until ingredients are heated through, cheese melts, and crust turns golden brown. Serve 1 per person, or for appetizer servings, cut each into 4 wedges.

NUTRITIONAL INFORMATION (PER APPETIZER SERVING): Calories 290; fat calories 110; total fat 13 grams; sat fat 7 grams; cholesterol 30 milligrams; sodium 500 milligrams; total carbohydrates 33 grams; fiber 2 grams; sugars 4 grams; protein 11 grams; vitamin A IUs 6%; vitamin C 0%; calcium 20%; iron 10%.

persimmon

CINNAMON

FUYU

HACHIYA

BEAUTY IS ONLY SKIN DEEP. That's good advice for impatient eaters of Hachiya persimmons, the heart-shaped variety that needs to be fully ripened to appreciate its tangy-sweet taste and jelly-like texture. Don't even think about eating it before it's ripe, and don't rely on color to judge ripeness. The skin is the same vivid orange color whether at the highly astringent, tannic unripe stage or the fully ripened, luscious point. Touch them. Ripe Hachiyas feel like overfilled water balloons. Their pulp can be scooped from the skin like jam from a cup.

Fuyu persimmons, the other well-known variety, are tomato-shaped and a lighter orange color. Because they are not astringent, they can be eaten when apple-like firm or when softened slightly. Sharon fruit, a Fuyu variety grown in Israel, is available December to February.

Cinnamon persimmons, a lesser known but glamorous Hachiya subvariety, have a tomato-like shape similar to the Fuyu, with skin a Fuyu-like shade of light orange. But inside, there's showy rust-colored speckling dappled throughout its sweet flesh, a pattern reminiscent of powdered cinnamon dusted onto a moist surface. Sweet, low in tannin and astringency, eat them when firm or softened slightly, as with Fuyu persimmons.

BUYING AND STORING

Cinnamon: Buy and store as with Fuyu. Can be eaten semifirm and used raw.

Fuyu: They can be eaten when firm or slightly soft. Look for fruit with a green (not brown) calyx. Skin should be a consistent light orange color, not yellow or green. Store in refrigerator up to 14 days or freeze up to 3 months.

Hachiya: Seldom sold ripe because they are supersoft and fragile. But they are easy to ripen at home, either at room temperature or placed in a loosely sealed paper bag with another fruit, such as an apple or banana. When ripe, store in refrigerator up to 10 days. Can also be frozen whole or in pulp form.

CINNAMON
Domestic only: *October–December*

FUYU AND HACHIYA
Domestic: *October–December*
Global: *May–June*

SHARON FRUIT
Global only: *December–February*

PREP

Hachiya: When very ripe, cut off top and scoop out pulp. Mash pulp by pulsing in food processor fitted with metal blade or push it through a large-mesh strainer. Discard skin.

Fuyu, Cinnamon, and Sharon fruit: Remove calyx and core. Peel if skin is thick. Eat fresh out of hand like an apple. Or cut into medium dice or thin wedges for salads or other cold dishes. Or cut into thin horizontal slices.

USE
Incorporate Hachiya pulp into jam, cookies, sorbet, pudding, smoothies, quick bread, and muffins. Use Fuyu raw, diced or sliced, in salad or salsa, or cooked in cake, chutney, or cooked sauce.

NUTRITIONAL INFO
$\frac{1}{2}$ cup is a good source of vitamins A and C; contains potassium and copper; good source of fiber.

SERVING SUGGESTIONS FOR RIPE HACHIYA PERSIMMONS
Lazy-way sorbet: Cut off and discard top. Place in plastic bag or container and seal. Freeze. Remove from freezer and leave at room temperature 5–10 minutes. Use a teaspoon to scoop semifrozen pulp from "shell."

Bright and light sauce: Place 1½ cups Hachiya pulp (about 4) in food processor fitted with metal blade. Add 1 tablespoon brandy and ½ teaspoon lemon juice. Process until smooth. Cover and refrigerate. Spoon over spice cake, gingerbread, ice cream, or rice pudding.

More pizzazz than pumpkin: Substitute persimmon pulp for pumpkin purée in pies, quick breads or cakes.

SERVING SUGGESTIONS FOR CINNAMON AND FUYU PERSIMMONS

Cheese tray splendor: Garnish cheese tray with thin Fuyu wedges.

Fall fruit salad: Gently toss Fuyu wedges with red grapes, pomegranate seeds, and apple wedges. Garnish with kiwi slices.

Autumn salsa: Combine 2 diced Fuyu persimmons, ½ cup diced onion, ½ cup diced tomatillo, ½ cup chopped cilantro, and 1 minced serrano chile. Season to taste with salt. Use to top grilled poultry, pork, or seafood. Or spoon over warm quesadillas. Store in airtight container up to 2 days in refrigerator. Best served at room temperature.

Hachiya

Fuyu

Cinnamon

green salad with fuyu persimmons, pomegranates, and blue cheese

Two things stand out in this salad. One, it is glorious to look at with its jewel-tone colors of bright green, ruby red, and pumpkin orange. Second, the flavors balance perfectly, with sweet-tart persimmons and pomegranates contrasting with the tangy slightly-sour edge of blue cheese and the subtle bitterness of the walnuts.

1 cup extra-virgin olive oil or safflower oil

4 ounces crumbled blue cheese

1/3 cup cider vinegar

Garlic salt to taste

Freshly ground black pepper to taste

2–3 firm Fuyu or Cinnamon persimmons

1 small bulb fresh fennel, washed, trimmed, thinly sliced

6–7 cups mixed baby lettuce

Seeds from 1/4 pomegranate (see Cook's Notes)

OPTIONAL: *1/4 cup toasted walnuts (see Cook's Notes)*

OPTIONAL GARNISH: Chives and unpeeled persimmon wedges

YIELD: 6 SERVINGS

COOK'S NOTES: The easiest way to remove seeds from a pomegranate is to place it on 2–3 paper towels and cut into quarters. Place in bowl of cold water, deep enough so that entire portion of pomegranate is underwater. Run fingers over membrane to remove seeds; it won't splatter because juices stay underwater. Bits of membrane will float to surface and can easily be discarded. Drain seeds.

To toast walnuts, place in single layer on baking sheet. Place in 350-degree oven for about 5 minutes; watch carefully because nuts burn easily. Cool.

Leftover dressing can be refrigerated, sealed, and used within 2 weeks.

1. In small bowl or 2-cup glass measuring cup, combine oil and cheese. Using fork, mash some of cheese against side of container, so it dissolves into oil. Add vinegar and stir. Add garlic salt and pepper; taste and adjust seasoning.

2. Using small knife, cut out green calyx from top of each persimmon. If persimmon skin seems tough, peel with vegetable peeler. Cut into 1/4-inch-wide wedges. Place in large bowl with fennel slices. Stir dressing and add 2–3 tablespoons to persimmons; toss to coat. Add lettuce and pomegranate seeds. Toss. Add enough dressing to lightly coat lettuce, making sure to include some crumbled cheese that may be at bottom of bowl of dressing. Taste. Add more garlic salt or pepper, as needed.

3. Divide among 6 salad plates. If desired, sprinkle on toasted walnuts. If desired, garnish with chives and place wedges of unpeeled persimmon on lip of plate. Serve immediately.

NUTRITIONAL INFORMATION (PER SERVING): Calories 140; fat calories 99; total fat 11 grams; sat fat 2 grams; cholesterol 5 milligrams; sodium 130 milligrams; total carbohydrates 9 grams; fiber 2 grams; sugars 2 grams; protein 2 grams; vitamin A IUs 35%; vitamin C 35%; calcium 8%; iron 8%.

pepino melon, also pepino

ELONGATED, WITH ONE POINTED END, pepino melon could be described as shaped like a long, slender heart. It can be the size of an egg or as large as a cantaloupe. The ivory to yellow to light green skin is thin and satiny smooth. It's marked with lengthwise purple streaks and blotches. Inside the edible skin, the flesh is yellow or coral, with the tender consistency of ripe mango. It's sweet and aromatic, a subtle blend of pear and very mild cantaloupe.

As with cantaloupes or honeydew melons, pepino melons have a central pocket filled with seeds. But pepino melon isn't really a melon. It's a member of the nightshade family, along with eggplant, tomato, and potato.

BUYING AND STORING

Size doesn't affect flavor. Ripe fruit gives slightly to gentle pressure. Skin color can also indicate ripeness. Look for yellow skin around purple streaking. If tinged with green, ripen at room temperature until it turns yellow. Refrigerate ripe fruit in crisper drawer up to 4 days.

Domestic: *none*
Global: *year-round*

PREP

Wash in cold water. Generally skin is tender, but if it is tough, peel with paring knife. Remove seeds if desired.

USE

Eat raw out of hand. Mild taste and bright color make it a perfect addition to fruit salad. Slice and use as garnish, or purée and combine with puréed mango and sugar syrup to make sorbet (see Meyer Lemon Sorbet, page 51).

Pepino Melon

NUTRITIONAL INFO

1 cup is a significant source of potassium.

SERVING SUGGESTIONS

Dessert simplicity: Cut pepino melon in half lengthwise and place on 2 plates, cut side up. Top each with scoop of ice cream and garnish with fresh mint sprigs. Or sprinkle halves with finely chopped crystallized ginger and top with generous squeeze of fresh lime or lemon juice.

Cheese course: Cut into slices and use to garnish cheese tray.

Coulis for crab cakes: Purée peeled and seeded pepino melon and fresh pineapple cubes in small batches in food processor fitted with metal blade. Add fresh lime juice to taste. Serve sauce (coulis) in a puddle under piping-hot crab cakes. Garnish, if desired, with sprig of fresh cilantro.

Spinach salad: Toss clean baby spinach with Simple Vinaigrette (page 310). Arrange on salad plates. Top with crumbled feta cheese and diced pepino melon.

pineapple

BABY HAWAIIAN

COMMON (GOLD)

SOUTH AFRICAN BABY

TOPPED WITH A BUSHY TUFT OF RIGID POINTED LEAVES, pineapple has a scalelike skin that varies in color from yellow to reddish-brown, green to greenish-brown. Beneath the prickly peel, below those spirals of fibrous "eyes," is a juicy-sweet treasure.

Images of these tropical beauties can be found in pre-Incan ruins in Central and South America, where pineapples are indigenous. Christopher Columbus's crew delighted in their sweet-tart flavor when they found them on the island of Guadeloupe in 1493. Spaniards later dubbed them piñas, or pine cones. The English name adds apple, proclaiming it a fruit rather than an inedible cone.

BUYING AND STORING

Generally, skin color isn't an indication of ripeness. First look at leaves on crown; they should be bright green, not dried or brown. Fruit should yield to light pressure and smell fragrant. Firm fruit will soften when left at room temperature for 2–4 days. But the sweetest fruit is picked when ripe; sugar content does not increase after picking. Refrigerate ripe pineapples up to 5 days. Or peel and cut into chunks and freeze on baking sheet.

Once frozen, store in airtight container; use frozen in smoothies and puréed cocktails.

Domestic: *year round*
Global: *year round*

PREP

Using a sharp, sturdy knife, cut off crown and bottom. Place cut side down on cutting board. Remove skin and "eyes" by cutting in strips from top to bottom, following the contour of the fruit. If cutting into chunks, cut into lengthwise quarters and remove core, cutting from top to bottom; cut quarters into chunks. South African Baby or Baby Hawaiian pineapples do not require coring.

USE

Eat raw cut into managable pieces or in fruit salads. Do not use in gelatin because a natural enzyme in fresh pineapple prevents setting. Or use cooked, grilled, sautéed, or broiled, or in baked goods.

South African Baby

Common (Gold)

BABY HAWAIIAN PINEAPPLE
Small version of Gold Pineapple, about 5–8 inches high. ▪
Sweet and aromatic with crunchy texture and edible core. Brown exterior.

COMMON
(gold)
Exterior looks like common pineapple, about 17–22 inches high. ▪ *Very, very sweet with brilliant yellow flesh. Golden exterior.*

SOUTH AFRICAN BABY
About 5–7 inches high. ▪
Supersweet, golden flesh, and very aromatic, with edible core. Great for serving 2. Golden exterior.

NUTRITIONAL INFO

1 cup diced is a significant source of vitamin C.

SERVING SUGGESTIONS

No-toil broil: Cut into rings and either grill on well-oiled grates or broil, turning to lightly caramelize each side. Serve with grilled meat or poultry. Or serve as dessert topped with ice cream.

Salad days: Add pineapple chunks to coleslaw or chicken salad. Or use in spinach salad dressed with a cilantro vinaigrette (combine 1/3 cup vegetable oil, 1/4 cup rice vinegar, 2 minced shallots, and 3 tablespoons finely chopped cilantro, plus salt and pepper to taste).

Curry: Add pineapple chunks to shrimp or chicken curry. The fruit's sweetness will balance nicely with the spicy sauce.

Breakfast sauté: Cook 3 cups of pineapple chunks in 2–3 tablespoons butter on medium-high heat until warm and starting to caramelize. Spoon over pancakes or waffles. Or serve with ham.

pineapple ginger beef

This delicious stir-fry entrée combines the sweet taste of fresh pineapple with beef and tangy Asian-style ingredients, such as ginger, oyster sauce, and plum sauce. Serve it over cooked rice. If desired, garnish with fresh cilantro.

BEEF

2 tablespoons oyster sauce (see Cook's Notes)

2 teaspoons cornstarch

3/4 pound flank steak, thinly sliced

SAUCE

2 teaspoons finely chopped crystallized ginger

1/4 cup water

1 tablespoon plum sauce (see Cook's Notes)

1 tablespoon soy sauce

2 teaspoons Asian sesame oil (see Cook's Notes)

1/4 teaspoon sugar

STIR-FRY

2 tablespoons vegetable oil

1 tablespoon minced fresh ginger

1/2 cup fresh pineapple chunks

1 teaspoon cornstarch dissolved in 2 teaspoons water

YIELD: 4 SERVINGS

COOK'S NOTES: Oyster sauce is a dark brown, rich, caramelized sauce made from oysters, brine, and soy sauce. Oyster sauce, Asian sesame oil, and plum sauce are sold in the Asian sections of most supermarkets.

1. Prepare beef: Combine oyster sauce and 2 teaspoons cornstarch in bowl. Add beef and stir to coat. Let stand 10 minutes.

2. Prepare sauce: Combine sauce ingredients in bowl; set aside.

3. Prepare stir-fry: Place wok or large, deep skillet over high heat until hot. Add oil, swirling to coat sides. Add beef and stir-fry until barely pink, about 2 minutes.

4. Add ginger and stir-fry 30 seconds.

5. Add pineapple and sauce; bring to boil. Add cornstarch mixed with water and cook, stirring, until sauce boils and thickens.

NUTRITIONAL INFORMATION (PER SERVING): Calories 310; fat calories 180; total fat 20 grams; sat fat 6 grams; cholesterol 60 milligrams; sodium 400 milligrams; total carbohydrates 8 grams; fiber less than 1 gram; sugars 2 grams; protein 24 grams; vitamin A IUs 0%; vitamin C 10%; calcium 2%; iron 20%.

pluot, plumcot, aprium

OVER THE PAST FEW YEARS, delectable apricot-plum hybrids (which are often trademarked) have become increasingly available in the marketplace. Their taste, texture, fragrance, and appearance can be similar to either apricots or plums. And often their sugar content is higher than either plums' or apricots'.

Supersweet, plump, and wrapped in smooth, party-dress colored skins, several varieties of these plum-apricot cousins have been developed. Generally, plumcots are a 50–50 cross between apricots and plums; often they are more like apricots than plums, with golden skin and bright-yellow flesh. Generally pluots are a 75 percent plum and 25 percent apricot cross; they look and taste more like plums than apricots. Generally apriums are 25 percent plum and 75 percent apricot; most often they have yellow skin and taste more like apricots than plums. Pluots make up about 98 percent of the yearly crop.

BUYING AND STORING

Look for plump fruit that is relatively firm yet gives slightly to gentle pressure. Avoid those with shriveling or soft spots. Ripen using Brown-Bag Ripening Technique (see page 309). Store ripened fruit up to 3 days in cool location or refrigerate loose in crisper drawer up to 7 days.

APRIUM:
Domestic: *May–June*
Global: *none*

PLUMCOT:
Domestic: *May–July*
Global: *none*

PLUOT:
Domestic: *May–September*
Global: *January–March*

Pluots are the most readily available of the plum-apricot hybrids. Here are some specific varieties:

PREP

Wash thoroughly with cold running water. Most are semifreestone, meaning they can be cut in half from top to bottom, following suture (lengthwise seam). Twist halves in opposite directions and fruit will break in half. Pits cling more stubbornly in some varieties than others. Some release by prying with a teaspoon; others need to be cut free with a paring knife.

USE

Eat raw out of hand, or pit, slice or dice, then use in fruit salad, salsa, or chicken salad. Or cook in poultry dishes or baked goods, such as pies, tarts, cakes, or custards. Or use for jam, preserves, or as a garnish.

DAPPLE DANDY
(sometimes labeled Dinosaur Egg, a trademarked brand) **Most common variety. Large with purple-red smooth skin dotted with yellow specks. Flesh ranges from golden to red.** ■ *Very sweet.*

EMERALD BAUT
Greenish-yellow skin with yellow flesh. ■ *Often the sweetest pluot.*

FLAVOR FALL
Dark purple skin with yellow flesh. Ripens late in season. ■ *Sweet.*

FLAVOR GATOR
Marbled red and yellowish-green skin with yellow flesh. ■ *Very sweet.*

FLAVOR KING
Red skin with yellow speckles, yellow flesh blushed with red. ■ *Delicious flavor profile, similar to Santa Rosa plums but without acidity.*

FLAVOROSA
Usually first of season variety. Medium sized with dark purple skin and red flesh. ■ *Very sweet with interesting plumlike flavors.*

FLAVOR QUEEN
Pale green to yellow skin with yellow flesh. ■ *Very sweet and complex flavor.*

NECTACOTUM
Red skin with yellow specks and red flesh with yellow blush. ■ *Very sweet and nectarine-like flavor.*

SWEET TREATS
Pale green to yellow skin with yellow flesh. ■ *Very, very sweet with interesting, complex flavor.*

NURITIONAL INFO

1 cup is a good source of vitamin C; significant source of vitamins A and K.

SERVING SUGGESTIONS

Couscous boost: Prepare packaged couscous according to directions. Add ⅓ cup chopped pluots (or apriums or plumcots), 2 tablespoons chopped fresh mint, and ½ teaspoon lemon juice.

Pluot-pineapple salsa: Combine 4 chopped pluots (or apriums or plumcots), 1 cup diced pineapple, 3 tablespoons cilantro, ¼ cup chopped sweet onion, 1 jalapeño chile (seeded, finely minced), 1 tablespoon vegetable oil, and 2 tablespoons fresh lime juice; toss. Serve over grilled fish, poultry, or pork.

Cheese-stuffed dessert: In food processor fitted with metal blade, process 4 ounces crumbled blue cheese with 3 ounces room-temperature cream cheese. Fill hollow portions of halved, pitted pluots (or plumcots or apriums) with generous amount of cheese mixture. Garnish with mint leaves.

Balsamic-dressed side dish: Cut each of 6 large pluots into eighths and place in medium bowl. In small bowl, stir 2 tablespoons balsamic vinegar and 1 tablespoon sugar until sugar dissolves. Pour over pluots and toss. Cut 8 large mint leaves into thin strips. Add to pluots and toss. Cover and chill. Serve next to grilled pork, duck, or salmon. Or to use as salad, arrange small amount of mixed greens on 6 salad plates. Top with thinly sliced tomato and season to taste with coarse salt and pepper. Spoon pluot mixture on top.

Flavor King

Flavorosa

Nectacotum

pomegranate

POMEGRANATE TRANSLATES FROM THE FRENCH as "apple with many seeds." Inside the fruit, seeds cluster like a glimmering carpet beneath thin yellow membranes. Shining like ruby-red crystal prisms, these seeds are filled with irresistible sweet-tart juice. Outside, the apple-sized fruit has a leathery shell that can range from pink to deep crimson, even russet brown. A frilly calyx cap gives them a regal appearance.

Native to Persia (now Iran) where they have been cultivated for more than 4,000 years, pomegranates have a long culinary history in the Middle East, India, and China. Now, New World chefs are using these wine-red seeds to garnish everything from green salads to game hens. The juice is used to tenderize lamb or to serve as a base for sorbet, jelly, or cocktails.

BUYING AND STORING

Choose fruit that is heavy for its size and shows no sign of deterioration. Generally, skin color is not an indication of ripeness. Early ripening varieties available in August and September have pink rinds; the seeds inside are deeply colored with a pleasing acidic edge. The Wonderful variety (the most common variety in the marketplace) ripens in September and October. It has a deep crimson rind and seeds with a nice balance of sweet and sour. Store whole fruit at room temperature for up to 1 week, or refrigerate up to 2 weeks. After 2 weeks, the fruit starts to dehydrate. Seeds can be refrigerated airtight up to 5 days or frozen up to 3 months. Juice may be refrigerated 1 week, or frozen up to 3 months.

Domestic: *August–December, Wonderful variety most common*

PREP

The trick to enjoying these jewel-like seeds is to find an easy way to remove them without creating pools of escaping juices and splatters. The foolproof way is to use the no-mess, "underwater" technique. Cut pomegranate into quarters over a paper towel. Fill a medium bowl with cold water. Hold a pomegranate quarter under the water, seed side down. Pull edges back, exposing seeds. Run fingers over seeds to remove them. Turn fruit over, still holding underwater, and pick out remaining seeds. Seeds will sink to the bottom of the bowl and small membrane pieces will float to the top. Discard membranes (they're bitter) and drain seeds. Pat dry with a paper towel.

To juice, place whole, unpeeled pomegranate on a hard surface; press the palm of your hand against the fruit, then roll gently to break all the juice sacs inside (you'll hear when they stop breaking). Carefully pierce in 1 place and squeeze out the juice; or poke in a straw and do the same, pressing the fruit to release the juice. Or, buy pomegranate juice at a health-food store or some supermarkets, then use seeds to add color, texture, and flavor to the dish.

NUTRITIONAL INFO

¾ cup seeds is a significant source of vitamin C; good source of vitamin B_6.

USE

Eat seeds raw out of hand or use as garnish for salads, oatmeal, meat dishes, or desserts. Use juice to make syrup for sorbets, sundaes, or savory sauces. Or use juice as part of braising liquid for meat; it gives the sauce irresistible jamminess.

SERVING SUGGESTIONS

Scarlet-speckled salad: Toss seeds in mixed green salad made with baby lettuces, crumbled blue cheese, and red-wine vinaigrette (see Simple Vinaigrette, page 310).

Sweet-tart syrup: To prepare pomegranate syrup, combine 1 cup pomegranate juice, 1 teaspoon lemon juice, and ½ cup sugar in medium saucepan. Bring to boil on high heat; reduce heat to medium-high and gently boil for 10 minutes or until slightly thickened. Serve on pancakes, waffles, French toast, and crepes. Or add to lemonade to make a tasty pink drink.

Couscous with color: Add visual drama, flavor, and crunch: before serving, top couscous with generous amount of seeds.

Pomegranate confetti salsa: Combine seeds from 3 pomegranates, 2 minced (cored and seeded) jalapeño chiles, 1 to 2 small (chopped)

Pomegranate

red onion, 1 tablespoon (chopped) cilantro, 1 teaspoon olive oil, 1 tablespoon fresh lime juice, plus salt and pepper to taste. Spoon over broiled fish, lamb, or pork.

pomegranate, orange, and dried cranberry salad with raspberry vinaigrette

Oranges, dried cranberries, pomegranate seed, and raspberries bring tangy sweetness to this mixed green salad. It makes the perfect accompaniment to rich meat (such as roast pork) or game birds (such as duck or goose). Or serve after the main course accompanied by a wedge of brie or cambozola.

1 pound baby greens

2 oranges, Cara Cara preferred, peeled, cut into sections

Seeds from 2 pomegranates (see Prep)

1 (3-ounce) package dried cranberries

1 cup fresh or frozen (thawed) raspberries

⅓ cup lime juice or Key lime juice

¼ cup raspberry vinegar

2 tablespoons honey

Salt to taste, coarse sea salt preferred

Pepper to taste

YIELD: 8 SERVINGS

1. Wash and dry greens; set aside. In medium bowl, gently toss orange sections, pomegranate seeds, and dried cranberries.

2. Combine raspberries, lime juice, vinegar, honey, salt, and pepper in blender. Whirl until creamy. Taste and adjust seasoning as needed.

3. Divide greens among 8 salad plates. Top each with fruit mixture. Drizzle vinaigrette over each salad. Serve.

NUTRITIONAL INFORMATION (PER SERVING):
Calories 150; fat calories 0; total fat 0 grams; sat fat 0 grams; cholesterol 0 milligrams; sodium 160 milligrams; total carbohydrates 37 grams; fiber 6 grams; sugars 15 grams; protein 2 grams; vitamin A IUs 30%; vitamin C 60%; calcium 6%; iron 20%.

quince

BASICALLY, QUINCE LOOK LIKE SQUATTY PEARS. But the surface is uneven, covered with subtle bumps that are shaped like shallow moguls on a powdery ski slope. Some have fuzzy skin; others are smooth; skin color varies from yellow to chartreuse.

Inside, the flesh is whitish-yellow with a texture similar to hard, underripe pears. Uncooked, they taste dry and astringent. Cooked, they become soft and flavorful, most varieties turning an appealing pink or red color. The fragrance is an alluring blend of pear and pineapple.

Quince

BUYING AND STORING

Look for firm fruit without spots or discoloration. In general, riper fruit have less fuzz. Store at room temperature for up to 1 week; left out, they will fill the room with "quince perfume." Or for longer storage, place in refrigerator for up to 3 weeks. Cooked quince wedges can be frozen up to 3 months (see Freezing, page 310).

Domestic: *September–December*
Global: *May–July*

PREP

Wash in cold water; if fuzzy, rub with clean towel. Cut into quarters; core and peel.

USE

Bake, sauté, braise, or poach. Use to make jelly or jam; if used underripe and green-tinged, they are higher in pectin and are superior for jam or jelly making. Or use braised (or baked) like apples in sweet or savory dishes. Quince paste is a popular dish in both Mediterranean and Mexican cuisines. Often it is paired with salty cheese.

NUTRITIONAL INFO

1 quince is a good source of vitamin C.

SERVING SUGGESTIONS

Quince 'n' cream: Poach quince wedges (peeled and cored) in brandy until tender. Spoon over ice cream or frozen yogurt.

Quince mix pastry: Combine quince slices (peeled and cored) with pear or apple slices in pies, cobblers, or crisps.

Baked: Place whole, cored quince in slow-cooker (if corer isn't sturdy enough to remove core, cut quince in half and core). Fill quince cavities with raisins mixed with sugar, cinnamon, and, if desired, chopped walnuts. Top each quince with 1/2 teaspoon butter. Add 3/4 cup water to bottom of pot. Cover and cook on low setting overnight or 8 hours. Serve warm, if desired, with cream or plain yogurt.

Non-apple applesauce: Cover quince slices (peeled and cored) with water or apple juice in saucepan; cover and simmer until tender. Drain and pulse in food processor until "saucy." Add sugar and ground cinnamon to taste.

ginger quince butter

This delectable spread can be slathered over pancakes, biscuits, waffles, or toast. Or dollop a spoonful on pork chops or ham slices.

3 quince, peeled, cored, and sliced

1 1/2 cups water

1 cup apple juice

3 tablespoons lemon juice

1/2 cup sugar

1/2 cup honey

1 tablespoon minced lemon zest, colored portion of peel

1 tablespoon minced fresh ginger

1 teaspoon ground cinnamon

1/2 teaspoon ground nutmeg

YIELD: ABOUT 2 CUPS

1. Place quince, water, and juices in medium saucepan. Bring to boil on high heat. Reduce heat to low and simmer about 30 minutes or until quince is very tender.

2. Stir in remaining ingredients. Increase heat to medium-high and bring to gentle boil, stirring constantly, for 5 minutes. Puree in blender or food processor. Can be refrigerated up to 1 week, or frozen in small containers up to 3 months (see Freezing, page 310).

NUTRITIONAL INFORMATION (PER TABLESPOON): Calories 40; fat calories 0; total fat 0 grams; sat fat 0 grams; cholesterol 0 milligrams; sodium 0 milligrams; total carbohydrates 10 grams; fiber 0 grams; sugars 8 grams; protein 0 grams; vitamin A IUs 0%; vitamin C 4%; calcium 0%; iron 0%.

rambutan

TO PICTURE RAMBUTAN, imagine a lychee that spent the night in Dr. Frankenstein's laboratory, being fitted top to bottom with hairlike protrusions. The bristles don't prohibit easy access to the luscious orb inside the shell, because they are soft and flexible. The shell ranges in color from crimson to orange to greenish-yellow and has a pebbly texture. It's easily penetrable with a small knife or sturdy thumbnail.

There are more than 50 varieties, but all contain a grayish-white globe that is juicy and surrounds an elongated, inedible pit. Less fragrant than lychees, rambutans have a sweet-tart tropical flavor, a pineapple-cherry taste with a subtle tart edge, and a grapelike texture.

BUYING AND STORING

Shells shouldn't have any ruptures, moisture, or mold on them. Spikes should be flexible and look fresh. Can store 1–2 days at room temperature, or refrigerate in perforated plastic bag for up to 7 days. For longer storage, freeze whole or shelled and pitted up to 3 months (see Freezing, page 310). If frozen whole, seeds are easier to remove than when fresh. Freezing causes texture change. They become slightly mushy but still taste delicious.

Domestic: *October–May*
Global: *August–October*

Rambutan

PREP

To peel, cut around "equator" with small paring knife or sturdy thumbnail, just deep enough to penetrate shell. Remove bottom half of shell and squeeze remaining shell. Edible, grapelike orb will pop from shell. To remove pit, cut in half lengthwise stopping at the pit; pull apart and cut out pit. Or, for easier pitting, try a Pitter (see page 309).

USE

Eat raw out of hand or include in fruit salads. Purée and use in jams, jellies, or sorbet (see Meyer Lemon Sorbet, page 51).

NUTRITIONAL INFO

1 cup is a good source of vitamin C.

SERVING SUGGESTIONS

Tropical pops: Eat frozen shelled and pitted rambutan as an ice-cold treat, much like frozen grapes.

Chocolate coated: Place shelled and pitted rambutan halves on paper towel. Melt coating chocolate (often coating chocolate is stocked next to berries in produce sections); it should be just warm enough to melt. Dip half of each rambutan in melted chocolate and place on waxed paper to dry. Or, if using a pitter to remove seeds, place a small piece of crystallized ginger in seed pocket and dip half in melted chocolate.

Mango marriage: Make a fruit salad with rambutans and other fruit, such as pineapple cubes, papaya cubes, and grapes. Prepare mango dressing in food processor. With machine running, add 2 tablespoons roughly chopped fresh mint; process until minced. Add 1 ripe (peeled and seeded) mango and process until puréed. Add 3–4 tablespoons fresh lime juice and 4 tablespoons sugar. Process until smooth and sugar dissolves. Place salad in individual bowls; drizzle dressing on top. If desired, garnish with toasted flaked coconut.

Lychee sub: Rambutan can be substituted for lychee in most recipes (see Lychee, page 58).

sapote, also zapote, custard apple

MAMEY

WHITE

ALTHOUGH THEY SHARE THE SAME SAPOTE LABEL, mamey sapotes and white sapotes look and taste quite different. Both sapote and cherimoya are referred to as custard apple in the produce industry, but the "true" custard apple is white sapote.

The crisp, applelike flesh that surrounds white sapote's seeds is bed-sheet white. It tastes like a combination of mango and banana, with a subtle hint of vanilla or coconut. The fruit looks something like a green-skinned apple that is gently pointed at one end. Seeds are inedible, and although the skin can be eaten, it is generally sour.

Usually quite large, mamey sapote are football-shaped and covered with rough skin that looks like the surface of a brown coconut. Inside, bright salmon-orange flesh surrounds an impressively large black seed. The texture is avocado-like and the taste is a blend of peach, apricot, and raspberry. Both seeds and skin are inedible.

White

Mamey

BUYING AND STORING MAMEY SAPOTES

Ripe fruit will yield to gentle pressure like a ripe plum. Ripen at room temperature up to 3 days. Refrigerate ripe fruit loose in crisper drawer up to 1 week. Freezes well.

BUYING AND STORING WHITE SAPOTES

Ripe fruit will yield to gentle pressure like a plum. Ripen at room temperature 1–2 days. Refrigerate loose in crisper drawer up to 14 days.

MAMEY SAPOTE
Domestic: *July–October*
Global: *none*

WHITE SAPOTE
Domestic: *year-round, peaks September–February*
Global: *none*

PREP FOR MAMEY SAPOTE

Cut in half lengthwise and scoop out flesh, discarding large seed and skin.

PREP FOR WHITE SAPOTE

Cut in half crosswise and scoop out flesh, discarding seeds. Skin is edible, but it can be somewhat tart.

USE

Both are eaten raw out of hand scooped from skin with small spoon (discarding skin). Squeeze a little fresh lime juice on top for best flavor. Great used in icy blender cocktails and shakes. Puréed, use as a dessert sauce, spooned over ice cream, yogurt, or cheesecake (or see dessert sauce in Serving Suggestions).

NUTRITIONAL INFO (MAMEY SAPOTE)

1 cup is a good source of vitamin A.

NUTRITIONAL INFO (WHITE SAPOTE)

1 cup is a significant source of vitamin A and a good source of vitamin C.

SERVING SUGGESTIONS

Sapote shake: In a blender, combine 6 ice cubes, 1/2 cup sweetened condensed milk, 1 cup sapote (peeled, seeded, diced), 1 teaspoon vanilla extract, and 1/4 cup milk. Whirl until smooth.

Freezer pleaser: Freeze ripe, halved sapotes in airtight container. For serving, leave at room temperature about 20 minutes and eat like sorbet. Cut in half, remove pit and spoon semifrozen flesh from skin with small spoon.

Fruit salad: Cut ripe sapote (peeled and seeded) into bite-sized chunks. Gently toss with kiwi slices (peeled) and fresh berries. Sprinkle with minced fresh mint and sugar (or orange liqueur). Toss very gently. Chill. Serve in chilled martini glasses garnished with small sprigs of fresh mint.

Sapote dessert sauce: Place about 2 cups ripe sapote chunks (peeled, seeded) in food processor fitted with metal blade. Add 2 tablespoons honey (lavender honey preferred) and 1 teaspoon finely grated fresh ginger. Process until puréed. Spoon around warm gingerbread or dense chocolate cake.

star fruit, also carambola

FIVE DEEP, LENGTHWISE PLEATS FORM STARS when this waxy-skinned yellow or yellowish-green fruit is sliced. The flesh is translucent, moderately juicy and crisp. Its flavor varies according to time of harvest and variety. It can be fragrantly sweet or wake-up tart. The taste is part grape, part plum, with a little crisp green apple thrown into the flavor mix.

There are two types of star fruit: domestic, grown in Florida, and Taiwanese. Domestic fruit is generally smaller and greenish-yellow. Fruit grown in Taiwan is about two times larger, deep yellow, and generally sweeter. Edible seeds inside flesh are small and tender.

Star Fruit

BUYING AND STORING

Look for firm fruit with a pleasant, flowery scent. Avoid fruit that is blemished or has soft spots. Store at room temperature until fully ripe and deep yellow. Refrigerate ripe fruit 1–2 weeks.

Domestic: *year-round*
Global: *year-round*

PREP

Wash with cold water. Skin is edible, but it sometimes is tough at the tips. If tips of ridges are brown or black, remove tips with vegetable peeler or paring knife. Slice horizontally to make star shapes.

USE

Generally eaten raw, but sliced star fruit can be used briefly simmered in simple syrup or quickly sautéed in stir-fries. Sliced star fruit makes a lovely star-shaped garnish for sweet and savory dishes and is a showy addition to fruit salad. Puréed, it can be used in sauces, soups, jams, or sorbets.

NUTRITIONAL INFO

1 cup cubed is an excellent source of vitamin C.

SERVING SUGGESTIONS

Building on a star: Use ¼-inch-thick slices as a base for appetizers. Top with chicken salad or sweet-spicy mango salsa.

Cocktail pizzazz: Use as a cocktail garnish. Make a shallow slit in a ¼-inch thick slice and gently insert slit on rim of cocktail glass.

Tart with splendor: Use a combination of sliced star fruit and berries to garnish individual fruit tarts. Fill baked pastry shells with cool pastry cream. Top with concentric circles of thinly sliced fruit.

Stars in sugar syrup: Poach ⅜-inch thick star fruit slices in simple syrup (2 cups water simmered with 1½ cups sugar until sugar dissolves). Add star fruit slices and gently simmer 3–5 minutes. Remove from heat. Cool. Spoon over ice cream, yogurt, or pudding.

tamarillo, also tree tomato

GOLD

RED

WITH SKIN THAT IS GLOSSY AND SMOOTH, a tamarillo looks like an egg-shaped, stem-on plum. About 2½ to 3 inches long, tamarillo has one variety that is scarlet, another that is golden. Inside the tough skin, swirls of small flat seeds form around a soft edible core. The red ones have black seeds that surround tiny green seeds; the yellow ones have greenish-white seeds. The flesh next to the skin is velvety like an apricot.

The taste has a pleasing acidity and is mildly astringent. They are related to tomatoes. Some describe the flavor as tomato-like; others say its sweet-tart taste is similar to plums. The gold variety often is a little sweeter than the red.

BUYING AND STORING

Look for fruit that are fragrant and give slightly to pressure. Ripen at room temperature. Because of their thick skin, they can be refrigerated for up to 4 weeks in plastic bag in crisper drawer. Or wrap individually in plastic and freeze.

Domestic: *none*
Global: *April–September*

PREP

Skin is tough and generally isn't eaten. Either cut in half lengthwise or scoop out flesh with spoon, or peel with paring knife. Skin can also be removed by submerging fruit in boiling water for 2 to 3 minutes; plunge in ice water, then slip skin off, grasping it at 1 end with paring knife. Or use vegetable peeler. Cut in wedges or slices. Or, if seeds are too hard to eat (generally only in red fruit), press through large-mesh sieve using wooden spoon. Note that red tamarillos can stain.

USE

Eat peeled, raw or cooked. Use in sweet or savory dishes: beverages, soufflés, cakes, sauces, salsas, or salads. Spoon strained fruit over ice cream, cake, or pudding, sweetening first with sugar if desired.

NUTRITIONAL INFO

1 cup is a significant source of vitamins A and C.

Red Tomarillo

Gold Tamarillo

SERVING SUGGESTIONS

Sauce for chicken or seafood: Cut 4 peeled tamarillos into wedges; place in heavy-bottomed medium saucepan with ½ cup vegetable broth and 1 tablespoon sugar. Bring to simmer on medium heat, covered. Simmer 15 minutes or until tender. Purée in 2 batches in blender, using caution because mixture is hot. Strain sauce over cooked chicken or seafood.

Tamarillo-tomato salad: In medium bowl, combine tomato wedges and gold tamarillo with chunks of fresh mozzarella cheese. Toss with vinaigrette made with 3 parts vegetable oil and 1 part white-wine vinegar. Season to taste with coarse salt. Garnish with fresh basil.

Cheesecake topper: Combine strained tamarillo (see Prep) with sugar and orange liqueur to taste; stir until sugar dissolves. Place individual servings of cheesecake on dessert plates. Spoon tamarillo sauce over cheesecake. Garnish with sprig of fresh mint.

Curry cuties: Use as garnish on plates next to spicy curry; the flavors are very complementary.

tamarindo,
also tamarind, indian date

THE FIBROUS, STICKY PULP inside the brittle, reddish-brown tamarind pod is sweet and sour, with an appealing flavor profile often described as sour apricot. The exterior looks like a 4- to 8-inch-long bean pod. It crackles and breaks away when pressure is applied and is discarded along with the mahogany-colored seeds inside the pulp.

The seeded pulp provides the complex tart-sweet flavor base in curries, chutneys, and soups. Before use, pulp is cooked in water, then pressed through a sieve.

BUYING AND STORING

Pods sold in produce section of Asian or Latin American markets and some supermarkets with large specialty produce sections. Store unpeeled pods at room temperature in zipper-style plastic bag up to 3 months. Also sold in paste (in cellophane-wrapped "bricks" or jars), powder, and syrup forms. (See Prep for homemade pulp storage). Store-bought "bricks" can be stored at room temperature up to 1 year.

Domestic: *none*
Global: *year-round*

Tamarindo

PREP FOR PODS

Remove and discard pods. Put pulp with seeds in saucepan and add enough water to completely cover. Simmer, covered, for 25–30 minutes, adding more water if necessary. Push pulp through medium sieve into bowl using back of wooden spoon. Discard seeds. Paste should have a ketchuplike consistency. Store, well sealed, in refrigerator up to 1 week. Or freeze small amounts in zipper-style plastic freezer bags (see Freezing, page 310).

USE

Tamarind pulp is used fresh, dried, candied, and pickled. It is used in soups, sauces, marinades, stews, candies, and cakes. It's used in Latin American, Indian, Southeast Asian, African, Indonesian, and Middle Eastern cuisine. It's one of the primary ingredients in Worcestershire sauce.

NUTRITIONAL INFO

1 cup provides moderate amounts of B vitamins, protein, phosphorus, iron, potassium, and niacin.

SERVING SUGGESTIONS

Chutney counterbalance: Use paste in raw or cooked chutney to balance spicy-hot and sweet elements.

Refreshing beverage: To make tamarind-flavored *agua fresca*, a drink much like lemonade, dilute tamarind paste (see Prep) with water and add sugar to taste. Serve chilled.

Vinaigrette for greens or game: Whisk 1 tablespoon tamarind paste (see Prep) with 3 tablespoons hot water until dissolved. Add 1 tablespoon honey, 3 tablespoons canola oil, and pinch ground cumin; whisk to combine. Stir in 1 tablespoon finely chopped red onion and salt and pepper to taste. Spoon over mixed greens or grilled duck, chicken, or pork. If desired, garnish with cilantro or fresh pineapple chunks.

Sour-sweet sorbet: Prepare simple syrup: combine 2 cups water and $3/4$ cup sugar. Bring to boil on high heat; reduce to medium-low and simmer 3–4 minutes or until sugar is completely dissolved. Cool. Leftover syrup can be stored airtight in refrigerator. Combine 1 cup tamarind paste (see Prep) with 2 cups cooled sugar syrup. Process in ice cream machine according to manufacturer's instructions. Serve as dessert after spicy meal. Accompany with cookies, if desired.

tangerine, mandarin

CLEMENTINE

FAIRCHILD

MURCOTT (HONEY)

PAGE

PIXIE

SATSUMA

TANGERINES ARE SO CONVENIENTLY WRAPPED. Their loose peel slips away from the brightly colored segments with only a gentle tug. The segments separate easily, too, and are less acidic than most citrus fruit. The flesh is juicy and fragrant, sweet with subtle tartness. Some have seeds, but most don't.

Most experts contend that tangerines are a subclass of mandarins, fruit that has been cultivated in China for thousands of years. (They were named for the brightly colored red-orange robes worn by noble mandarins.) Tangerines may have gotten their name when mandarins were introduced to Europe via Tangiers (Morocco).

BUYING AND STORING

Look for fruit that is heavy for its size, without soft spots. Store at room temperature up to 1 week, or refrigerate wrapped in plastic bag 10–12 days. Juice can be frozen.

ALL VARIETIES OF TANGERINES/MANDARINS
(except pixie and clementine)
Domestic: *December–February*
Global: *none*

PIXIE
Domestic: *December–June*
Global: *none*

CLEMENTINE
Domestic: *November–March*
Global: *June–August*

Pixie

Page

PREP

Peel skin and separate segments. If seeds are present, remove with tip of small paring knife.

USE

Eat raw out of hand or in fruit salads; stir into yogurt or dip in warm melted chocolate. Use juice in dressings or marinades. Use zest in sauces, desserts, and marinades.

NUTRITIONAL INFO

1 cup is an excellent source of vitamin C; significant source of thiamin.

SERVING SUGGESTIONS

Citrusy couscous: Toss tangerine segments (cut into ½-inch pieces if large, seeded if necessary) into cooked couscous. Garnish with thinly sliced green onion and toasted slivered almonds.

Dressed up roasted or grilled vegetables: To prepare tangerine vinaigrette, combine 1 teaspoon minced tangerine zest, ½ cup tangerine juice, 1 large clove garlic (finely minced), and 2 tablespoons rice vinegar. Whisk in 2 teaspoons Asian sesame oil and 1 tablespoon finely sliced chives or green onion. Add salt and pepper to taste; spoon over roasted or grilled vegetables.

Easy tangerine sorbet: To make a tangy-sweet dessert, substitute tangerine juice for lemon juice in sorbet (see Meyer Lemon Sorbet, page 51).

Fish bliss: Lightly season firm-flesh fish fillets with mixture made with equal parts ground cumin, finely minced tangerine zest, salt, and black pepper. Grill or broil. Meanwhile, boil 1½ cups tangerine juice until reduced to ½ cup. Off heat, stir in ⅓ cup butter, 1–2 tablespoons at a time. Spoon over cooked fish.

Murcott

Satsuma

Fairchild

CLEMENTINE
Hybrid between mandarin and bitter orange. Range in size from small to medium. Deep red-orange skin, almost spherical. Generally seedless. ■ *Varies from sweet to moderately sweet with subtle tart edge. Juicy.*

FAIRCHILD
Deep orange, lightly dimpled skin. Small, almost spherical with small segments. Generally seedless. ■ *Moderately sweet with chewy, dense texture. Orange flavor with little bright tangerine tartness.*

MURCOTT
(sometimes called Honey in California, but in Florida, Honey is different variety) Dark orange, lightly dimpled skin. Small and oblate shape (very flat at top and bottom). Generally seedless. ■ *Highly acid profile. Tastes lemony-orange.*

PAGE
Deep orange skin that is thicker than most. Looks like a small orange. Generally seedless. ■ *Very juicy with bright, tangy flavor.*

PIXIE
Well-defined bumps on light orange skin. Subtly collared with ridge at stem end. Generally seedless. ■ *Very easily peeled and not too juicy, making them great for lunchboxes. Straight orange flavor.*

SATSUMA
Bright orange, lightly dimpled skin. Small and oblate shape (very flat at top and bottom). Generally seedless. ■ *Lemon-orange aroma with tangy-tart refreshing flavor.*

tangerine soufflés

These beautiful soufflés showcase the sweet-tart taste of tangerines. They are delectable on their own, but for added glamour, accompany them with either raspberry sauce (coulis) or a custard sauce (crème anglaise).

Butter for greasing dishes

Sugar for dusting dishes

³⁄₄ cup whole milk

1¹⁄₂ tablespoons cornstarch

3 tablespoons freshly-squeezed tangerine juice

2 teaspoons finely minced tangerine zest (colored part of peel)

4 egg yolks

6 egg whites

pinch salt, kosher preferred

¹⁄₃ cup sugar

GARNISH: powdered sugar

OPTIONAL GARNISH: tangerine wedges and sprigs of fresh mint

YIELD: 8 SERVINGS

1. Adjust oven rack to middle position. Preheat oven to 350 degrees. Lightly butter 8 (8-ounce) soufflé cups. Lightly dust with sugar and invert to remove excess sugar.

2. In heavy-bottomed, large saucepan, combine milk and cornstarch. Stir until blended. Place on medium heat and scald (bring to just below boil). Remove from heat. Stir in tangerine juice and zest. Let cool 5 minutes. Whisk in egg yolks and set aside.

3. Place egg whites in large bowl of electric mixer. Beat on medium speed until frothy. Add salt and increase speed to high, and beat until soft peaks form. Add sugar, about 1 tablespoon at a time, beating 20 seconds between additions. Beat until stiff and glossy.

4. Add about one-third of egg white mixture to yolk mixture; fold together. Gently fold yolk mixture into egg white mixture. Gently spoon mixture into prepared soufflé cups, filling them to within ⅛ inch of top. Place cups on rimmed baking sheet. Bake in middle of preheated oven about 20 minutes or until tops are golden brown and soufflés have risen above rims of dishes.

5. Dust lightly with powdered sugar: Place powdered sugar in small sieve and shake over top of soufflés. Place each dish on a dessert plate. Garnish plate with wedge of tangerine and mint sprig, if desired. Serve immediately or soufflés will deflate.

NUTRITIONAL INFORMATION (PER SERVING): Calories 110; fat calories 13.5; total fat 1.5 grams; sat fat 1 gram; cholesterol 105 milligrams; sodium 80 milligrams; total carbohydrates 14 grams; fiber 0 grams; sugars 12 grams; protein 5 grams; vitamin A IUs 4%; vitamin C 4%; calcium 4%; iron 2%.

uniq fruit, ugli fruit

UNIQUE IN ITS APPEARANCE AND APPEALING FLAVOR, this citrus fruit looks downright rumpled. The mottled green and yellow skin looks ill-fitted and bumpy. But its bizarre packaging doesn't affect the treasure inside. It peels away easily to reveal juicy, sweet sections that are most often seedless. This tropical fruit ripens without the rind being fully yellow.

A cross between grapefruit and mandarin, Uniq fruit has grapefruit's juicy texture, but without its hallmark acidity. The highly fragrant flesh is a lovely yellow hue.

BUYING AND STORING

Look for those with skin that is more yellow than green. Brown blemishes on skin don't affect taste. Refrigerate loose in crisper drawer up to 2 weeks.

Domestic: *none*
Global: *November–July*

PREP

Pull peel to break; peel will easily slide away from flesh. It's very easy to pull into segments. If recipe requires membranes surrounding segments to be removed, leave peeled fruit whole and cut between membranes with small, sharp knife (holding fruit over bowl to catch juices).

USE

Eat raw out of hand or in fruit salads. Or use to garnish rice dishes or couscous. Delicious on top of cream-filled fruit tarts.

NUTRITIONAL INFO

1 cup is an excellent source of vitamin C.

SERVING SUGGESTIONS

Uniq salad with minty attitude: Peel 4 Uniq fruit and while holding over salad bowl, remove membranes covering sides of segments (see Prep). Add segments to bowl and drizzle with 1 tablespoon orange liqueur. Toss. Place 3 tablespoons sugar and ¼ cup fresh mint leaves in food processor fitted with metal blade; pulse until mint is minced. Sprinkle over fruit. Toss. Cover and chill up to 8 hours.

Ice cream or spicy pork? This tangy topping can be ladled over ice cream or spooned on the plate next to roast pork. Make a simple sugar syrup by bringing 4 tablespoons water and 3 tablespoons sugar to boil; boil 1 minute and stir in 3 tablespoons dried cranberries. Cool. Stir in 2 tablespoons dark rum or coconut rum. Toss with 4 Uniq fruit, peeled and membranes removed (see Prep). Refrigerate, well-sealed, up to 2 days.

Uniq Fruit

uniq fruit, avocado, and red onion salad

This tangy salad can be made with a variety of greens. If you like, use baby arugula or baby spinach instead of the mixed baby greens. Or leave out the avocado and garnish salad with a wedge of blue cheese or creamy brie.

2 Uniq fruit

2 teaspoons seasoned rice vinegar

Salt and pepper to taste

¼ cup olive oil, extra-virgin preferred

¼ medium red onion, cut into thin slivers

2½ cups mixed baby lettuces

1 ripe avocado

1. Over large bowl, peel Uniq fruit and remove membranes, allowing juices to go into bowl. Place sectioned Uniq fruit in separate bowl. Add vinegar, salt, and pepper to juice in large bowl. Whisk in oil. Add onions and marinate at room temperature for 1 hour.

2. Add lettuce and toss. Taste and adjust seasoning as needed. Divide among 4 plates. Peel avocado and cut into wedges. Garnish with avocado wedges and Uniq fruit segments.

YIELD: 4 SERVINGS

NUTRITIONAL INFORMATION (PER SERVING): Calories 230; fat calories 180; total fat 20 grams; sat fat 3 grams; cholesterol 0 milligrams; sodium 310 milligrams; total carbohydrates 15 grams; fiber 5 grams; sugars 8 grams; protein 2 grams; vitamin A IUs 50%; vitamin C 15%; calcium 2%; iron 2%.

watermelon

BABY (MINI), RED SEEDLESS

ORANGE, SEEDLESS

RED, SEEDED OR SEEDLESS

YELLOW, SEEDED OR SEEDLESS

THEY CAN BE OBLONG OR SPHERICAL, clothed in rind that is solid, striped, or speckled. Some have classic red flesh; others have orange or yellow flesh. But all varieties of ripe watermelons share common flavor and texture traits. They are seductively sweet and have a juicy crunch.

Over the past few years, seedless varieties have become commonplace. Shiny black seeds have disappeared in these varieties, replaced instead with "seeds" that aren't developed. They are small, empty white "pips" (that surround seeds in seeded varieties). Some, orange-fleshed and Baby (Mini) varieties, are only available seedless.

Baby melons are a small, convenient size for refrigerators and ice chests, usually only about 5 to 8 inches in diameter. They have a thicker rind and a longer shelf life. There are many "baby" varieties; some have solid dark green rind and others are variegated. Interior flesh and flavor remain consistent.

ALL VARIETIES
Domestic: *April–October, peak from June–August*
Global: *October–May*

BUYING AND STORING

Available whole or cut into halves, slices, or quarters. For cut watermelons, choose those with sweet fragrance and dense flesh; avoid those with flesh that has pulled away from seeds. Whole watermelons should feel heavy for their size. Look at area where melon has rested on ground during growing period. A creamy yellow area indicates ripeness at harvest. Avoid those with cracks or soft spots. Some contend that a thudding sound made by tapping with palm of hand is a sign of ripeness.

Keep at room temperature up to 1 week. Or refrigerate, whole, up to 2 weeks. Or cut and cover cut surface with plastic, or store pieces in airtight container up to 2 days. Remove rind and cut into wedges or balls; freeze up to 3 months, well sealed.

ALL VARIETIES EXCEPT ORANGE
Domestic: *May–October, peak from June–August*
Global: *October–May*

ORANGE, SEEDLESS
Domestic: *April*
Global: *none*

PREP

Wash and cut into wedges, or cut off both ends, then in half through equator. Place wider cut edge on work surface. Using sturdy knife, cut off rind, cutting from top to bottom. If desired, reserve rind for pickling. Cut into desired shape. Or, to use watermelon rind as a container, cut in half lengthwise and remove flesh. Run knife around inner edge of rind; cut into wedges, then scoop out with large spoon.

USE

Eat raw in fruit salad, beverages, cold soup, or sorbet. Rind can be pickled in mixture of salt, water, vinegar, sugar, and spices.

NUTRITIONAL INFO

1 cup is a good source of vitamin C, significant source of vitamin A.

SERVING SUGGESTIONS

Fruit bonanza: Prepare fruit salad with bite-sized chunks of watermelon, cantaloupe, orange, jicama, and cucumber. Toss with generous amount of fresh lime juice and sprinkle with small amount of chile powder.

Watermelon vinaigrette: In blender or food processor, combine 2 cups peeled watermelon cubes, 1 cup fresh raspberries, and 2 tablespoons rice vinegar. Process until smooth. Taste and add sugar and/or salt, if desired.

Edible containers: Cut seedless watermelon into 1½-inch cubes. Using melon baller, scoop out a ¾-inch-deep "bowl" in each cube. Fill with spicy fruit salsa (see Mango Salsa, page 62) that is cut into fine dice. Serve chilled garnished with fresh mint leaves or cilantro leaves.

Star garnish: Cut peeled, seedless watermelon into 1-inch-thick slices. Use cookie cutters to cut out shapes.

Red

Orange

Baby

Yellow

watermelon margaritas

Mexican *aguas frescas* are refreshing drinks. One version uses strained, puréed seedless watermelon mixed with water, fresh lime juice, and sugar. Frozen cubes of seedless watermelon are also delicious in a wide variety of blender beverages, including these thirst-quenching Watermelon Margaritas.

1 seedless watermelon, red-flesh preferred, large enough to yield 4 cups peeled cubes

Fresh lime juice and coarse salt (such as kosher), for coating glass rims

½ cup fresh lime juice

1 tablespoon sugar

½ cup tequila

2 tablespoons orange liqueur

GARNISH: lime wedges

YIELD: 4 SERVINGS

1. Remove rind from watermelon and cut flesh into 1-inch cubes. Place in single layer on rimmed baking sheet. Freeze until solid, at least 1 hour.

2. To salt rims, place lime juice and coarse salt in separate shallow bowls. Dip lip of 4 margarita glasses in lime juice, then in salt. Set aside.

3. In blender, combine ½ cup lime juice, sugar, tequila, and liqueur. Add a few frozen watermelon chunks and whirl. Keep adding chunks, a few at a time, until drink has thick, smooth consistency. Pour into prepared glasses and serve.

NUTRITIONAL INFORMATION (PER SERVING WITHOUT SALT): Calories 160; fat calories 0; total fat 0 grams; sat fat 0 grams; cholesterol 0 milligrams; sodium 0 milligrams; total carbohydrates 21 grams; fiber 1 gram; sugars 16 grams; protein 1 gram; vitamin A IUs 20%; vitamin C 35%; calcium 2%; iron 2%.

yuzu

YUZU, A PEBBLY-SKINNED JAPANESE CITRUS (sometimes labeled Japanese citron), is rare in the United States and is only occasionally available, in the fall. A cross between a sour mandarin orange and a primitive citrus called *ichang papeda*, it's prized both for its juice and perfumy zest (colored portion of skin). About the size of a tangerine, yazu has green skin that turns yellowish-orange when it's ripe. The flesh is heavily seeded.

Highly fragrant with intense lemon-lime-tangerine-grapefruit flavors, its juice is often included in *ponzu*, a traditional Japanese dipping sauce. Bottled yuzu juice is sold at Japanese markets. Frozen juice, as well as *yuzu kosho* (a paste made with yuzu zest, salt, and chiles) is also sold at some Japanese markets.

BUYING AND STORING

Typically dark green when harvested early in the season, yuzu is also used when fully matured in a yellowish-orange skin late in the season. Choose fruit that seems heavy for its size. Refrigerate in plastic bags up to 2 weeks or loose at room temperature up to 1 week.

Domestic: *September–November*
Global: *none*

PREP

If using zest, remove it before cutting yuzu (see Zester, page 309). When juicing, for best results first bring yuzu to room temperature or microwave for 10 seconds. Or roll on counter, pressing down with palm.

USE

Minced zest and/or juice can be used in sauces, soups, and salad dressings, and in desserts, beverages, and entrées. Strips of yuzu peel can be candied and used to garnish both sweet and savory dishes.

NUTRITIONAL INFO

1 cup is a good source of vitamin C.

SERVING SUGGESTIONS

Yuzu-rita: Use fresh yuzu juice in an ice-cold margarita, substituting it for half of the lime juice.

Meringue-topped tart or pie: Substitute fresh yuzu juice and zest for lemon juice and zest in tart or pie recipes.

Tangy vinaigrette for seafood: Combine ¼ cup orange juice, 2 tablespoons yuzu juice, 1 teaspoon finely minced yuzu zest, 1 teaspoon minced ginger, and 2 tablespoons soy sauce in small bowl. Whisk in ½ cup canola oil or vegetable oil. Add salt to taste. If desired, add a pinch of sugar and whisk to dissolve. Drizzle over grilled seafood (such as scallops, shrimp, or octopus) and garnish with a little thinly sliced green onion (including dark green portion). Or, use this vinaigrette on mixed baby greens (choose one that includes either mizuna or tatsoi, if available). Garnish with toasted sesame seeds.

Simple ponzu sauce: Combine ¼ cup fresh yuzu juice with ¾ cup seasoned rice vinegar and ⅓ cup soy sauce. Stir to combine. Serve as a dipping sauce with sashimi or tempura.

Yuzu

vegetables

ARTICHOKE

Baby, Cocktail

Thorned

Thornless

AVOCADO

Cocktail

Common

Large Green-Skinned

BEAN

Edible Pod Beans

Chinese (Chinese Long, Yard-Long)

Dragon Tongue

French (Haricot Vert)

Green (String , Blue Lake)

Purple Wax

Yellow Wax

Shell Beans

Fava (Broad Bean)

Soybean (Edamame)

BEET

Baby Candy Cane (Chioggia)

Baby Gold

Baby Red

Candy Cane (Chioggia)

Gold

Red

BITTER MELON

Chinese

Indian

BROCCOLINI

CABBAGE

Common (green)

Napa

Red

Savoy

CARDONI

CACTUS LEAF

CELERY

Common

Chinese

CELERY ROOT

CHARD

Common (green)

Rainbow

Red Swiss

CHILE

Anaheim (green, red)

Banana Wax

Cherry Bell

Chilaca

Cubanelle, Hungarian Wax

Fresno (green, red)

Habanero (green, orange, red, yellow)

Hatch

Jalapeño (green, red)

Manzana

Pasilla, Poblano (green, red)

Scotch Bonnet

Serrano (green, red)

Thai, Bird's Eye (green, red)

Yellow

CHOY (WITH CURVED STALKS)

Baby Bok Choy

Bok Choy

Choy Sum, Flowering Cabbage

Gai Choy, Chinese Mustard

CORN

Baby

Bicolor

Common (yellow)

Red

White

CUCUMBER

Armenian

Common

Hot House, English

Japanese

Lemon

Persian, Baby

Pickling

EGGPLANT

Baby Purple (Indian)

Baby White

Chinese

Common (purple, Globe, Italian, American)

Graffiti

Japanese

Thai

White

ENDIVE

Belgian

Curly

Frisée

Escarole

Red Belgian

FENNEL

FIDDLEHEAD FERN

GAI LAN

GALANGAL, GINGER, TURMERIC

GARLIC

Common (purple, white)

Elephant

Green (Spring)

Rocambole

GOBO ROOT

GREENS

Beet

Collard

Dandelion

Kale (common green, flowering, purple, white)

Mustard (green, red)

Spinach

Turnip

HEARTS OF PALM

HORSERADISH, WASABI

JICAMA

KOHLRABI

Green, Baby Green

Purple, Baby Purple

LEEK

Baby

Chinese

Leek

Ramp, Wild

LEMON GRASS

LOTUS ROOT

MALANGA

MICROGREENS

Bulls Blood

Mizuna

Popcorn

Rainbow

Red Beet

Tatsoi

MUSHROOM

Chanterelle, Girolle

Common White, Button

Cremini, Crimini, Italian Brown

Enoki

Lobster

Morel

Oyster

Porcini, Cèpes

Portobellini

Portobello, Portabella

Shiitake, Chinese Golden Oak

Wood Ear

NIRA GRASS

Common (green), Chinese Chive

Yellow, Garlic Chive

OKRA, CHINESE OKRA

ONG CHOY

ONION

Boiler (gold, red, and white)

Cipolla, Large Italian Flat

Cipolline, Italian Flat

Green, Scallion, Spring

Maui

Mexican BBQ

Pearl (gold, red, and white)

Red, Spanish

Sweet: Oso Sweet, Texas Sweet, Vidalia, Walla Walla

White

Yellow (common)

PARSLEY ROOT

PARSNIP

PEA

Black-eyed, Cowpea

English, Green

Pea Shoots, Snow Pea Leaves

Sno, Snow, Chinese Snow, Mangetout

Sugar Snap

POTATO

Creamer Purple, Purple

Creamer Red, Red

Creamer Ruby Gold

Creamer White, White

Creamer Yellow Dutch

Fingerling French

Fingerling Purple Peruvian

Fingerling Ruby Crescent

Fingerling Russian Banana

Russet

Yukon Gold

PUMPKIN

Baby (orange, white)

Common (orange)

Fairytale

Mini (orange, white)

Sweet, Pie

White

RADICCHIO

Common

Treviso

RADISH

Black

Common (red)

Daikon (Japanese)

Easter Egg

French Breakfast

Icicle

Lo Bok (Korean)

Watermelon

RAPINI

RHUBARB

RUTABAGA

SALICORNIA

SALSIFY

SHALLOT

SUMMER SQUASH, SQUASH BLOSSOM

Edible Skin

Baby Crookneck, Crookneck

Baby Gold Bar, Gold Bar

Baby Scallopini, Scallopini

Baby Summer Green (Pattypan), Summer Green

Baby Summer Yellow (Pattypan), Summer Yellow

Baby Zucchini, Zucchini

Eight Ball

Tatuma

Nonedible Skin

Chayote (Mirliton)

Cucuzza

Mo Qua

Pul Qua (Opo)

Winter Melon

Squash Blossom

SUNFLOWER CHOKE

SWEET POTATO

Asian (Japanese, Okinawa)

Boniato (Cuban)

Orange Flesh (Beauregard, Jewel, and Garnet)

Yellow Flesh (Jersey)

TARO ROOT

Large

Small

TINDORA

TOMATILLO

TOMATO

Beefsteak

Cherry (orange, red, and yellow)

Common, "On the Vine" or Hothouse (orange, red, and yellow)

Grape

Green

Heirloom

Roma (Plum)

Teardrop, Pear (orange, red, and yellow)

TUNG HO

WATER CHESTNUT

WINTER SQUASH

Acorn (green, gold, and white)

Banana

Buttercup

Butternut

Carnival

Delicata

Gold Nugget

Hubbard (blue and orange)

Kabocha

Orangetti

Red Kuri

Spaghetti

Sweet Dumpling

Turban

YUCA ROOT

YU CHOY SUM

artichoke

BABY, COCKTAIL

THORNED

THORNLESS

SOMETIMES CONE SHAPED, SOMETIMES SPHERICAL, artichokes are the unopened flower buds of a thistle-like plant. Tapering leaves tightly overlap around a tweedy choke, while the fleshy heart at the base holds everything together. There are thorn-free varieties, as well as several thorned varieties.

In general, artichokes grown in summer and fall are more conical than those grown in spring. Those grown in summer or fall tend to have a more purplish tinge to their outer petals.

Tough until cooking tames them, they taste buttery sweet, with an alluring nuttiness and subtle bitterness. Those that grow at the end of the plant's central stem are large. Their hearts are generous, but only about a quarter of the lower portion of their leaves are edible.

Artichokes that come from lower lateral shoots are babies, ranging in size from unshelled walnuts to goose eggs. Choke-free with more tender leaves, the entire baby artichoke is edible when properly trimmed and cooked.

BUYING AND STORING

Look for deep green artichokes that feel heavy for their size and are tightly closed. To test for freshness, press leaves against each other; a squeaking sound is a sign of freshness. Refrigerate (unwashed, untrimmed) in crisper drawer in tightly closed plastic bag up to 1 week.

Domestic: *year-round, but peaks twice a year, March–May, September–November*
Global: *none*

PREP FOR LARGE ARTICHOKES

Wash in cold water. Using sharp knife (not carbon steel), cut off stem at base and, if they have thorns, cut off top 1 inch from tip. If desired, use kitchen scissors to trim tips of remaining leaves, about ½ inch from tips. Remove small bottom leaves. To "boil", stand upright in deep, nonreactive saucepan. Squeeze lemon juice over cut tops to prevent discoloration. Add enough water to come halfway up side of artichoke(s) and a pinch of salt. Bring to boil on high heat.

BABY, COCKTAIL
Grown on lower sides of stalk.
Entirely edible when properly
trimmed. ▪ *Tender with more
delicate taste. All are small but
sizes vary. Size does not affect taste.*

THORNED
Meaty, more loosely packed
leaves. ▪ *Generally described
as best; most pronounced
flavor profile.*

THORNLESS
Often more densely packed
leaves. ▪ *Milder flavor than
thorned variety.*

Partially cover and reduce heat to gentle boil; cook until fork tender at base, 35–45 minutes. Artichokes can also be grilled or steamed. Trimmed into wedges, they can be deep-fried.

When served whole, grasp leaf by tip and tug between almost-closed teeth to scrape away the luscious meat. Using the tip of a teaspoon, pluck hairlike choke from heart. The choke-free heart will be bowl-shaped and can be enjoyed in its entirety.

To prepare for stuffing, spread leaves apart at the center and pull out the small leaves; use teaspoon to remove and discard fuzzy choke.

PREP FOR BABY ARTICHOKES

Wash in cold water. To make entirely edible, use sharp knife (not carbon steel) to cut off stem at base and cut to remove top ½ inch of leaves. Remove a few outer leaves; bend them back until they snap (the edible portion at bottom will stay

Thorned

Baby

intact). Trim sides of base with paring knife as if peeling an apple.

USE

Most often cooked, but trimmed hearts can be eaten raw when cut into strips and dressed with an herby vinaigrette. Boil, microwave, or steam until heart is fork tender; serve hot, room temperature, or cold. Or cut into quarters and deep-fry.

Serve whole and cooked accompanied by dipping sauce; mayonnaise is classic, but plain yogurt, lemon juice, or a mixture of melted butter and soy sauce are good, too. Or serve large, whole cooked artichokes stuffed (see Prep) with seafood salad or rice. Cooked baby artichokes are very versatile and are delicious marinated, then tossed with cooked fingerling potatoes.

NUTRITIONAL INFO

1 cup is good source of vitamin C and folate.

SERVING SUGGESTIONS

Grilled delight: Cut cooked, large artichokes in half lengthwise. Remove and discard choke. In bowl, combine 1/4 cup each balsamic vinegar, water, and olive oil; stir in 1 1/2 tablespoons soy sauce. Place artichoke halves in heavy, zipper-style plastic bag; add vinegar mixture. Marinate in refrigerator overnight. Drain and reserve marinade. Grill halves cut side down until lightly browned, 5–7 minutes. Turn and drizzle with a little marinade. Grill until lightly charred, 3–4 minutes. Baby artichokes can be prepared in similar manner, but require less grilling time.

Babies in pasta, couscous or rice: Cut cooked baby artichokes into quarters. Toss with well-seasoned (salt, pepper, and either minced lemon zest or capers) pasta, couscous, or rice.

Salad with cheesy topping: Cut cooked baby artichokes into lengthwise quarters. Place on salad plates. Drizzle with extra-virgin olive oil and top with crumbled queso fresco cheese or grated Parmesan, and minced fresh basil or Italian parsley. Season with a little salt and generous amount of freshly ground black pepper. Serve with lemon wedges for optional use.

Artichoke pesto: Finely chop cooked artichoke hearts (from large artichokes) or entire cooked baby artichokes (see Prep). Stir into favorite basil pesto, either homemade or store bought. Use to dress pasta, rice, or cooked vegetables, or spread on thin slices of toasted French bread (crostini) for appetizers.

avocado, also alligator pear

COCKTAIL

COMMON (HASS, BACON, ZUTANO, GWEN, PINKERTON, FUERTE, REED)

LARGE GREEN-SKINNED

SOME VARIETIES HAVE BUMPY, LIZARD-LIKE SKIN. Others are covered with smooth, slender skin. Some skins are black, while others are green. They can be pickle-shaped, pear-shaped, or contoured like plump little blimps.

But all avocados share three common traits. One, as they ripen their fat content increases. Two, they only ripen off the tree. And three, when they are ripe, they have a creamy texture and a rich, nutty taste.

Common: Generally the variety of these avocados isn't specified in the marketplace. The Hass variety accounts for 85 percent of California's avocado crop. They are fairly large, pear-shaped, and have a thick, pebbly skin. Other common varieties include Bacon (medium-sized pear shape with smooth, thin skin), Fuerte (large pear shape with smooth, thin skin) and Gwen (large, oval, with green, bumpy skin), Pinkerton (long pear shape with moderately pebbly surface and small pit), and Zutano (small pear shape with shiny skin).

Large Green-Skinned

Hass

Cocktail avocados: Only about 2 inches long, except for the skin, these pit-less pickle-shaped avocados are entirely edible. A cocktail avocado results when a bud on an avocado tree isn't correctly pollinated. These avocados usually have a shorter shelf life.

Large Green Skinned: This variety is very large, oval-shaped with moderately pebbly surface that stays green, even when ripe. They are called Reed in California and Choqoette in Florida. Most are grown in Florida. They have a milder, less nutty taste.

BUYING AND STORING

Push the skin to determine ripeness. If it is hard, it will require 2–6 days for ripening (see Brown Bag Ripening, page 309). If it yields slightly to gentle pressure, it's ripe and good for slicing or dicing. If it leaves a small dent when pressed, it's very ripe and good for mashing. If it leaves a large dent when pressed, it is overripe and will probably be discolored. Refrigerate ripe avocados loose in crisper drawer up to 5 days.

Domestic: year-round
Global: year-round

PREP

Cut in half lengthwise; twist halves in opposite directions to separate. Use teaspoon to pry out pit. If mashing, scoop flesh out with small spoon. If dicing, place avocado in 1 hand cut side up (as a safety precaution, place a potholder or thick kitchen towel underneath avocado). Using a small knife, make parallel cuts about ½ inch apart going side to side (do not cut through rind). Make parallel cuts about ½ inch apart going top to bottom (do not cut through rind). Scoop out with bowl of small spoon getting as close to rind as possible.

If slicing, remove skin. Some varieties have skin that peels easily; others are stubborn. Use a paring knife to grasp skin at small end and pull to opposite end. Or score skin into shallow, lengthwise strips and pull off from top to bottom.

To prevent discoloration, squeeze lemon or lime juice on cut avocado. Cover mashed avocado with plastic wrap pressed snugly on surface (to press out air). Some contend that placing the pit in the mixture also helps.

USE

Eat raw or use as garnish on warm dishes. Use avocado halves as containers for seafood salads. Add to salads, sandwiches, and hamburgers.

NUTRITIONAL INFO FOR COCKTAIL AND COMMON (GREEN HAS SLIGHTLY REDUCED NUTRITIONAL PROFILE)

1 cup is good source of vitamin C, folate, vitamin B_6, and potassium.

SERVING SUGGESTIONS

Guacamole reigns: Maybe the simplest version is best. Dice ripe avocados (see Prep) and place in bowl. Toss with fresh lime juice, diced red onion, a splash of tequila, a gentle squeeze of hot sauce, and coarse salt; gently toss. Serve with tortilla chips.

Endive-fennel-'cado salad: Gently toss chunks of peeled avocado, wide slices of Belgian endive, and thin slivers of fennel with enough mustardy vinaigrette to lightly coat (see Simple Vinaigrette, page 310). Taste and adjust seasoning. Arrange peeled orange slices on salad plates. Top with salad. Season with freshly ground black pepper.

Cream o'cado soup: In a food processor fitted with metal blade, process until smooth: 2 ripe peeled and pitted avocados; 2 cups vegetable broth or reduced-sodium chicken broth; 1 tablespoon cider vinegar; 4 dashes hot pepper sauce; 1 cup heavy whipping cream or plain, whole milk yogurt; ½ teaspoon lemon zest; and salt to taste. Chill thoroughly. Taste, adding a little lemon juice, salt, or white pepper, as needed. Serve in 6 chilled bowls. Garnish with either crumbled bacon or chopped tomatoes.

No mayo: Substitute avocado for mayonnaise on sandwiches or burgers.

green goddess salad dressing

This version of green goddess dressing substitutes mashed avocado for most of the mayonnaise. It can be made in advance and refrigerated up to 5 days. Use to top mixed greens or as a dip for raw vegetables.

4 canned anchovies, drained

1 tablespoon chopped fresh Italian parsley

4 tablespoons chopped fresh chives

3 tablespoons tarragon vinegar

1 cup mashed avocado

1 cup sour cream

¼ cup mayonnaise

1½ tablespoons freshly squeezed lemon juice

1 drop hot pepper sauce

Salt and freshly ground black pepper to taste

OPTIONAL FOR THINNING: milk

1. Place all ingredients (except milk) in blender and whirl until smooth. Or to use food processor (fitted with metal blade), process anchovies, parsley, and chives until finely minced. Add remaining ingredients (except milk) and pulse until smooth. Taste and adjust seasoning as needed. Place in bowl and cover tightly. Refrigerate. Use as dip.

2. To use as a salad dressing, stir in enough milk to reach a thinner consistency.

YIELD: ABOUT 3½ CUPS

NUTRITIONAL INFORMATION (PER TABLESPOON): Calories 20; fat calories 18; total fat 2 grams; sat fat .5 gram, cholesterol 0 milligrams; sodium 45 milligrams; total carbohydrates 1 gram; fiber 0 grams; sugars 0 grams; protein 0 grams; vitamin A IUs 2%; vitamin C 2%; calcium 0%; iron 0%.

bean

edible-pod beans

CHINESE (CHINESE LONG, YARD-LONG)

DRAGON TONGUE

FRENCH (HARICOT VERT)

GREEN (STRING, BLUE LAKE)

PURPLE WAX BEAN

YELLOW WAX BEAN

shell beans

FAVA (BROAD BEAN)

SOYBEAN (EDAMAME)

FRESH BEANS COME IN A WIDE VARIETY OF SHAPES AND COLORS, from lanky, magenta-speckled pods to plump, fuzzy-skinned crescents. They don't belong to one specific plant species, but all have one thing in common: the beans inside the pods are immature and tender. Left to mature, they would grow to full size and harden. They fall into two categories: edible-pod beans and shell beans. Shell beans have pods that aren't particularly pleasing to eat.

French

Fava

Soybean

Dragon Tongue

BUYING AND STORING

Beans with edible pods should snap crisply when broken and should be flexible. If seeds can be detected through pod, they are probably too mature and will be tough. Shell bean pods should be plump and green, not yellowed. If sold shelled, beans should look plump, shiny, and moist. Refrigerate in pods up to 1 week in crisper drawer, except for Chinese beans, which are more perishable and should be refrigerated no more than 5 days . Store shelled fava beans in refrigerator in single layer (because they are delicate) up to 3 days covered loosely with plastic wrap. Refrigerate shelled or unshelled soybeans in unopened vacuum pack up to 5 days. Once opened, refrigerate in airtight container up to 3 days. Shelled, cooked soybeans and shelled fava beans can be frozen in airtight containers.

CHINESE BEANS
Domestic: *June–November*
Global: *November–June*

DRAGON TONGUE, FRENCH (HARICOT VERT), GREEN BEAN, PURPLE WAX, YELLOW WAX
Domestic: *year-round*
Global: *December–April*

FAVA
Domestic: *March–September*
Global: *October–March*

SOYBEAN, EDAMAME
Domestic: *none*
Global: *year-round*

PREP FOR CHINESE, DRAGON TONGUE, GREEN, FRENCH (HARICOT VERT), PURPLE WAX, AND YELLOW WAX BEANS

Wash with cold water. Snap off ends by hand or cut off with paring knife. Leave whole or cut crosswise on diagonal into 2-inch lengths. Blanch until cooked tender crisp (except Chinese beans, which retain their signature firmness) 2–8 minutes. Drain and refresh with cold water.

PREP FOR FAVA BEANS

All fava beans must be cooked. When mature, beans should be shelled, cooked, and skinned. First remove beans from pods. Snap off stem end and pull string toward opposite end; use thumbnail to open along seam and push out beans. Blanch 1 minute; drain and place in ice water. Drain and use thumbnail to break skin; squeeze to pop bean from skin. Most recipes call for further cooking, often simmering them in water with herbs, garlic, and a little olive oil for about 5 minutes. Note that people who have inherited a particular enzyme deficiency can experience a serious reaction to fava beans.

PREP FOR SOYBEANS

Always sold cooked, either frozen or fresh-cooked in vacuum packs, both in pods and shelled. If in pod, remove beans from pod. Pull string and pop beans out with thumbnail; discard pod.

CHINESE

Very long and slender, these are dense beans that can grow to be 3 feet long but are usually harvested at about 18 inches. ■ *Not as sweet or crisp as green beans. Mild taste with hint of asparagus flavor in beans. Cooked, they are chewy-firm. Blanch and use in stir-fries.*

DRAGON TONGUE

Cream-colored skin with purple streaks and flecks, about 4–5 inches long. Wider than green beans. ■ *Tender and sweet, similar to green bean. Bright purple markings fade with cooking, so for most dramatic appearance, serve raw with creamy dip.*

FRENCH

(haricot vert)

Generally more slender than a pencil, these green beans have soft, velvety skin and are about 5 inches in length. ■ *Green bean taste with added sweetness. Very tender, yet crisp when briefly cooked.*

GREEN

(blue lake, string)

Straight and about 4–6 inches long, these bright-green beans are plump and have a velvety feel. Generally stringless. ■ *They have pleasant, beany sweetness and tender-crisp texture.*

PURPLE WAX

Red to reddish-purple, sometimes with dark coppery tint. ■ *Similar to green bean and will turn green when cooked.*

YELLOW WAX

Green bean shape, but skin is light yellow to deep yellow and very thin. Size varies. ■ *Flavor profile milder than green bean. Very tender seeds.*

FAVA

Tough, inedible green pod encloses 4–7 plump beans. Pods vary in length from 4–13 inches. Beans are bright green and kidney shaped. Must be cooked. ■ *Smaller, less mature beans are pale green, sweeter and more tender. Larger beans become starchier, require longer cooking, and must be peeled.*

SOYBEAN

Fuzzy, green, crescent-shaped pods about 2–3 inches long. Gray-green beans. Must be cooked. ■ *Beans have appealing mild flavor with a subtle nuttiness.*

USE FOR CHINESE, DRAGON TONGUE, GREEN, FRENCH (HARICOT VERT), PURPLE WAX, AND YELLOW WAX BEANS

Edible-podded beans are most often cooked: either blanched, simmered, or steamed. Include in stir-fries, salads, stews, or casseroles. To serve with creamy dips, blanch just enough to take away the raw taste, 30–60 seconds, drain, and refresh with cold water.

USE FOR FAVA AND SOYBEAN

Use as appetizer or snack, or include in soups, salads, or stir-fries. Include in rice or pasta dishes.

NUTRITIONAL INFO FOR CHINESE, DRAGON TONGUE, GREEN, FRENCH (HARICOT VERT), PURPLE WAX, AND YELLOW WAX BEANS

1 cup is a good source of vitamin C; significant source of vitamin A and folate.

NUTRITIONAL INFO FOR FAVA

1 cup is an excellent source of folate and a significant source of protein and iron.

NUTRITIONAL INFO FOR SOYBEAN

1 cup is a excellent source of protein, iron, calcium, and vitamin C.

SERVING SUGGESTIONS

Beans 'n' bacon: This side dish is good enough to be an entrée. Blanch about 1 pound (edible-pod) beans until tender-crisp. Drain, refresh with cold water, and set aside. In large, deep skillet, fry 2 strips bacon until crisp; drain on paper towel. Drain off all but 1 tablespoon drippings. On medium-high heat, stir-fry beans until heated through. Toss in 2 chopped tomatoes, salt, and pepper. Crumble bacon on top. If desired, spoon over cooked brown rice.

Beans niçoise: Cold, cooked green beans or French beans are an essential ingredient in a classic salade niçoise. To make a vegetarian version, arrange cold, cooked beans (any edible-pod bean except Chinese, or a mixture) on platter. Surround with small tomatoes (halved), either grape or cherry, and cooked fingerling potatoes. Top with Simple Vinaigrette (page 310) augmented with chopped fresh basil or tarragon.

Garnish with hard-cooked eggs (halved) and olives.

Elegant fava succotash: Use proportions that suit your taste, but be sure to include plenty of fava beans. In large, deep skillet, heat a little olive oil and butter on medium-high heat. Add corn kernels (fresh or frozen), shelled and skinned fava beans (see Prep), and canned hominy (drained). Stir-fry until heated through. Toss in generous amount of minced fresh basil and a smidgen of white wine vinegar (to taste). Season with salt and pepper.

Soybean Greek salad: Place vinaigrette (see Simple Vinaigrette, page xx) in bottom of salad bowl; add sliced red onion, pitted black olives, cucumber slices, crumbled feta cheese, and a good handful of shelled, cooked soybeans. Add chopped fresh basil or tarragon and toss. Add bite-sized lettuce pieces and vine-ripened tomato wedges. Toss again and taste; adjust seasoning as needed.

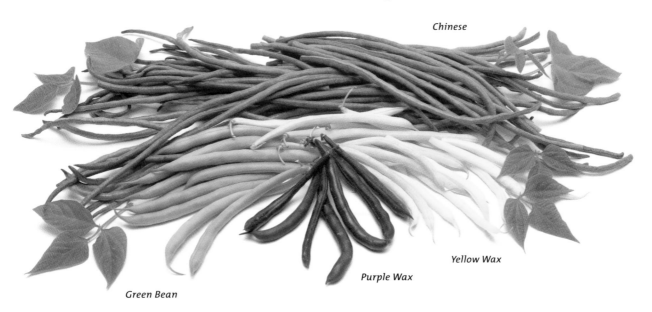

Chinese

Yellow Wax

Purple Wax

Green Bean

beet, also table beet

BABY CANDY CANE
(CHIOGGIA)

BABY GOLD

BABY RED

CANDY CANE (CHIOGGIA)

GOLD

RED

FLAVORWISE, BEETS ARE A CROSS between carrots and earthy wild mushrooms. Colorwise, they are a feast for the eye: glorious yellows, snappy magentas, or striped like a peppermint lollipop. Available in both small "baby" and grown-up sizes, these bulb-shaped wonders are best when cooked fresh rather than eaten from the can. Beet greens (leaves) are edible and are best when harvested when 4–6 inches high (see page 200).

Table beets shouldn't be confused with sugar beets, a large root vegetable used in sugar production.

BUYING AND STORING

Look for beets with crisp, fresh-looking greens. Bulbs should be firm with fairly smooth skin. Small and medium bulbs are generally more tender. Remove all but 1 inch of (greens') stem. Refrigerate in plastic in crisper drawer up to 3 weeks. Store greens in plastic in crisper up to 2 days. Wash just before cooking. Tiny baby beets can be the exception. Because they can be steamed whole with stems attached, store untrimmed and refrigerate; use within 1 day.
Domestic: *year-round*
Global: *none*

PREP

Cut (greens') stem 1 inch from top of bulb. Wash bulb and greens separately. Generally, do not peel unless using raw; peel slips off easily once cooked. The peeling process is much tidier once beets are cooked; because there is less bleeding. If using raw, peel wearing rubber gloves to protect hands from staining.

USE

Eat raw, peeled and finely grated in salad, or cook. Can be roasted, steamed, baked, or boiled. To bake, wash beets with 1-inch stems attached and wrap (still wet, 3 to a packet) in heavy-duty aluminum foil. Bake in 400-degree oven until fork tender, 30–60 minutes, depending on size. When cool enough to handle, slip off peel. Cooked beets can be served hot or cold. Beet greens can be slowly braised like turnip greens (see page 202).

NUTRITIONAL INFO

1 cup is a good source of vitamin C and potassium; significant source of folate.

Gold

Red

Baby Candy Cane

Baby Red

Baby Gold

SERVING SUGGESTIONS

Beets 'n' goat: Goat cheese and beets are an incredible team. Slice peeled and cooled cooked beets (see Use) on top of mixed green salad dressed with a Simple Vinaigrette (see page 310). Sprinkle with soft goat cheese. If desired, sprinkle with toasted pistachios or walnuts. Candy cane beets look especially elegant in this salad.

Asparagus and gold beets: Cut cooked, cooled, and peeled gold beets (see Use) into thick wedges (or cut babies in half). Place in nonreactive bowl with vinaigrette of choice. Cook asparagus (blanch, roast, or grill). Place a few stalks of asparagus on each salad plate. Spoon beets and vinaigrette on top. Garnish with slivers of red onion.

BABY CANDY CANE, CANDY CANE, CHIOGGIA
Slice crosswise to reveal concentric rings of magenta and cream-colored flesh. Babies about 1 inch long. ■ *Milder flavor profile than red variety.*

BABY GOLD, GOLD
Bright orange-yellow. Babies about 1 inch long. Regular can be 6 times larger. ■ *Sweeter, more delicate flavor than red. Baby beets don't require peeling.*

BABY RED, RED
Deep magenta. Babies, generally about 1 inch long. Regular can be 6 times larger. ■ *Large red can have earthy, bitter edge. Baby reds are sweeter.*

Warm, herbed and buttered: Cautiously peel warm cooked beets (see Use); slice (or cut babies in half). Toss with butter and minced fresh tarragon. Add salt to taste.

Send them to Harvard: Harvard beets is a classic recipe. In medium saucepan, combine ¼ cup sugar, 1 tablespoon cornstarch, and pinch of salt. Stir in ⅓ cup cider vinegar and ½ small onion (minced); cook over medium-high heat until thickened, stirring frequently. Remove from heat and add 3 cups cooked, peeled, and sliced beets (see Use). Stir and cook on medium heat until heated through.

magenta soup

This colorful soup can be prepared 2 days ahead and reheated. Because one of the goals is to produce a purplish-red color, use red beets. In this instance, for best color and flavor, start with raw beets.

1½ pounds red beets (see Cook's Notes)

3 tablespoons butter

1 tablespoon olive oil

1 cup chopped red cabbage

4 celery stalks, trimmed, chopped

1½ cups roughly chopped red onions

1 jalapeño chile, seeded, minced (see Cook's Notes)

About 6 cups chicken broth or vegetable broth, low-sodium preferred

2–3 tablespoons fresh lime juice

salt, if needed

GARNISH: sour cream

GARNISH: finely sliced chives

COOK'S NOTES: To prevent staining hands, use rubber gloves when working with raw beets. Use caution when working with fresh chiles. Wash work surface thoroughly upon completion and do NOT touch face or eyes.

1. Peel beets and chop. Melt butter and oil in large pot or Dutch oven on medium-high heat. Add beets, cabbage, celery, onion, and chile; stir to coat with butter and oil. Cook, stirring occasionally, until onion softens, about 10–12 minutes; do NOT brown; reduce heat if necessary.

2. Off heat, cautiously pour in broth. Bring to boil on high heat. Reduce heat to medium-low; cover and simmer 1 hour or until beets are very tender. Remove from heat.

3. Purée in small batches in food processor fitted with metal blade, or blender, reserving 1 cup of broth. Use caution when processing hot liquids, holding lid down tightly with potholder and working with small amounts.

4. Return puréed mixture to pot. Add reserved broth if mixture is too thick. Stir in lime juice; reheat soup on medium-high heat. Taste andd add salt if needed. Ladle into bowls. Top each serving with spoonful of sour cream and sprinkle with chives.

YIELD: 6 SERVINGS

NUTRITIONAL INFORMATION (PER SERVING): Calories 180; fat calories 70; total fat 8 grams; sat fat 4 grams; cholesterol 15 milligrams; sodium 290 milligrams; total carbohydrates 17 grams; fiber 4 grams; sugars 10 grams; protein 9 grams; vitamin A IUs 10%; vitamin C 35%; calcium 6%; iron 15%.

bitter melon, also bitter gourd

CHINESE

INDIAN

NEVER EATEN RAW, bitter melon isn't a true melon. It looks like a pebbly skinned cucumber with tapered ends. The apple-green peel is littered with wartlike bumps. Inside, the flesh is creamy white and rather dry, with inedible seeds that look similar to cucumber seeds.

Bitter melon has a high quinine content that gives it a bitter taste. When skin is green, it has a somewhat sour taste. As the melon ripens, the exterior turns yellow-orange, and the melon's bitterness increases. Chinese bitter melon is about 6–10 inches long. Indian bitter melon is about half the size of the Chinese variety and isn't as readily available. It has more bumps on the skin and is more perishable. Both varieties have similar tastes.

Chinese Bitter Melon

Indian Bitter Melon

BUYING AND STORING

Look for firm bitter melons that are free of blemishes or soft spots. Store in perforated plastic bag in vegetable drawer of refrigerator for about 1 week.

Domestic: *year-round*
Global: *year-round*

PREP

Peel. Either cut crosswise into rounds or cut in half lengthwise. Remove and discard seeds and spongy core with bowl of spoon. Cut into similar-sized pieces to ensure uniform cooking. The melon's bitterness decreases when blanched for a few minutes. Or salt lightly and set aside for 30 minutes, then rinse in cold water. When using salting technique, melon is sometimes left unpeeled.

USE

Eat cooked. It can be stir-fried, braised, pickled, steamed, or curried. Use in chutney or soups, or add to a traditional Chinese dish that includes pork, onions, ginger, and black bean sauce.

Chinese and Indian bitter melons can be used interchangeably, but traditionally in Indian cooking, bitter melon is served at the beginning of the meal, either alone or combined with lentils or potatoes, seasoned with cumin and turmeric.

NUTRITIONAL INFO

1 cup is an excellent source of vitamin C; good source of potassium.

SERVING SUGGESTIONS

Souped up: Add blanched pieces to chicken vegetable soup. If desired, garnish with chopped cilantro.

Stuffed slices: Peel and cut raw into ⁵⁄₈ -inch-thick rounds; seed and core. Combine ½ pound ground pork, ¼ pound minced shelled shrimp, and 2 minced green onions; season with salt and pepper. Stuff each slice with mixture, pressing it in place. Heat 2 tablespoons vegetable oil in deep, nonstick skillet. Fry about 5 minutes per side or until stuffing is completely cooked and bitter melon is tender. Drain on paper towels. Drizzle with sauce made of equal parts soy sauce and rice vinegar (and a squeeze of Asian hot sauce, if desired).

Stir-fry with a bitter attitude: Add peeled, blanched and patted dry bitter melon cubes to vegetable stir-fries.

fried bitter melon 'salad'

This alluring salad combines crisp slices of deep-fried bitter melon with a sweet-spicy dressing. It should be prepared just before serving.

2 bitter melons, washed, peeled, cut into ¼-inch-thick rounds, cored

Salt

Peanut oil

2 tablespoons freshly squeezed lime juice

½ teaspoon sugar

3 shallots, peeled, thinly sliced

2 fresh jalapeño chiles, thinly sliced (see Cook's Notes)

3 tablespoons coconut milk, use thick part at top of can if possible

COOK'S NOTES: Use caution when working with fresh chiles. Wash hands and work surface thoroughly upon completion and do NOT touch eyes or face.

1. Place bitter melon slices on baking sheet lined with paper towels. Sprinkle with salt on both sides. Let sit 30 minutes on paper towels; pat dry.

2. Heat 1 inch oil in large, deep skillet. Deep-fry bitter melon slices until golden brown. Don't crowd pan; fry in batches if necessary. Drain on paper towels.

3. In large bowl, combine lime juice and sugar; stir to dissolve sugar. Add shallots, chiles, and coconut milk. Stir to combine. Add fried bitter melon slices and gently toss.

YIELD: 6 SERVINGS

NUTRITIONAL INFORMATION (PER SERVING): Calories 50; fat calories 40.5; total fat 4.5 grams; sat fat 1 gram; cholesterol 0 milligrams; sodium 5 milligrams; total carbohydrates 3 grams; fiber 1 gram; sugars 1 gram; protein 1 grams; vitamin A IUs 4%; vitamin C 60%; calcium 2%; iron 2%.

broccolini

DEEP GREEN STALKS, long and slender, support clusters of tender buds. Broccolini's buds look like compact broccoli florets. But the taste of bud and stalk is sweeter than broccoli and has an alluring hint of mustard. When it's cooked, the peppery edge disappears, replaced by increased sweetness. The stalks are less fibrous than broccoli and never require peeling.

Many incorrectly assume that broccolini, a trademarked name, is a cross between broccoli and asparagus, when in fact it is a cross between broccoli and gai lan (also known as Chinese broccoli).

BUYING AND STORING

Generally sold in small bundles. Look for bright green stalks and buds, crisp stalks, and tightly closed buds. Refrigerate, unwashed, in perforated plastic in crisper drawer up to 10 days.

Domestic: *year round*
Global: *none*

PREP

Completely edible. If stalk looks dry or discolored at cut end, trim about 1/8 inch off bottom. Rinse under cold running water. Pat dry gently with paper towels if stir-frying. Leave whole or cut on diagonal into 1 1/2-inch lengths.

USE

Serve raw with creamy dips. Or blanch, stir-fry, sauté. or steam. Include in pasta dishes or omelets, salads, slaws, or soups.

NUTRITIONAL INFO

1 cup is an excellent source of vitamin C; significant source of potassium and vitamin A.

Broccolini

SERVING SUGGESTIONS

Chili and olive oil sauté: Cut broccolini stalk on diagonal into 1½-inch lengths, reserving florets in separate pile. Heat a little olive oil in deep skillet on medium-high heat. Add broccolini stalks and cook, stirring frequently, until broccolini is almost tender-crisp. Add more olive oil, if needed. Add florets and minced garlic (to taste). Season with smidgen of dried red chili flakes and salt. Cook, stirring frequently, until tender-crisp. If desired, top with grated Parmesan cheese.

Asian flourish: Blanch whole broccolini 1–2 minutes. Drain and refresh with cold water; gently pat dry. In large, deep skillet heat a combination of vegetable oil and Asian sesame oil on medium-high heat. Add broccolini and stir-fry until tender-crisp and heated through. Add equal parts hoisin sauce and oyster sauce, enough to lightly coat; gently toss. Serve as is or over cooked rice or rice noodles.

Pasta salad with feta and tomatoes: Cut broccolini on diagonal into 1½-inch lengths. Blanch 3–4 minutes; drain and refresh with cold water. Drain. Toss with cooked penne pasta and enough olive oil (extra-virgin preferred) to lightly coat. Add crumbled feta, halved cherry tomatoes (or grape tomatoes), and chopped fresh basil. Season to taste with garlic salt and pepper. Taste; add a squeeze of fresh lemon juice, if desired.

Couscous or rice: Prepare couscous or rice. Cut broccolini on diagonal into 1½-inch lengths. Blanch 3–4 minutes; drain and refresh with cold water. Drain. Toss with hot couscous or rice. Garnish with chopped fresh Italian parsley or mint. Add toasted slivered almonds, if desired.

cabbage

COMMON (GREEN)
NAPA
RED
SAVOY

THERE'S NOTHING BORING ABOUT CABBAGE. As there are more than 400 varieties, shapes can range from spherical to elongated. Leaves, deeply veined and superimposed layer upon layer, can be smooth or curly, firm and sturdy, or delicately limp. Colors run the gamut from almost-white green to deep forest green to reddish-purple.

Raw or properly cooked, cabbage has an appealing texture and spicy-sweet taste. But cooked too long or with too much water, it loses nutrients and takes on an unpleasant odor.

BUYING AND STORING

Look for firmly packed, crisp leaves, avoiding those with soft spots, cracks, or discoloration. Heads should feel heavy for their size. Store in plastic bag in vegetable drawer of refrigerator up to 2 weeks. Can be blanched and frozen up to 3 months (see Freezing, page 310).

Domestic: *year-round*
Global: *year-round*

PREP

Remove any wilted or discolored leaves. To shred, cut in half from bottom to top, then cut each half in half to make quarters. Cut core off each quarter (leaving a little attached so wedge stays together). Discard core. Place cut side down on cutting board. Using large knife, cut into shreds according to desired thickness.

Or to prepare single leaves for stuffing, cut base of each leaf and carefully peel away from head.

Blanch 2–3 minutes in boiling water. Cool and, if necessary, shave off thick part of central rib to make leaf pliable.

Use stainless-steel knife when cutting red cabbage to prevent discoloration (carbon steel will turn red cabbage blue). Also, cook cabbage in nonreactive pans, not aluminum or cast iron). To prevent discoloration when using raw red cabbage in salad, sprinkle with a tiny bit of vinegar or toss immediately after shredding with vinaigrette that contains vinegar or lemon juice.

USE

Eat raw or cooked. Braise, simmer, steam, or stir-fry. Use leaves as "wrappers" for stuffing.

NUTRITIONAL INFO

1 head (about 4 cups shredded) is an excellent source of vitamin C; significant source of vitamins A and B_6; good source of pantothenic acid.

COMMON
(green)
Generally round, firmly packed heads. Pale green outer leaves and white interior leaves. White central core and tightly packed leaves. ■ *Sturdy with crunchy texture. Strongest spicy-sweet flavor profile when cooked.*

NAPA
(celery cabbage)
Some are barrel-shaped, others are long and cylindrical. Leaves have more delicate texture than green and are pale green and crinkled at edges. ■ *Mild, subtle cabbage taste and crisp texture.*

RED
Similar to green cabbage in shape and texture. Color is reddish-purple. ■ *Sturdy with crunchy texture. Almost as strong flavor profile as green cabbage when cooked.*

SAVOY
Looser heads with ruffled, deep-green leaves. ■ *More delicate texture and milder flavor profile than green or red cabbage*

SERVING SUGGESTIONS

Perfect partner for poultry or game: Braised red cabbage can bring out the best with salty meats. In large, nonreactive saucepan, combine 1 tablespoon butter and 2 tablespoons vegetable or canola oil over medium-high heat. Add 1 onion (chopped) and 1 large tart apple, peeled, cored, and thinly sliced. Cook 5 minutes, stirring occasionally. Add 1 medium head shredded red cabbage, 1 cup water, ⅓ cup red-wine vinegar, and ¼ cup sugar. Bring to boil; reduce heat to medium-low, cover and cook until cabbage is tender, about 30 minutes, stirring occasionally. Season with salt and pepper.

Spuds with crunch: Shred cabbage and cook until tender-crisp in small amount of water in covered saucepan. Drain well and stir into well-seasoned mashed potatoes.

Stir-fried cabbage: Add shredded cabbage to vegetable stir-fries. Cabbage adds a delectable texture, and its flavor teams well with soy sauce and ginger.

Creamy, bacony braise: Shred 1 medium head savoy or green cabbage. On medium-high heat, cook 4 strips bacon (chopped) in large, deep skillet until crisp. Add cabbage and cook until wilted, stirring occasionally, about 4 minutes. Add ½ cup whipping cream or half-and-half and reduce heat to medium-low. Cook, stirring occasionally, for 12–14 minutes, or until cabbage is creamy. Season with salt and pepper.

spicy 3-cabbage slaw

This spicy coleslaw teams beautifully with grilled meat or poultry; it's also delectable paired with grilled mushrooms. If you prefer a less spicy version, reduce the amount of chile paste. If you don't have 3 types of cabbages on hand, use just 1 or 2, and increase the total amount to total 1½ pounds.

¼ cup rice wine vinegar

2 tablespoons Asian sesame oil (see Cook's Notes)

1 tablespoon sugar

1 teaspoon chile paste (see Cook's Notes)

½ cup mayonnaise

Salt to taste

Freshly ground pepper to taste

½ pound Napa cabbage, cored, shredded

½ pound red cabbage, cored, shredded

½ pound green cabbage, cored, shredded

⅔ cup thinly sliced red onion

YIELD: 6–8 SERVINGS

Napa

COOK'S NOTES: Asian sesame oil and chile paste are available at Asian markets or in the Asian specialty section of many supermarkets. Refrigerate sesame oil after opening.

1. In large mixing bowl, add vinegar, sesame oil, sugar, chile paste, and mayonnaise; stir to combine. Season with salt and pepper.

2. Add cabbage and red onion. Toss to coat cabbage with dressing. Refrigerate 1–2 hours. Taste and add salt or pepper as needed.

NUTRITIONAL INFORMATION (PER SERVING): Calories 110; fat calories 72; total fat 8 grams; sat fat 1 gram; cholesterol 5 milligrams; sodium 270 milligrams; total carbohydrates 10 grams; fiber 1 gram; sugars 3 grams; protein 1 gram; vitamin A IUs 4%; vitamin C 40%; calcium 4%; iron 4%.

Green

Savoy

Red

cardoni, also cardoon

AN ARTICHOKE COUSIN, a full-grown cardoni plant looks like a lofty thistle. But unlike artichokes, the edible part is the lengthy, silvery-gray stalk rather than the flower. The elusive flavor is somewhat like a combination of artichoke and celery. And although when harvested it looks something like broad, flattened celery, the texture is drier, the surface coarser and more deeply grooved. When it's cooked, the texture is meaty like an artichoke heart.

But flavor, texture, color, and size vary considerably. Some are bitter, but most are mild. Some are limp, but most are crisp. Some are pale green, but most are gray.

BUYING AND STORING

Small and medium stalks are the tenderest. Large stalks are generally pithy. Often the edges are browned and require trimming. Wrap base in moist paper towels and place in plastic bag. Refrigerate in vegetable drawer up to 2 weeks (if very fresh when purchased).

Domestic: *October–April*
Global: *none*

PREP

Discard leaves using caution, because they can have thorns. Trim any discolored area on stalk. Wash and trim stalks with vegetable peeler or small knife. Cut in half crosswise.

To remove bitterness, blanch in boiling, salted water with a little lemon juice until tender, about 15–25 minutes. Drain, refresh with cold water, and pat dry. Use small knife to remove strings (see Celery Prep, page 151).

USE

Can be deep-fried, braised, boiled, or baked. Delicious in salad, soup, or vegetable gratin.

NUTRITIONAL INFO

3 cups contains significant amounts of iron and calcium.

Cardoni

SERVING SUGGESTIONS

Soupy but scrumptious: Blanch cardoni (see Prep), trim, and cut into 1-inch pieces (about 2 cups). Heat 1 tablespoon olive oil in large, deep skillet on medium-high heat. Add 1 onion (chopped) and 1 large clove garlic (minced). Cook until softened but not browned, about 3–4 minutes. Add 1 (15-ounce) can diced tomatoes with juice, blanched cardoni, 2 teaspoons minced fresh oregano, salt, and pepper. Bring to boil on high heat; reduce heat to medium and simmer 5 minutes. Serve in shallow bowls spooned over cooked rice.

Marinated: Blanch cardoni (see Prep), trim, and cut into 1-inch pieces (about 2 cups). Place in glass or ceramic bowl. Cover with favorite homemade or store-bought vinaigrette (see Simple Vinaigrette, page 310). Cover and refrigerate overnight. Serve cold garnished with drained capers, minced Italian parsley, and olives. Accompany with slices of rustic bread.

Dippers: Blanch cardoni (see Prep), trim, and cut lengthwise into sticks to use for dipping. Bagna cauda is a traditional dip for these in Italy. It's a warm mixture of olive oil, butter, minced anchovies, lemon, salt, and pepper. Cardoni also tastes delicious with a wide variety of dips.

Cardoni bake: Blanch cardoni (see Prep), trim, and cut into 1-inch pieces. In a baking dish, toss with olive oil (enough to lightly coat) and a mixture of minced fresh thyme and Italian parsley. Season with salt and pepper. Bake in 350-degree oven until very tender and heated through, about 15–20 minutes. Sprinkle with grated Parmesan cheese.

cactus leaf, also nopal, nopalito, cactus paddle

EAT FLESHY CACTUS PADDLES LITTERED WITH BARBED NODES? That may sound like more trouble than it is worth. But get rid of those thorns and these prickly pear leaves are absolutely delectable, combining the flavor and texture of green beans and green bell pepper sprinkled with a little lemon juice.

A common vegetable in Mexico, they are sold in the United States in Latin American markets, supermarkets with large Latin American produce sections, and some farmers markets. Apple green to deep green, they are about 8 inches long, 4 inches wide, and about ½ inch thick.

BUYING AND STORING

Look for leaves that are somewhat rigid. If leaves are limp or wrinkled, those are signs that leaves aren't fresh. Medium-size leaves, about 8 inches long, are best; larger leaves may be tough and smaller ones cook down to nothing. Refrigerate tightly wrapped in plastic up to 1 week. Some Latin American markets sell them sealed in plastic bags, trimmed and cut into 1/4-inch strips. They can be frozen, well-sealed, either cooked or raw, up to 3 months (see Freezing, page 310).

Domestic: *year-round*
Global: *year-round*

PREP

Before use, remove thorns. Often, cactus leaves sold at supermarkets have most of the barbs removed. Either way, it is best to wear gloves to protect hands. Trim off edge around paddle. Scrape or cut off tiny spines from both sides, or peel with vegetable peeler. Rinse thoroughly to remove any stray spines and some of the sticky fluid that will be extruded. May be cleaned 1–2 days ahead; cover and refrigerate, well sealed.

USE

Generally cooking directions say to cut into 3/4-inch squares or 1/2-inch strips, then simmer in water about 20 minutes or until tender. Similar to simmered okra, a somewhat slimy substance is exuded. Rinsing simmered cactus leaves helps to eliminate much of this sliminess. But to help mitigate the slime factor, grill or roast instead. The texture won't be as tender, but it won't be sticky.

To grill, brush whole, well-trimmed leaf with vegetable or canola oil and sprinkle with a little salt. Grill over medium coals, turning frequently until completely limp. Cool and cut into strips. Or grill strips of raw, well-trimmed leaf in same manner on vegetable grid.

To roast, toss strips with vegetable oil or canola oil. Preheat oven to 375 degrees. Place strips on rimmed baking sheet, and place in preheated oven for 17–20 minutes.

Use cooked cactus leaves (cut into either strips or squares) in egg dishes, soups, and stews, or cold in salsas and salads.

NUTRITIONAL INFO

1 cup is a good source of vitamin A; significant source of vitamin C.

SERVING SUGGESTIONS

Sublime scramble: Scrambled eggs with cactus leaves is a traditional Mexican dish. Sauté chopped white onion in butter until softened. Add strips of cooked cactus leaves and beaten eggs. Cook until set, stirring frequently on medium heat. Season with salt and pepper. If desired, top with grated cheese and salsa.

Enchilada filling: Add cooked strips to vegetable-cheese filling for enchiladas.

Veggie soup: Add pieces to vegetable soup, along with either tomato salsa or tomatillo salsa. Garnish with crumbled tortilla chips.

Cactus quesadillas: Place strips of cooked cactus leaves and a few spinach leaves on flour tortilla. Cover with shredded Jack cheese, leaving 1-inch margin around edge. Top with second tortilla and brush top tortilla lightly with vegetable oil. Invert into heated, nonstick skillet; cook until lightly toasted. Brush top tortilla lightly with oil; turn and cook until toasted and cheese melts.

nopalitos salad

Grilled meats and fish pair nicely with this refreshing salad. If desired, mount it on a bed of fresh romaine lettuce.

2 pounds fresh cactus leaves, grilled (see Use)

Salt and pepper, to taste

1 large ripe tomato, chopped

½ cup chopped onions

2 medium serrano chiles, seeded, chopped (see Cook's Notes)

½ cup chopped cilantro

½ cup grated Parmesan cheese

½ cup red wine vinegar

½ cup olive oil

OPTIONAL GARNISH: avocado slices

YIELD: ABOUT 10 SERVINGS

COOK'S NOTES: Use caution when working with fresh chilies. Wash work surface thoroughly upon completion and do NOT touch face or eyes.

1. Cool grilled cactus leaves and cut into ¼-inch-by–2-inch strips.

2. In medium-large bowl, combine all ingredients. Toss and taste, and adjust seasoning as needed. May be served as a side dish or in warm tortillas, folded like tacos. If desired, top with avocado slices.

NUTRITIONAL INFORMATION (PER SERVING WITHOUT AVOCADO): Calories 140; fat calories 105; total fat 12 grams; sat fat 2 grams; cholesterol 5 milligrams; sodium 320 milligrams; total carbohydrates 5 grams; fiber 2 grams; sugars 2 grams; protein 3 grams; vitamin A IUs 15%; vitamin C 30%; calcium 20%; iron 4%.

Cactus Leaf

celery

COMMON
CHINESE

REFRESHING AND SLIGHTLY SWEET, common celery may be taken for granted as an aromatic, thought of as a team player to flavor sauces, stocks, or soups, or included as part of a no-surprise raw vegetable platter served with dip.

But common celery becomes the star when it's braised or sautéed and served, more or less on its own. It sweetens slightly and becomes more herbaceous.

Chinese celery's stalks are daintier and thinner than those of its common cousin. It's stalks are generally hollow, somewhat limp, and topped with abundant leaves. Slightly more aromatic, it is rarely eaten raw. Most often, it's added to soup or stir-fries, braised chicken, or rice dishes.

Common

Chinese

BUYING AND STORING

Look for common celery with stalks that are shiny and crisp, avoiding those with brown spots or yellow leaves. To store, trim base and remove any damaged stalks. Rinse in cold water and place in plastic bag. Place in refrigerator vegetable drawer up to 2 weeks. If needed, refresh by chilling in ice water. Can be frozen and used in cooked dishes.

Look for Chinese celery with crisp, fresh-looking leaves, and avoid those with droopy leaves or brown spots. To store, place in perforated plastic bag and refrigerate. Do not wash until ready to use.

Domestic: *year-round*
Global: *year-round*

PREP

For common celery, wash stalks under cold running water. Tough strings on large, outer stalks can be removed; use paring knife to barely cut into celery (on stringy side at base). Pull knife away, catching strings between thumb and blade, and pull toward leaves. Discard strings. Cut into sticks, slice, or dice, as needed.

For Chinese celery, remove and discard any yellow leaves. Wash in tub of cold water. If gritty, you may need to drain water and repeat process. Shake to remove water. Chop or slice as needed. Often leaves are reserved for last-minute addition to soup or used as garnish.

USE

For common celery, use raw or cooked. Raw and chopped, add to salads, such as tuna, shrimp, chicken, or potato salad, or use plentiful amount in poultry stuffing. Add to stir-fries and soup, or braise as a vegetable side dish.

For Chinese celery, use cooked. Chop and add to stir-fry, soup, or casseroles, generally close to end of cooking. Delicious in fried rice.

NUTRITIONAL INFO

1 cup is a good source of vitamin A.

SERVING SUGGESTIONS

Edible swizzle stick: Use, leaf-attached, as garnish for tomato juice–based drinks, such as Bloody Marys.

Victor: Celery Victor is a classic braised celery dish that's served cold. Cut 2–3 common celery hearts (inner, tender portion of bunch) into 4-inch-long stalks, removing and reserving leaves. Braise in enough vegetable broth or chicken broth to cover (bring to boil on high heat, then lower to simmer, and cover until tender, about 10 minutes). Chill. Top drained, chilled celery with favorite vinaigrette, either homemade (see Simple Vinaigrette, page xx) or store-bought. Garnish with chopped chives and reserved celery leaves.

Canapé canoes: Stuff common celery sticks with deviled eggs or deviled ham (or deviled turkey).

Mac and cheese: Sauté generous amount diced celery in combination of butter and vegetable oil until tender-crisp. Add to favorite macaroni and cheese recipe, along with a pinch of celery seed.

chicken and chinese celery stir-fry

The rather neutral flavor of skinned and boned chicken breast allows the delicious aromatic nature of Chinese celery to shine. If Chinese celery isn't available, substitute common celery. As with all stir-fry dishes, make sure all ingredients are measured and ready to go before you heat the wok.

2 large boneless, skinless chicken breasts, about 12 ounces, patted dry

Salt

1 tablespoon vegetable oil or canola oil

2 garlic cloves, minced

2 teaspoons minced fresh ginger

3 Chinese celery stalks, leaves trimmed and reserved, stalks cut in ½-inch slices

2 tablespoons soy sauce

1 tablespoon cornstarch mixed with 2 tablespoons water

1. Cut chicken into 1-inch chunks and season with a little salt.

2. Heat oil in wok on high heat. Add garlic and ginger and stir-fry 30 seconds.

3. Add chicken; stir-fry until browned, about 5–7 minutes. Add celery; stir-fry until chicken is thoroughly cooked and celery has softened.

4. Add soy sauce and cornstarch mixture. Stir-fry until sauce thickens. Serve with cooked rice. Chop about 3 tablespoons celery leaves and use as garnish on top of stir-fry mixture.

YIELD: 4 SERVINGS

NUTRITIONAL INFORMATION (PER SERVING WITHOUT RICE): Calories 150; fat calories 40.5; total fat 4.5 grams; sat fat 1 gram, cholesterol 50 milligrams; sodium 900 milligrams; total carbohydrates 4 grams; fiber less than 1 gram; sugars 0 grams; protein 21 grams; vitamin A IUs 15%; vitamin C 25%; calcium 10%; iron 25%.

celery root,
also celeriac, knob celery

GNARLY, KNOBBY AND, WELL, JUST PLAIN UGLY. Celery roots are lopsided spheres speckled with whorls and crevices. Their dimensions range from baseball- to cantaloupe-size. Get past the appearance, and this irresistible root vegetable has the zesty flavor of celery and parsley. It has a refreshing, clean taste, deeper than celery, but without the strings.

Hidden beneath the scruffy brown skin is luscious white flesh, dappled with light-caramel tinges. For hundreds of years, this pallid-but-alluring interior has been prized in European purées, gratins, soups, stuffing, stews, and salads.

BUYING AND STORING
Look for relatively small, firm bulbs with a minimum of crevices and rootlets, avoiding any with soft spots. Best if they feel heavy for their size. Refrigerate root in plastic bag for 7–10 days.
Domestic: *August–June*
Global: *None*

PREP
Peel and soak briefly in acidulated water (cold water with a good squeeze of lemon juice) to prevent discoloration.

Celery Root

USE
To eat raw, peel, then grate or shred and use in salad. To cook, peel, then slice, dice, or grate; boil, braise, or blanch until tender but not mushy.

SERVING SUGGESTIONS

Celery root remoulade—main course or salad: Peel celery root and cut it into wedges to fit into feed tube of food processor fitted with grating disk; grate the wedges. Blanch 2 minutes in boiling water (to cover) with a squeeze of lemon juice; drain, pat dry (but if you wish, you can use it raw). Then toss it with mixture of ¼ cup mayonnaise, 2 tablespoons sour cream, 1–2 teaspoons lemon juice (use less if boiled in water with lemon juice, more if you're using raw), 2 tablespoons minced parsley, and 1 tablespoon Dijon mustard; use just enough dressing to coat. Taste and season with salt and pepper. If desired, serve on bed of mixed baby lettuces or watercress and garnish with cooked shrimp.

Avant-garde lasagna: Instead of pasta, use thinly sliced, blanched (tender-crisp) celery root.

The "best" mashed potatoes—Celery Root and Potato Teamwork: Cook peeled and cubed celery root (either 1 large or 2 small) in large pot of boiling, salted water 5 minutes. Add 4 large peeled and cubed baking potatoes; boil 15–20 minutes, or until tender. Drain and return to pot; cook on medium heat until potatoes look dry, about 1–2 minutes. Remove from heat and mash with ½ stick butter (¼ cup), about 4 tablespoons milk, salt, and pepper.

Celeriac of the sea: Add finely chopped raw celery root to your favorite tuna salad, along with a tablespoon of minced fresh parsley or tarragon.

triple "c" soup

This creamy soup is a "triple crown" combination of celery-flavored ingredients: celery root, celery, and celery seeds. Balanced with other vegetables, such as sweet carrots and leeks, it makes a delicious first course. Add a garnish of baby shrimp or sautéed scallops or caviar, and it becomes a luncheon entree.

¼ cup (½ stick) butter

1 medium celery root, peeled, cut into 1-inch chunks

5 stalks celery, trimmed, cut into 1-inch pieces

1 medium carrot, peeled, cut into ½-inch chunks

1 medium leek, white part only, washed and sliced

2 medium onions, chopped

2 tablespoons minced fresh Italian parsley

3 tablespoons minced fresh dill

OPTIONAL: 2 teaspoons minced fresh tarragon
¼ teaspoon whole celery seeds

1 teaspoon salt

4 cups chicken broth or vegetable broth

2 Yukon gold or russet potatoes, peeled and cut into 1-inch slices

2 cups half-and-half or 1 cup milk and 1 cup cream or 2 cups nonfat evaporated milk

Freshly ground pepper and salt, to taste

OPTIONAL GARNISHES: Small cubes of orange bell pepper, or cooked baby shrimp, or sautéed scallops, or caviar, or fresh dill, or parsley

1. In large pot or Dutch oven, melt butter over medium-high heat. Add celery root, celery, carrot, leek, and onions. Cook 1 minute, stir, and reduce heat to low. Cover and cook 10–15 minutes, stirring occasionally, until vegetables start to soften.

2. Remove lid and add herbs, celery seeds, salt, and chicken broth; increase heat to medium-high. Simmer 15 minutes, reducing heat if necessary to maintain simmer.

3. Add potatoes and half-and-half (or cream and milk). Cover and simmer on low heat 20 minutes, or until potatoes are tender.

4. Carefully, because mixture is hot, purée in 3 or 4 batches in food processor fitted with metal blade. Taste and add more salt or pepper, as needed. Ladle into soup bowls and garnish as desired.

YIELD: 8–10 SERVINGS

NUTRITIONAL INFORMATION (PER SERVING): Calories 180; fat calories 90; total fat 10 grams; sat fat 6 grams; cholesterol 35 milligrams; sodium 480 milligrams; total carbohydrates 17 grams; fiber 3 grams; sugars 5 grams; protein 6 grams; vitamin A IUs 25%; vitamin C 20%; calcium 10%; iron 6%.

chard

COMMON (GREEN)

RAINBOW

RED SWISS

SMOOTH OR CURLY, LIGHT TO DARK GREEN, chard's sizable leaves have a fairly mild, spinachlike flavor. Both stem and leaf are edible. Stem color varies according to variety. They can be pink, red, orange, gold, flashy purple, pink-and-white striped, or creamy white.

The flavor of those colorful stems is gentler than their robust leaves. Some recipes call for using just the leaves; others use both stem and leaves, most often directing cooks to cook stems first, then add leaves during the last few minutes.

common (green)

Red Swiss

COMMON

(green)

Creamy white stalk, ribs and veins, with medium-sized ruffled, glossy dark-green leaf. ■ *Leaves have mild, spinachlike flavor, the bitterness balanced with sweetness. Stems have less prominent vegetal taste.*

RAINBOW

Stalks (and ribs and veins) come in a wide variety of colors, including orange, pink, red, or gold or purple or pink and white stripes. Leaves vary in color; they can be smooth or ruffled. ■ *Mixture of colors result in flavor variations from very mild to more robust.*

RED SWISS

Deep red stalk, ribs, and veining. Leaves are moderately puckered. ■ *Slightly milder flavor profile than green chard.*

BUYING AND STORING

Look for stems that are fairly stiff, without brown spots. When bundles are wrapped too tightly, it causes damage. Larger leaves are generally milder and more tender. Store in plastic, unwashed and dry, in crisper up to 10 days. Stems with leaves removed can be refrigerated a few days longer.

Domestic: *year-round*
Global: *none*

PREP

Wash just before using; rinse under generous amount of cold running water. Trim leaves from stems and thick ribs with kitchen scissors or knife, or fold leaf next to rib and pull away rib. If stems are thick, peel away strings as with large celery stalks (see Celery Prep, page 151). Stems are generally cut into 1/2–3/4-inch slices, often on the diagonal.

USE

Use leaves raw or cooked; when raw they have a rougher texture than spinach, so use them sparingly in salads, finely shredded and combined with more tender greens. Stems should be cooked. Chard leaves and stems can be steamed, braised, boiled, or sautéed. All varieties are interchangeable in recipes.

NUTRITIONAL INFO

1 cup is an excellent source of vitamin A; significant source of vitamin C.

SERVING SUGGESTIONS

Boil, toss, and eat: Add stems (cut into 1/2-inch pieces) to boiling water. Boil 5 minutes. Add shredded leaves and boil 4–5 minutes. Drain well; toss with enough extra-virgin olive oil to very lightly coat. Season with salt and pepper. For added zip, toss with pinch of dried red pepper flakes. If desired, serve over cooked rice.

Chard with ginger rice: Heat 3 tablespoons vegetable oil in large saucepan on medium-high heat. Add 1 onion (chopped) and cook until softened, about 3 minutes. Add 1 clove garlic and 1 cup uncooked long-grain white rice; stir to coat rice with oil. Cook, stirring occasionally, until golden. Add 2 cups vegetable broth or chicken broth, 1 teaspoon minced ginger and 1 cup chopped chard leaves. Bring to boil; cover and reduce heat to low. Simmer, covered, 18 minutes. Remove lid and toss. Season with salt and pepper. If desired, garnish with minced cilantro.

Shock treatment: Boil chard leaves in water for 2 minutes. Drain and place in bowl of ice water. Drain well; pack in plastic bags and freeze up to three months.

Omelet filling: Heat 2 tablespoons vegetable oil in large, deep skillet on medium-high heat. Add ½ cup diced red onion; cook until softened, about 3 minutes. Add 3 cups shredded chard leaves and toss. Cover and cook 4–5 minutes, stirring occasionally. Remove lid and cook until all liquid evaporates. Remove from heat and season with salt and pepper. Use as omelet filling, adding goat cheese, if desired.

warm pasta "salad" with chard

Shredded chard gives pasta a flavor boost. In this dish, chopped chicken, sautéed mushrooms, and smoked mozzarella also add their share of interesting tastes and texture. If you prefer, use cooked, sliced Italian sausage instead of chicken.

8 ounces fusilli (corkscrew) or farfalle (bow) pasta

4 tablespoons olive oil, divided use

8 ounces shiitake mushrooms, stems removed and discarded, sliced

8 ounces cremini mushrooms, quartered

2 cloves garlic, minced

3 tablespoons red-wine vinegar, divided use

⅓ cup chicken broth, low-salt preferred

1 cup cubed cooked boneless, skinless chicken

2 tablespoons minced fresh Italian parsley

1½ cups shredded chard leaves

Salt and freshly ground black pepper, to taste

½ cup (½-inch) cubes smoked mozzarella cheese

GARNISH: 1 lemon, cut in quarters from top to bottom

1. Bring large pot of water to boil on high heat. Cook pasta al dente, according to package directions. Drain.

2. Meanwhile, heat 2 tablespoons olive oil in large, deep skillet. Add mushrooms and cook until lightly browned. Add garlic, 1 tablespoon vinegar, and broth; simmer 5 minutes. Add chicken, toss, and remove from heat. Stir pasta into mushroom mixture.

3. Whisk 2 tablespoons olive oil, 2 tablespoons vinegar, and parsley. Toss chard with vinaigrette; add to mushroom-pasta mixture and toss. Taste and add salt and pepper as needed.

4. Divide among 4 small plates. Top with cubes of smoked mozzarella. Place lemon quarter on each plate; diners can add lemon juice, if desired. Serve.

YIELD: 4 FIRST-COURSE SERVINGS

NUTRITIONAL INFORMATION (PER SERVING): Calories 480; fat calories 180; total fat 20 grams; sat fat 6 grams; cholesterol 40 milligrams; sodium 240 milligrams; total carbohydrates 50 grams; fiber 3 grams; sugars 4 grams; protein 27 grams; vitamin A IUs 25%; vitamin C 15%; calcium 25%; iron 20%.

chile, also chile pepper, chili

ANAHEIM (GREEN, RED)

BANANA WAX

CHERRY BELL

CHILACA

CUBANELLE, HUNGARIAN WAX

FRESNO (GREEN, RED)

HABANERO (GREEN, ORANGE, RED, YELLOW)

HATCH (ONLY SEASONAL VARIETY)

JALAPEÑO (GREEN, RED)

MANZANA (ORANGE, RED)

PASILLA, POBLANO (GREEN, RED)

SCOTCH BONNET

SERRANO (GREEN, RED)

THAI, BIRD'S EYE (GREEN, RED)

YELLOW

IT'S HARD TO IMAGINE THE WORLD'S CUISINES without the delectable fiery bite of chiles. But before explorers ventured into the Western Hemisphere in the late fifteenth century, chiles existed only in the warm areas of the Americas.

Capsaicin is the incendiary substance in chiles that produces the sensation of heat. Because the amount of capsaicin varies greatly from one chile variety to another, pharmacist Wilbur Scoville developed a system for measuring a pepper's power. In this system capsaicin content is measured in parts per million, then converted into Scoville units. One part per million is 15 Scoville units. Bell peppers weigh in with zero Scoville units, while the habanero registers a scorching 100,000–300,000 Scoville units.

It should be noted that chiles of the same variety (even when picked from the same plant) can vary greatly in their hotness.

BUYING AND STORING

Choose those that are firm and glossy without shriveling or soft spots. Jalapeños sometimes have "scar cracks" at stem ends, but other varieties should be free of cracks. Refrigerate unwashed and wrapped in paper towels inside plastic bag up to 10 days.

ALL CHILES EXCEPT HATCH
Domestic: *June–October*
Global: *year-round*

HATCH CHILES
Domestic: *June–September*
Global: *none*

PREP

Cooks with delicate skin should use gloves when working with chiles. Wash hands and work surface thoroughly upon completion and do NOT touch face or eyes. To use raw, remove stem. Most often, recipes advise the removal of seeds and veins to reduce heat; cut chile into quarters lengthwise, then cut out veins and seeds. Cut into desired shape.

To roast small chiles, place in dry skillet on medium heat, turning until sporadically blackened and slightly softened. Most often small roasted chiles are not peeled.

To roast larger chiles, use barbecue, gas flame, or broiler. Place on hot grill or flame from gas burner, turning with tongs as they blister. Or, under broiler, place on rimmed baking sheet and broil, about 6 inches below heated broiler element, turning as they blister (note that chiles roasted in oven have softer texture). Either way, when blistered and moderately blackened, place in bowl or on plate and cover with plastic wrap or kitchen towel, or place in plastic bag. Let sit 5 minutes, then uncover. To peel and seed, wear rubber gloves if hands are sensitive. When cool enough to handle, peel skin (or rub off skin if easier). Core with small knife, cut in half, and scrape out seeds. If necessary, rinse briefly with cold water, but water rinses away delicious juices. Sometimes, a moist hand can remove loose

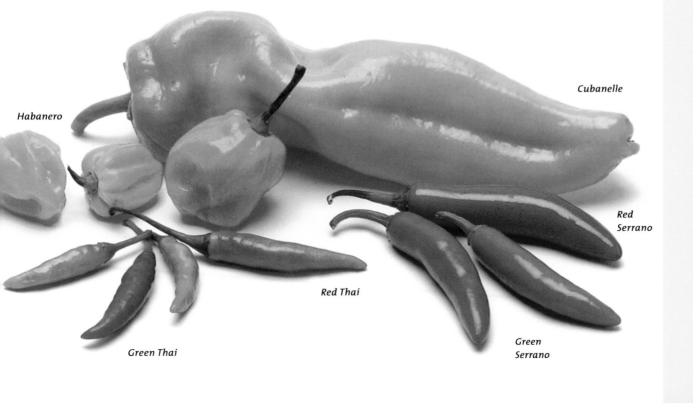

Habanero

Cubanelle

Red Serrano

Red Thai

Green Thai

Green Serrano

SCOVILLE UNITS

0–4,000: Mild
4,000–15,000: Medium
15,000–50,000: Hot
Greater than 50,000: Very hot

ANAHEIM

(green, red)
Elongated, tapered, and rather flat, about 6 inches long and 2 inches wide with apple-green skin and flesh. Sometimes called long green chiles or *chile verde*. Mild, sweet flavor. Red when fully matured (but seldom available).
■ *500–1,500*.

BANANA WAX

Elongated, tapered, 3–5 inches in length with light yellow skin and medium-thick flesh. Sweet, gentle flavor. ■ *1,000–3,000*

CHERRY BELL

Almost spherical with about 1-inch diameters, deep red skin and thick flesh. ■ *500–3,500*

CHILACA

Elongated, slightly flattened, and generally curved, about 6–9 inches long with 1-inch diameter, deep brown skin and dark green flesh. When dried, called *chile negro*. ■ *1,000–2,500*

CUBANELLE, HUNGARIAN WAX

These two chiles are very similar and are often marketed interchangeably. In Southeast, marketed as Cubanelle; on West Coast, marketed as Hungarian Wax. Elongated and tapered, about 5–7 inches long. Greenish-yellow skin and thick flesh. ■ *500–1,000*

FRESNO

(green, red)
Tapers from broad shoulders to rounded end, about 3 inches long and 1 inch at widest portion. Glossy red or green skin (red most common, green is rare) with thick flesh. Often mistaken for red jalapeño. ■ *3,000–15,000*

HABANERO

(green, orange, red, yellow)
Lantern-shaped, about 2 by 2 inches. Can have orange, red, yellow, or green skin and flesh, but orange is most common. Often credited as "hottest chile." The Red Savina is the hottest variety of habanero. ■ *100,000–300,000 (Red Savina has measured up to 576,000)*

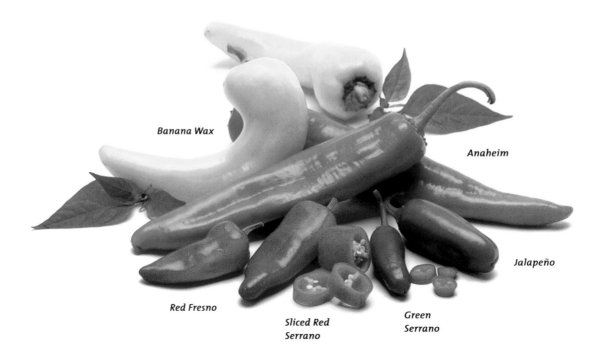

Banana Wax

Anaheim

Jalapeño

Red Fresno

Sliced Red Serrano

Green Serrano

HATCH

Similar to Anaheim chile, but generally curved and often hotter. Thick flesh. Named for town in southern part of New Mexico where grown. Most often picked green, but turns red when fully matured. ■ *1,000–8,000*

JALAPEÑO (GREEN, RED)

Tapered from broad shoulders, about 2–4 inches long; deep green skin and thick flesh. Turns red when fully mature, but most often sold green. Some cooks look for white lengthwise streaking, saying it indicates fully developed flavor. (Red seldom available). ■ *2,500–10,000*

MANZANA

(orange, red)
Often shaped like a large habanero chile with about 2-inch diameter (but doesn't have hot flavor profile like habanero). Yellowish-orange or red skin with thick flesh. Seeds are generally black. Red variety is rare. ■ *10,000–60,000*

PASILLA, POBLANO

(green, red)
Labeled Pasilla on the West Coast, these fresh chiles are called Poblano elsewhere in the U.S. Dark forest-green flesh and skin (turns red when fully mature, but seldom seen red in marketplace). Thick flesh has rich, green bean–like flavor. Red is rare. ■ *1,000–3,000*

SCOTCH BONNET

(yellow, red, green, orange)
Similar in shape to habanero but often slightly smaller. Can be green, orange, red, or yellow. ■ *100,000–300,000*

SERRANO

Thin and bullet-shaped, generally 1–2 inches long with deep green skin and flesh (turns red when mature, seldom available). ■ *15,000–30,000*

THAI, BIRD'S EYE

(green, red)
Often called bird chiles, these small, narrow chiles are tapered and about 1-inch long with ¼-inch diameters. Green Thai chiles turn red when fully mature. ■ *40,000–100,000*

YELLOW

Plump, sweet, can be 3 inches long with 1-inch diameter. Waxy yellow skin and thick flesh. ■ *2,500–6,000*

Pasilla (Poblano)

Cherry Bell

Hatch

Yellow

debris. Holding chile in sink (but not under running water), rinse hand and run wet hand over surface. Repeat until seeds and skin are removed. Cut into desired shape. Can be refrigerated airtight up to 2 days, or frozen.

USE

Use in salsas, bean salads, and sauces. Stuff with meat or cheese mixtures. Use in curries, stews or casseroles. To reduce mouth burn, milk, ice cream, sour cream, and yogurt are soothing remedies. And remember to add small doses to dishes; taste, then add more as needed. It is easier to add than subtract.

NUTRITIONAL INFO

1 cup is an excellent source of vitamin C; significant source of vitamins A, K, B_6, and folate.

SERVING SUGGESTIONS

Mango-habanero sauce: Heat 1 tablespoon vegetable oil in large saucepan on medium-high heat. Add 4 ripe mangos (peeled, seeded, and diced), 1 small onion (diced), and 1 habanero chile (seeds and veins removed, minced). Cook, stirring frequently, until onion softens, about 6 minutes. Add ¼ cup fresh lemon juice, ¼ cup ketchup, and 3 tablespoons sugar. Bring to boil, stirring constantly. Reduce heat to low; simmer 30 minutes. Remove from heat and cool. Whirl in blender is batches until smooth. Season to taste with salt and pepper. Serve room temperature with fish or pork. Delectable drizzled over tacos, especially *carnitas* (shredded pork) tacos.

Creamy topping: Place 2 cups roasted (peeled and seeded) Anaheim, Hatch, or Pasilla (Poblano) that have been cut into ⅛-inch-wide strips with ⅓ cup heavy whipping cream or crème fraîche in large, heavy-bottomed saucepan. Simmer until thickened. Spoon over grilled fish or chicken or cooked rice. Season with salt to taste.

Lime 'n' jalapeño dressing: In blender or food processor fitted with metal blade, process 1 medium clove peeled garlic and about 15 large fresh mint leaves; pulse until minced. Add 3 tablespoons fresh lime juice, 1 minced (seeded) jalapeño, ⅓ cup vegetable oil, 1 teaspoon sugar, and salt to taste; process until well combined. Toss with cooked rice noodles, adding enough dressing to generously coat. Garnish with toasted sesame seeds and sprig of fresh mint. If desired, cooked shrimp or chicken can be added.

Salsa and black bean dip: Toss ¼ cup finely chopped red onion with 4 diced medium tomatoes, 2 teaspoons fresh lime juice, splash balsamic vinegar, 1–2 minced (seeds and veins removed) jalapeño chiles (or use serrano for hotter version). Toss. Rinse 1 (15-ounce) can black beans; drain and add to mixture. Add 4 tablespoons chopped cilantro. Toss. Add salt to taste. Serve with tortilla chips, or on tacos or quesadillas.

potato and chile gratin

Anaheim chiles add a just-right spiciness to this creamy side dish. If a little more heat is desired, sprinkle ½ teaspoon minced serrano on the first layer of potatoes. Serve with baked chicken or roast pork. If desired, garnish with sprigs of fresh cilantro.

Butter for greasing pan

4 large baking potatoes, such as russets, peeled, thinly sliced

1½ cups grated cheddar cheese

2 Anaheim chiles, roasted, peeled, seeded, and diced

1 cup chicken broth

1 cup heavy whipping cream

Salt and pepper to taste

1. Grease 7-by–11-inch baking pan with butter. Preheat oven to 400 degrees.

2. Layer ⅓ of potatoes, ½ cheese, and ½ chiles. Repeat layers. End with final layer of potatoes.

3. In medium bowl, combine broth, cream, salt, and pepper; pour over potatoes. Bake in middle of preheated oven 45 minutes, or until potatoes are tender, liquid is absorbed, and top is browned. Let stand 5 minutes before serving.

YIELD: 6–8 SERVINGS

NUTRITIONAL INFORMATION (PER SERVING): Calories 340; fat calories 162; total fat 18 grams; sat fat 11 grams; cholesterol 65 milligrams; sodium 350 milligrams; total carbohydrates 34 grams; fiber 4 grams; sugars 3 grams; protein 11 grams; vitamin A IUs 25%; vitamin C 35%; calcium 20%; iron10%.

choy (with curved stalks)

BABY BOK CHOY

BOK CHOY

CHOY SUM, FLOWERING CABBAGE

GAI CHOY, CHINESE MUSTARD

ONG CHOY
(SEE SEPARATE LISTING, PAGE 231)

YU CHOY SUM
(SEE SEPARATE LISTING, PAGE 307)

THESE VERSATILE VEGETABLES ADD CRUNCH AND COLOR to a wide variety of dishes. Their curved, bright-white to apple-green stalks are topped with dark green leaves. Joined at the base in a bulb-like cluster, stalks graduate from large to small, from hearty outer ribs to more petite heart.

Stalks are crunchy and very juicy, with a gentle mustard-like edge balanced by subtle sweetness. The flavors of the leaves vary, from mild to very spicy, sweet to peppery.

BUYING AND STORING

Look for crisp stalks and leaves; leaves should be bright green. Avoid those with brown spots or wilted leaves. Refrigerate, unwashed, in perforated plastic bags up to 5 days.

BOK CHOY, BABY BOK CHOY, CHOY SUM (FLOWERING CABBAGE)
Domestic: *year-round*
Global: *year-round*

GAI CHOY
Domestic: *year-round*
Global: *none*

PREP

Trim and discard ¼ inch at base. Pull stalks apart and rinse several times in tubs of cold water. Shake dry. In most instances, baby bok choy is used with leaves attached, either halved or quartered. With mature bok choy, choy sum, and gai choy, cut leaves from stem. Cut stem into ½-inch slices. Cut leaves into 2-inch slices.

USE

Stir-fry, steam, microwave, braise, or boil. Stems require longer cooking than leaves, so cook stems until just barely tender-crisp and add leaves. Stem of gai choy is often pickled.

NUTRITIONAL INFO

1 cup is a good source of vitamins A and C.

SERVING SUGGESTIONS

Fried rice: Cut baby bok choy into eighths, lengthwise. Stir-fry in hot vegetable oil or peanut oil. Stir into fried rice.

BABY BOK CHOY, BOK CHOY
About 16 inches from base to leaf tops, bok choy has wide white, thick curved stalks and broad deep green leaves with white veins. Baby bok choy is about 7 inches long. Immature stalks are tinged with apple green, leaves are oblong, deep green with smooth edges. Shanghai bok choy is same size as baby bok choy but has thinner, white stems. It's often labeled baby bok choy. ■
Stalks are juicy, crisp, and mild, more celerylike than cabbagey. Leaves have mild spinach-cabbage flavor. Baby bok choy is less fibrous and more tender.

CHOY SUM
(flowering cabbage)
About 12 inches long with slender, white curved stalks. Outer stalks join at base, interior stalks attach higher up the stalk and tend to be meatier with less defined curve. At the heart is a cluster of green buds that can develop into yellow flowers. Stalks are topped with elongated, deep green leaves. ■
Stalks are juicy and crisp with mild radishlike flavor. Leaves have alluring hint of bitterness balanced with sweetness. Buds have a mustard tang.

GAI CHOY
(chinese mustard)
About 11 inches long, curved stalks are deep apple green. Dark green leaves pucker into folds and have ragged edges. ■
Stalks are crunchy and less juicy than bok choy or choy sum. They have a slight mustardlike bite. Leaves are peppery with a pronounced mustard taste.

Steamed and seasoned: Steam over boiling water until tender crisp. In bowl combine 3 tablespoons vegetable or canola oil, 1 teaspoon Asian sesame oil, ¼ cup mirin or dry sherry, 2 teaspoons soy sauce, 3 tablespoons rice vinegar, and smidgen of Asian hot sauce; stir to blend. Add drained vegetable and toss. Season to taste, if needed, with salt.

Simmered in soup: Add to vegetable soups during the last 10 minutes of cooking (adding stems four minutes sooner than leaves). Asian soups that contain ginger and tofu have special appeal.

Choy Sum

lion's head stew

This soup is a twist on a classic Chinese soup. Squint and the turkey meatballs floating among colorful baby bok choy may look like lions' heads. If you prefer, sliced stems and chopped leaves of mature bok choy, choy sum, or gai choy can be substituted for baby bok choy (see Prep). If you like, sliced fresh mushrooms can be added in step 4 along with bok choy.

2 teaspoons minced fresh ginger

Pinch sugar

½ teaspoon salt

1 tablespoon cornstarch

¾ teaspoon soy sauce

1 teaspoon dry sherry

1 tablespoon egg white

½ teaspoon Asian sesame oil

6 ounces ground turkey

2 green onions, minced, white and light green portion only

Cornstarch for coating meatballs

1 teaspoon cornstarch

1 teaspoon soy sauce

1 teaspoon water

Canola oil or vegetable oil, for frying

1 tablespoon minced fresh ginger

12 ounces baby bok choy, halved lengthwise, thoroughly washed, well-drained

2 cups chicken broth

Optional for serving: cooked rice

1. In medium-large bowl, combine first 8 ingredients; stir to combine. Add turkey and green onion. Gently mix with hands and form into 1¼-inch balls (overworking mixture will cause toughness).

2. Heat about ⅜-inch oil in large, deep skillet on medium-high heat. Roll meatballs in cornstarch, lightly coating entire surface. Brown on all sides and drain on paper towels.

3. In small bowl combine 1 teaspoon cornstarch, 1 teaspoon soy, and 1 teaspoon water; set aside.

4. In large deep skillet or wok, heat 2 tablespoons canola or vegetable oil on high heat. Add 1 tablespoon minced ginger and baby bok choy. Stir-fry for 30 seconds. Cautiously add broth and meatballs. Lower heat to medium and gently simmer 10 minutes. Stir in reserved cornstarch mixture and gently stir. Simmer until slightly thickened. Serve in bowls, either with or without rice.

YIELD: 4 SERVINGS

NUTRITIONAL INFORMATION (PER SERVING WITHOUT RICE): Calories 260; fat calories 189; total fat 21 grams; sat fat 2.5 grams, cholesterol 30 milligrams; sodium 290 milligrams; total carbohydrates 6 grams; fiber 1 gram; sugars 2 grams; protein 13 grams; vitamin A IUs 80%; vitamin C 70%; calcium 10%; iron 6%.

corn

BABY

BICOLOR

COMMON (YELLOW)

RED

WHITE

BEFORE NEW SUPERSWEET HYBRIDS OF CORN WERE DEVELOPED, cooks followed the pick-it, cook-it rule. They knew that corn's sugar started to convert to starch as soon as it was harvested, so for the sweetest taste, corn needed to be consumed within minutes or, at most, hours of picking. But new hybrids are extremely sweet, juicy, and very crisp, and shelf life is extended to up to one week. Varieties include yellow (common), white, red, and bicolor.

Baby corn is whitish-yellow. Once shucked, these bantam beauties are entirely edible, cob and all. Their flavor profile is sweet but with a distinct vegetal edge, something like a sugary green bean.

BUYING AND STORING

For the freshest taste, it's best to buy any variety of corn in husks. Look for plump kernels and green husks, avoiding any that look dried out. To check kernels, pull back portion of husk. Baby corn should have green silks that are slightly sticky. Except for baby corn, refrigerate (with husks intact) in plastic bag in crisper drawer up to 7 days, but for freshest taste eat as soon as possible. Baby corn can be stored in same manner, but it should be used within 4 days. To freeze all but baby corn, blanch (on cob) in boiling water 2 minutes; drain and refresh in cold running water. Pat dry and remove kernels from cob (see Prep). Place in single layer on rimmed baking sheet. Freeze. When frozen, place in airtight freezer bag and return to freezer. If freezing baby corn, remove husk and freeze without blanching.

BABY, BICOLOR, WHITE, YELLOW
Domestic: *May–September*
Global: *November–April*

RED
Domestic: *July–September*
Global: *none*

PREP

Unless grilling, pull off and discard husks. Pull off silks, running cupped hand over top of corn, or use dry, soft vegetable brush to remove silk between kernels. If grilling, either pull husks back and leave them attached and use as handle for turning (place on grill with kernels on grill and husks extending over side of grill, off heat) or pull back husks, remove silk, and return husks to original position.

Common (yellow)

White

Red

Baby

BABY
Immature, whitish-yellow kernels. About 2–4 inches long. ■ *Tender, with subtly sweet vegetal flavor profile. After husked, entirely edible—cob and all.*

BICOLOR
A mixture of white and yellow kernels. ■ *Retains sweetness of white and yellow hybrid varieties.*

COMMON
(yellow)
Plump bright yellow kernels. Tightly packed on cob. ■ *Juicy, tender, and very sweet.*

RED
Red kernels that can be streaked with creamy white. When cooked kernels change color; boiling turns them blue,

microwaving turns them purple and roasting turns them maroon. ■ *Sweet like the hybrids. Similar to white corn in taste.*

WHITE
Creamy-white kernels that are often slightly smaller than Yellow variety. ■ *Very tender and very sweet.*

If you want only kernels, cut them off cob. Stand ear upright, resting tip on rimmed baking sheet. Using sharp knife, start at top of cob cutting down slowly, between base of kernels and cob (leave about ¼ of kernel base attached to cob). Rotate cob and repeat, until all kernels have been removed; discard cob.

USE FOR ALL VARIETIES EXCEPT BABY

Generally eaten cooked, cold, warm, room temperature, or hot. Can be cut off cob and tossed into salads. Cook on the cob by grilling, roasting (see Crowd corn, below), or boiling (about 2 minutes; do not salt water when boiling, as it will toughen corn). For kernels, sauté, simmer, blanch, or roast. Add to soup, salads, or stir-fries, or include in muffins, pancakes, or polenta.

USE FOR BABY

Generally cooked. Use on the edible cob in stir-fries, salads, and as garnish. Baby corn is perfect for pickling. For grilling, husk and brush with olive oil; grill briefly, just until lightly marked.

NUTRITIONAL INFO

1 cup is a good source of protein and excellent source of vitamin B_6.

SERVING SUGGESTIONS

Crowd corn: This casual roasted approach is great for large backyard gatherings. It is essential that corn is fresh and moist. Place 8 ears of corn (not baby) with husks in single layer on rimmed baking sheet. Stack 6 on top in a second layer. Bake in middle of preheated 350-degree oven for 30 minutes. Have guests husk their own corn; silks will come very easily off the kernels. Provide lime wedges, pepper mill, and flavored butter (mix soft butter with minced fresh basil and seasoned salt).

Risotto: Add corn kernels (not baby) or whole shucked baby corn to risotto 5 minutes before end of cooking time.

Corn and tomato salad: Heat 1 tablespoon olive oil or vegetable oil in large skillet on medium-high heat. Add ½ red onion (chopped); cook, stirring occasionally, until softened, about 2 minutes. Add 3 cups corn kernels (not baby) and cook 2–3 minutes, stirring frequently. Remove from heat and season with salt and pepper. In medium bowl, combine 1 tablespoon rice vinegar, 1 teaspoon extra-virgin olive oil, and 2 teaspoons minced fresh basil. Toss. Add 2 cups cherry tomatoes (cut in halves); toss. Add corn mixture; toss. Taste and adjust seasoning as needed, adding a little fresh lime juice if needed. Place a handful of baby spinach on 4 salad plates. Top each with corn mixture and serve.

Mexican-style corn on the cob with cheese and lime juice: Preheat grill. Soak 4–6 ears corn (not baby) in husks in cold water to cover 10 minutes (you may need to weigh them down to keep them submerged). Drain and grill about 10 minutes. When cool enough to handle, remove husks; return to grill for about 5–8 minutes or until nicely browned in spots. Combine ¼ cup mayonnaise with ⅛ teaspoon cayenne. Brush on hot corn. Roll in ⅔ cup shredded Cotija or feta cheese. Serve accompanied with lime wedges.

california succotash

This elegant version of succotash is a great side dish with grilled beef, pork, or poultry. In fact, it's so delicious that it could be a meal in itself. Succotash has a long history in Southern cooking and takes its name from the Narragansett Indian word *msickquatash,* which translates as "boiled whole kernels of corn."

4 tablespoons (½ stick) butter, divided use

1 (29-ounce) can hominy, drained

7 ears yellow corn, cut off cobs (about 6 cups)

2 cups canned small red beans, rinsed and drained

4 cups frozen lima beans, defrosted

About 14 large fresh basil leaves

1 cup olive oil, extra-virgin preferred

¼ cup white wine vinegar

Salt and pepper to taste

GARNISH: sprigs of fresh basil

1. Melt 2 tablespoons butter in large Dutch oven or large, deep skillet. Add hominy, and cook over medium heat until it is lightly browned. Add corn and red beans; stir to combine and cook 1 minute. Remove from heat. Pour into large bowl.

2. Return pan to medium heat. Melt remaining 2 tablespoons butter. Add lima beans and cook until beans are lightly browned. Add to hominy mixture.

3. Place basil in blender or food processor fitted with metal blade; pulse to mince. Add oil and vinegar; pulse to blend. Season to taste with salt and pepper. Add to hominy mixture and toss thoroughly.

4. Mound on large platter. Garnish with sprigs of basil. Serve warm or at room temperature.

YIELD: 12 SERVINGS

NUTRITIONAL INFORMATION (PER SERVING): Calories 370; fat calories 207; total fat 23 grams; sat fat 5 grams; cholesterol 10 milligrams; sodium 290 milligrams; total carbohydrates 35 grams; fiber 5 grams; sugars 2 grams; protein 7 grams; vitamin A IUs 10%; vitamin C 25%; calcium 2%; iron 10%.

cucumber

ARMENIAN

COMMON

HOT HOUSE, ENGLISH

JAPANESE

LEMON

PERSIAN, BABY

PICKLING

NEUTRAL BUT NOISY, cucumbers may be on the bland side, but their crisp texture is ready for endless flavoring variations, both simple and complex. Most often served on the chilly side, they have a cold crunch combined with a fragrance that is pleasingly grassy.

All varieties are mildly flavored, but their packaging is amazingly varied. Some are yellow, bumpy, and round; others are pale green, deeply ridged, and seductively curved. Some have seeds, some don't. Some need peeling, some don't.

BUYING AND STORING

Look for firm cucumbers without shriveling or discoloration. Check ends for desired rigid texture; ends generally are first area to soften. Refrigerate, unwashed and uncut, in crisper drawer up to 1 week, but check sooner for softening, especially when unwaxed.

ARMENIAN
Domestic: *July–August*
Global: *none*

COMMON, BABY (PERSIAN), HOT HOUSE
Domestic: *year-round*
Global: *year-round*

JAPANESE
Domestic: *year-round*
Global: *November–April*

LEMON
Domestic: *sporadically in spring months*
Global: *none*

PICKLING
Domestic: *May–August*
Global: *November–May*

PREP

Peel if desired with vegetable peeler or paring knife. To remove seeds, cut in half lengthwise. Run bowl of spoon from end to end to scoop out seeds. Cucumbers can be sliced, diced, or grated. Some recipes call for salting and draining cucumbers to remove some interior watery liquid. Generally this is required before tossing with a dressing. To do that, peel, seed (if necessary) and

ARMENIAN

Long and often twisted, with furrowed yellow-green skin. ▪ *Aromatic with mild, sweet flavor and subtle hint of citrus. No peeling required. Contains a few small seeds.*

COMMON

Sometimes called "plain" or "pole" cucumbers, they are 6–9 inches long with dark green flesh. Usually coated with wax to prolong shelf life. ▪ *Mild flavor. Peeled and often seeded before use.*

HOT HOUSE, ENGLISH

Grown in greenhouses and often sealed in plastic wrap. Thin skin, 12–15 inches long. Some are ridged, others smooth. Most are seedless. ▪ *Mild flavor. No seeding required. Often served with thin skin intact.*

JAPANESE

Narrow and thin, dark green skin with wart-like bumps. Very small seeds. ▪ *Sweet, delicate flavor. Both skin and seeds generally eaten.*

LEMON

Pale yellow, about the same shape and size as a lemon. As they age, skin turns deeper yellow. Small seeds. ▪ *Delicate, sweet-edged flavor. Seeding optional. Peeling is optional.*

PERSIAN, BABY

Thin skinned, slender and relatively small. About 5–6 inches long. ▪ *Juicy, sweet, and finely textured. No peeling required. Contains a few small seeds*

PICKLING

About 4 inches long, dark green skin. Extremely crunchy. ▪ *Pickled whole, unpeeled.*

Common

Pickling

Japanese

Hot House

Baby

slice; place in colander in sink and sprinkle with salt. Toss and let rest 1 hour. Shake colander and pat cucumbers dry with paper towels.

USE

Generally eaten raw but can be sautéed and served warm with chopped dill as a side dish. Use in salads and slaws, and as garnish on cold soups such as gazpacho. Or for a tasty snack, combine cold peeled cucumber chunks with pineapple chunks, then top with lime juice.

NUTRITIONAL INFO

Cucumbers are more than 90 percent water; 2 cups are a significant source of vitamin C and potassium.

SERVING SUGGESTIONS

Simple salad: Slice and salt cucumbers (see Prep). Toss with crème fraîche and chopped fresh tarragon, or plain yogurt and minced dill. Or toss with tomato wedges, slivers of red onion, and Simple Vinaigrette (page 310).

Cuke-scented salad dressing: In measuring cup (with handle), combine 1 cup extra-virgin olive oil with 4 ounces crumbled feta cheese. Using tines of fork, smash about ⅓ of cheese against side of cup. Stir in ⅓ cup cider vinegar, 1 tablespoon balsamic vinegar, 2 tablespoons minced Italian parsley, and 1 cup finely chopped, peeled (and seeded if necessary) cucumber. Add garlic salt to taste. Use to dress mixed greens or grilled vegetables, or as dip for grilled slices of rustic bread.

Sandwich crunch: Sliced cucumbers can add appealing crisp texture to sandwich fillings. One suggestion is grilled eggplant, sliced tomato, Provolone cheese, and sliced cucumber. Spread bread with mixture of plain yogurt, mayonnaise, and minced basil.

Cuke cups: Turn cucumbers into containers for cold sake shots or appetizer fillings. Cut peeled hothouse cucumber into 1½-inch slices. Using a melon baller, scoop out center ¾ inch deep. Lightly salt and invert on paper towel for 15 minutes. One filling might be chopped smoked salmon, minced shallot, and minced parsley tossed with a smidgen of extra-virgin olive oil; garnish with chives.

vietnamese cucumber, noodle, and shrimp salad

In hot weather, this tangy salad makes an irresistible, cooling entrée. For variety, substitute slivers of cold cooked chicken or chunks of cold cooked firm-fleshed fish, such as halibut or salmon.

DRESSING

⅓ cup Asian fish sauce (see Cook's Notes)

¼ cup rice vinegar (not seasoned)

2 large garlic cloves, minced

3–4 tablespoons sugar

2 tablespoons fresh lime juice, plus more if needed

½ teaspoon dried red chile flakes or Asian hot sauce, or to taste

SALAD

6 ounces dried rice-stick noodles

1 pound cooked, shelled and deveined shrimp

1 hothouse cucumber, unpeeled, halved lengthwise, thinly sliced

4 green onions, trimmed, thinly sliced

1 cup fresh mint leaves, chopped

⅓ cup chopped cilantro

Salt to taste

GARNISH: 3 tablespoons coarsely chopped peanuts

GARNISH: Sprigs of fresh mint and lime wedges

COOK'S NOTES: Asian fish sauce and dried rice-stick noodles are sold in Asian markets and Asian specialty section of some supermarkets.

1. Place large pot water on high heat and bring to boil.

2. Meanwhile, in large bowl, stir all dressing ingredients. Set aside.

3. Cook noodles about 3–4 minutes or until al dente; drain and refresh with cold water. Drain, shaking colander to remove excess water. Cut noodles into roughly 3-inch lengths. In large bowl, combine noodles, dressing, shrimp, cucumbers, green onion, mint, and cilantro. Toss gently. Add salt to taste and more lime juice if needed.

4. Divide among 4 shallow bowls. Sprinkle with peanuts. Garnish with sprigs of fresh mint, cilantro and lime wedges.

YIELD: 4 SERVINGS

NUTRITIONAL INFORMATION (PER SERVING): Calories 380; fat calories 45; total fat 5 grams; sat fat 1 gram; cholesterol 220 milligrams; sodium 2120 milligrams; total carbohydrates 52 grams; fiber 3 grams; sugars 13 grams; protein 32 grams; vitamin A IUs 20%; vitamin C 25%; calcium 10%; iron 35%.

eggplant

BABY PURPLE (INDIAN)

BABY WHITE

CHINESE

COMMON (PURPLE, GLOBE, ITALIAN, AMERICAN)

GRAFFITI

JAPANESE

THAI

WHITE

THE PEAR-SHAPED OR SOMETIMES ALMOST CYLINDRICAL, dark-purple-skinned eggplant is the most common variety found in supermarkets. But a staggering number of other varieties exist. Eggplant can be egg-size to football-size, covered in skin that is creamy white, apple green, or all shades of purple; shape, size, texture, and color can greatly differ.

Commonly thought of as a vegetable, this member of the nightshade family (along with tomatoes) is really a fruit.

BUYING AND STORING

Look for those that are heavy for their size and smooth-skinned without cracks or discoloration. Bruises on surface indicate flesh below will be discolored. A medium-sized common purple eggplant, about 4–6 inches in diameter, will generally be milder, and have more tender skin and fewer seeds, than a more mature, larger one. Store whole, unwashed, in plastic in crisper drawer 4–5 days. Larger varieties will last longer, up to 7 days.

BABY PURPLE (INDIAN), BABY WHITE
Domestic: *April–September*
Global: *November–January*

CHINESE, JAPANESE, THAI
Domestic: *April–November*
Global: *November–March*

COMMON (PURPLE)
Domestic: *March–November*
Global: *November–April*

GRAFFITI
Domestic: *none*
Global: *September–December*

WHITE
Domestic: *March–June*
Global: *none*

PREP

Wash in cold running water and pat dry. Trim off cap and stem end using a stainless steel-knife (don't use a carbon steel knife, it will discolor eggplant). Can be cooked peeled or skin-on. Generally the larger the eggplant, the tougher the skin, so large eggplants are often peeled,

BABY PURPLE
(Indian)
Egg-shaped and egg-sized with dark purple skin. Heavily to moderately seeded, but seeds are tiny. ▪ *Sweet and very tender.*

BABY WHITE
Golf ball–sized and spherical with creamy white skin. Heavily to moderately seeded, but seeds are tiny. ▪ *Firm, dense texture with mild, subtly sweet flavor. Even though skin is fairly thick, it is usually cooked unpeeled.*

CHINESE
Long and thin with light purple skin and purple calyx. Very lightly seeded. ▪ *Mild and holds shape when cooked.*

COMMON
(purple, globe, Italian, American)
Either an elongated pear-shape or almost cylindrical, these medium to large eggplants have glossy, deep purple skin. Can be heavily or moderately seeded. ▪ *Flavor profile varies from mild to moderately bitter and can be slightly astringent. Skin can be tough and is often peeled.*

GRAFFITI
Classic shape of common purple eggplant, but skin is either ivory with purple streaks or purple with ivory streaks. Moderately seeded. ▪ *Skin can be tough and is often peeled. Taste is similar to common purple varieties.*

JAPANESE
Long and thin with light purple or dark purple skin and bright green calyx. Very lightly seeded. ▪ *Firm, mild, and slightly sweet. Skin is very thin and generally left unpeeled. Holds shape well when cooked.*

THAI
Generally lime green with lighter green striations at bottom and about the same size as a golf ball. Heavily seeded, but seeds are tiny and have a pleasant taste. ▪ *Sweet and dense, with subtle hint of artichoke. Generally eaten unpeeled.*

WHITE
Looks like common purple eggplant, but with ivory skin. Moderately to heavily seeded. ▪ *Firm and moist with mild taste, but can sometimes have very slight bitter edge. Generally peeled because skin is very tough.*

especially those with white skin, which is usually thicker. All eggplants are generally peeled when used for soup. Peel with paring knife or vegetable peeler.

To eliminate bitterness, astringency, and excess water in larger eggplants (and to prevent eggplant from absorbing too much oil), many cooks slice and salt eggplant 30–40 minutes before cooking. To do this, line rimmed baking sheet with paper towels. Arrange eggplant slices on towels in single layer and lightly salt on both sides. Let sit for 30–40 minutes. Rinse with cold water and thoroughly pat dry.

When including Chinese or Japanese eggplant in stir-fries, casseroles, or pasta dishes, to maintain the vibrant color of the skin cut eggplant into desired shape, then dip in hot oil for 10 seconds; remove and drain on paper towels, then proceed with recipe.

USE

Always cooked; grill, bake, boil, braise, microwave, sauté, or steam. Eggplant is often used as a meat substitute. Use mashed in dips and spreads, or add diced and sautéed to omelets, pasta sauce, or vegetable medleys. Small rounded eggplants are great for stuffing.

NUTRITIONAL INFO

2 cups are a significant source of folate and potassium.

SERVING SUGGESTIONS

Grill: Cut large unpeeled eggplant into ¾-inch thick crosswise slices or, for smaller eggplants, cut in half lengthwise (Japanese or Chinese should also be scored at 2-inch intervals, but be careful not to cut all the way through). Brush surfaces with olive oil and grill over medium coals until cooked through, turning as needed. Olive oil may be augmented with chopped garlic, minced parsley, and a smidgen of dried red pepper flakes or top with Ginger dipping sauce, page 192.

Pan-fried: Cut unpeeled common (purple), Chinese, or Japanese eggplant into ¾-inch thick slices. Dip in flour or fine dry bread crumbs. Beat egg with a little cold water. Dip eggplant slices in egg mixture, then back in either flour or bread crumbs again. Season with salt and pepper. Fry in small amount of hot vegetable or olive oil on medium heat until brown. Turn and cook until tender and nicely browned. Serve hot.

Chinese

Common (Italian)

Graffiti

Baby (Indian)

Thai

Japanese

Oven roast for baba ghanoush: Pierce skin of medium or large eggplant several times with fork. Place 2 pounds eggplant on rimmed baking sheet and bake in 375-degree oven until soft, generally 25 minutes for medium eggplants or 40 minutes for large. Test for doneness by inserting a small knife; it should feel soft and tender. When cool enough to handle, cut in half, scoop pulp into sieve and drain 5 minutes (discard skin). Place eggplant in food processor fitted with metal blade. Add 1 clove minced garlic, 2 teaspoons lemon juice, 2 tablespoons tahini, 2 teaspoons olive oil, and salt and pepper to taste. Process until coarsely chopped and place in bowl. Cover and chill. Garnish with chopped fresh parsley. Serve with pita wedges or crackers.

Stuffed babies: Cut baby purple or baby white eggplants in half lengthwise. Cut off a small slice on rounded bottom to stabilize them, then use mellon baller to scoop out a part of the flesh. Chop flesh and sauté in a little olive oil until softened; toss with seasoned rice or fried rice. Place eggplants on rimmed baking sheet. Fill cavities with rice mixture. Bake in 350-degree oven until eggplants are tender and rice is heated through, about 20 minutes.

ratatouille

Ratatouille is derived from the French word *touiller,* which means to mix or stir together. It's a classic dish that combines eggplant with tomatoes, summer squash, and bell peppers. This version can be made with or without sausage. Ratatouille can be prepared a day in advance and refrigerated, then reheated before serving.

OPTIONAL: 1 pound hot or sweet Italian sausage (see Cook's Notes)

About 2 tablespoons olive oil, plus more as needed

5 Japanese or Chinese eggplants (unpeeled, cut into ½-inch slices) or 1 large purple (common) eggplant (peeled, cut into quarters lengthwise, and then into ½-inch slices)

2 large onions, cut in half and thinly sliced

2 yellow bell peppers, cored and seeded, cut into strips

1 red bell pepper, cored and seeded, cut into strips

4 medium-large ripe tomatoes, about 1 pound, cut into 1-inch chunks

Pinch of ground fennel seed

3–4 yellow zucchini or yellow pattypan squash, sliced

⅔ cup coarsely chopped fresh basil

Salt and pepper to taste

FOR SERVING: cooked rice or pasta

GARNISH: grated Parmesan cheese

COOK'S NOTES: If using ratatouille as a filling or topping, cut vegetables smaller and reduce the cooking time. If using it cold, omit sausage. If omitting sausage, start with Step 3. Place 2–3 tablespoons olive oil in pan and add vegetables as directed.

1. Line microwave-safe plate with 3 layers white paper towels. To reduce fat, poke holes in sausage on all sides with fork. Place in single layer on towels and cover with paper towel. Microwave on high power 4 minutes. When cool enough to handle, remove sausage and cut into 1½-inch slices.

2. Heat 2 tablespoons olive oil in Dutch oven or large, deep skillet. Add sausage and cook on medium-high heat, stirring or shaking pan frequently, to brown sausage on all sides. Remove sausage with slotted spoon.

3. Add eggplant, onion, and bell pepper to pan. Add 1–2 tablespoons of olive oil if pan looks dry. Cook on medium heat about 8 minutes, stirring or shaking pan frequently, until vegetables start to soften.

4. Add sausage, tomatoes, fennel, and squash. Cover and simmer on low until vegetables are tender, about 15 minutes.

5. Add basil and season to taste with salt and pepper. If there is a lot of juice, strain off solids (using slotted spoon or pouring mixture through colander, reserving juices). Cook juices on high heat until reduced by two-thirds. Return vegetables to reduced juices.

6. Place rice or pasta in shallow bowls. Ladle ratatouille on top. Sprinkle with Parmesan cheese. Serve.

YIELD: 6 SERVINGS

NUTRITIONAL INFORMATION (PER SERVING WITH SAUSAGE): Calories 450; fat calories 135; total fat 15 grams; sat fat 4 grams; cholesterol 50 milligrams; sodium 560 milligrams; total carbohydrates 57 grams; fiber 4 grams; sugars 7 grams; protein 24 grams; vitamin A IUs 35%; vitamin C 230%; calcium 8%; iron 25%.

endive

BELGIAN

CURLY

ESCAROLE

FRISÉE

RED BELGIAN

DELECTABLE RAW OR COOKED, Belgian endive, curly endive, escarole, and red Belgian endive are members of the chicory tribe. Each variety packs an appealing hint of bitterness.

Torpedo-shaped, Belgian endive is pale green; the lighter the color, the milder the taste. The red variety, burgundy with thin creamy-white ribs, tends to be slightly bitterer but pleasing none the less. Curly endive takes bitterness up a notch but balances it with gentle sweetness. It looks like a bushy head of deep-green lettuce with frilly, tickle-producing edges. Frisée, a subvariety of curly endive, has smaller, more delicate leaves that are creamy-yellow at the base and turn an apple green toward their tops. Escarole offers a little bitter kick, too. It looks like lettuce, but the leaves are thicker and less pliable, white at the ribs and dark green toward the softly frilled edges.

Belgian

Red Belgian

BELGIAN

Torpedo-shaped, 4–6 inches long. Color ranges from almost white to yellow-green. ■ *Appealing crunchiness. Light-colored tastes mildest, slightly sweet with soft bitterness.*

CURLY

Loose heads with yellow-white heart and tightly ruffled deep-green edges. ■ *Chewy texture. More assertive bitterness.*

FRISÉE

Popular, subvariety of curly endive. Smaller, with delicate, ragged edges. ■ *More tender texture. Sweetness balances bitterness.*

ESCAROLE

Looks like thick, sturdy butter lettuce with curled, ragged edges. ■ *Chewy texture. Refreshing, with slight bitterness. Inner leaves are more tender and less bitter. Tastes similar to chard.*

RED BELGIAN

■ Same shape as Belgian endive, but color is burgundy red. ■ *Appealing crisp texture. Can be slightly more bitter than white or light green Belgian endive.*

Escarole

Curly

Frisée

BUYING AND STORING

Look for crisp, firm heads of Belgian endive or red Belgian endive, without brown edges. Choose whiter Belgian endive for milder flavor. For curly endive or escarole, choose heads that are crisp and free of brown spots or wilting.

For storage, place Belgian endive or Red Belgian endive in perforated plastic bag (or loosely wrap in moist paper towel or cloth and place in plastic bag) and refrigerate 5–7 days. Longer storage increases bitterness. For escarole and curly endive, refrigerate, unwashed, in perforated plastic bag (or wrap in damp paper towels or cloth and place in plastic bag) up to 1 week. Bitterness does not increase with storage.

Domestic: *year-round*
Global: *none*

PREP FOR BELGIAN
OR RED BELGIAN ENDIVE

Prep just before serving raw or cooking. Pull off and discard any outer leaves that are discolored or wilted. If cooking whole, trim base (root end), leaving enough behind so that head stays together. If using raw for canapé "boats" (see Use), trim bases so that leaves can be separated; pull leaves apart.

PREP FOR CURLY ENDIVE, ESCAROLE, OR FRISÉE

Just before use, rinse briefly in cold water; avoid soaking. Remove tough, lower ribs near base if serving raw. For salads, tear into bite-sized pieces.

USE FOR BELGIAN ENDIVE
OR RED BELGIAN ENDIVE

Leaves make convenient and crunchy canapé boats to use in place of crackers, chips, or breads. Their gentle, curved shape surrounds the filling on three sides. Or chop and serve raw in salads, adding milder lettuce for flavor balance.

USE FOR CURLY ENDIVE OR ESCAROLE

Delectable in bean soups that contain chopped vegetables, such as minestrone. Or to serve cooked, cut into quarters and simmer in broth or water until tender-crisp, then season with grated Parmesan cheese. Or use as frilly-edged liner for salad bowls or cold platter presentations.

NUTRITIONAL INFO

1 cup is an excellent source of vitamins A, C, potassium, and pantothenic acid; good source of thiamin, calcium, magnesium, zinc, and copper; significant source of riboflavin and iron.

SERVING SUGGESTIONS

Boats or scoopers: Use individual Belgian endive leaves as scoops for dips. Or use as appetizer boats to hold a filling, such as soft goat cheese mixed with minced fresh herbs (such as basil or Italian parsley). Filling can be piped onto endive using a pastry bag or, more simply, just spooned onto leaf. Garnish each with a toasted pistachio or walnut half. Or team them with fillings such as cream cheese mixed with smoked salmon or chopped walnuts and Gorgonzola cheese. Or leave whole and braise or steam and serve with chicken, seafood, or game.

Easy escarole soup: Cook 1 onion (chopped) and 3 medium carrots (finely chopped) until softened in 1 tablespoon olive oil in Dutch oven or large, deep skillet on medium-high heat, about 5 minutes. Chop 1 head escarole into 1-inch pieces. Add to onion mixture, toss and cook 2 minutes. Add 1 cup water and simmer, partially covered, for 8 minutes or until escarole is tender. Add 1 can cannellini beans. Gently stir and bring to simmer. Add salt and pepper to taste. For spicier version add pinch dried red chile flakes. Garnish each bowl with Parmesan cheese.

Braised Belgian endive (either variety): Preheat oven to 375 degrees. Cut in half lengthwise. Heat small amount butter and oil in large, deep ovenproof skillet on medium-high heat. Add endive halves, cut side down. Lightly brown, about 3–5 minutes. Turn endive and add vegetable broth or chicken broth about 1/2-inch deep. Cover and place in preheated oven for about 15 minutes or until endive is fork tender. Serve warm or at room temperature. Can be garnished with grated Parmesan cheese, if desired.

endive combo salad

2 Belgian endive, cut into thin crosswise slices

About 1 cup escarole, torn into bite-sized pieces

1 small head butter lettuce, torn into bite-sized pieces

Enough extra-virgin olive oil to barely coat leaves, about 2–3 tablespoons

1 teaspoon red-wine vinegar

1 teaspoon balsamic vinegar

1 1/2 tablespoons drained capers

1/3 cup toasted pine nuts (see Cook's Notes)

Salt to taste

2 ounces cold, soft goat cheese

COOK'S NOTES: To toast pine nuts, place in small skillet on medium heat. Brown lightly, shaking handle to redistribute nuts as they toast. Watch carefully because they burn easily.

1. Place endive, Escarole, and butter lettuce in bowl. Drizzle with enough olive oil to barely coat leaves; toss to coat. Drizzle with vinegars and toss. Add capers and cooled, toasted pine nuts. Toss. Taste and add salt.

2. Divide among 4 salad plates. Pinch goat cheese into dime-sized nuggets and place on salads.

YIELD: 4 SERVINGS

NUTRITIONAL INFORMATION (PER SERVING): Calories 130; fat calories 99; total fat 11 grams; sat fat 2.5 grams; cholesterol 5 milligrams; sodium 450 milligrams; total carbohydrates 5 grams; fiber 3 grams; sugars 1 gram; protein 5 grams; vitamin A IUs 8%; vitamin C 4%; calcium 4%; iron 6%.

fennel

NO WONDER FENNEL ROOKIES ARE CONFUSED. Sometimes supermarkets label it "anise" or "sweet anise," but it's not. Because it has its feathery, dark green tops, folks mistake it for dill, but it's not. Fennel is a green-tinged but almost white bulb with celery-like stalks sprouting at the top. The stalks are adorned with fernlike, dark green leaves.

It has a gentle, sweet flavor reminiscent of anise or licorice. Eaten raw, it has a pleasing crunch; blanched, it has a texture like cooked asparagus. It's available both in mature sizes, with stalks about 14–18 inches long, as well as immature "baby" sizes, with stalks about 5–8 inches long. Baby fennel is especially sweet, with an intense anise aroma.

Fennel

BUYING AND STORING

Choose bulbs that are unblemished, without browning; should be fragrant, firm, and rounded. Green feathery leaves at top should be bright green. Refrigerate, unwashed and dry, wrapped in plastic bag up to 5 days. Baby fennel is more difficult to find; sometimes available in supermarkets with large specialty produce items.

Domestic: *year-round*
Global: *none*

PREP

Wash with cold water. Cut off fern-like greenery at top (reserve it for garnish or last-minute flavor enhancer). Trim at base, removing and discarding any brown layers. To cut into crosswise strips, cut bulb in half lengthwise; place cut side down and cut in half lengthwise again (if there is a core in center, generally it is small and doesn't need to be removed, but if it's large, cut it out and remove it with a small paring knife). Cut into crosswise slices. Or for braising, cut fennel into halves or quarters.

USE

Eat raw, plain or pickled, or cooked. Can be braised, sautéed, baked, or grilled. Called *finocchio* in Italian and *fenouil* in French, this aromatic vegetable is an essential ingredient in many mouthwatering Mediterranean dishes. In France, whole fish are grilled over fennel stalks (for a similar effect, oven bake fish over sliced fennel). In Italy, diced fennel is used in pasta sauces or steamed and tossed with fresh herbs and Simple Vinaigrette (page 310). It's also eaten raw as a digestive aid.

NUTRITIONAL INFO

1 cup is a significant source of vitamin C and potassium.

SERVING SUGGESTIONS

Licorice-kissed salad: You really get the taste of licorice in this delicious salad made with raw fennel, apples, pecans, and blue cheese. In a large bowl, toss 1–2 large trimmed, sliced fennel bulbs; 1 large, tart, green apple (cored and thinly sliced); 3 cups Bibb lettuce (torn into bite-size pieces); ¼ cup toasted walnuts; and 2 ounces of crumbled blue cheese. Toss with enough olive oil to lightly coat the ingredients. Add 1 teaspoon cider vinegar and garlic salt to taste; toss. Serve.

Fennel, not celery: Substitute fennel for celery. It's especially delicious in tuna or salmon salad or in fish-based casseroles.

Grilled glory: Toss ¼-inch-thick fennel slices with enough olive oil to just barely coat. Grill over medium-hot fire (using vegetable grid), turning frequently, until cooked tender-crisp. If desired, toss with more olive oil, extra-virgin preferred. Season with salt and pepper. Can be eaten hot or cold.

Cream o' fennel soup: Simmer 2 fennel bulbs (trimmed and diced), 2 medium leeks (white part only, chopped), and 1 large russet potato (peeled and diced) in 6 cups chicken broth (or vegetable broth) until tender (about 30 minutes). Cautiously purée in batches in food processor or blender. Can be served as is, or for a richer version, stir in ⅓ cup heavy whipping cream or half-and-half. Season to taste with salt and white pepper. Ladle into bowls and garnish each bowl with a sprig of fennel leaves and/or crumbled bacon.

fish fillets with fennel and orange

This easy fish entrée can be prepared with salmon, red snapper, or sea bass fillets. You can use any orange variety you prefer. Tangerines would also be delicious.

3 tablespoons olive oil or vegetable oil, divided use

2 medium fennel bulbs, trimmed, cut in crosswise strips (see Prep); reserve leaves for garnish

Salt and pepper to taste

1 orange, Cara Cara preferred, cut in segments (see Cutting Citrus Into Segments, page 310), reserve juice from segmenting process (see Cook's Notes)

4 (5–7-ounce) fish fillets, such as salmon, red snapper, or sea bass

2 tablespoon minced fresh Italian parsley

COOK'S NOTES: If using Cara Cara oranges, there may not be enough juice produced when segmenting (the juice stays in the segments). You need about 3 tablespoons of juice for the recipe, so use orange juice from another orange, if necessary. So you may need 2 Cara Cara oranges.

1. In large, deep skillet, heat 2 tablespoons oil on high heat. Add fennel, salt, and pepper. Lower heat to medium and cook until fennel browns slightly, about 3 minutes. Add reserved orange juice, cover, and simmer on medium low until tender, about 2 minutes. Set aside.

2. Heat 1 tablespoon oil in large, nonstick ovenproof skillet on medium-high heat. Add fillets and cook about 3 minutes on each side, browning well. Delicate fillets will be cooked through at this point, but thicker fillets will need additional cooking. Place skillet in 350-degree oven until cooked through, about 3–5 minutes.

3. Place fish on 4 plates. Stir parsley into fennel; spoon over fish. Garnish with orange segments.

YIELD: 4 SERVINGS

NUTRITIONAL INFORMATION (PER SERVING):
Calories 390; fat calories 189; total fat 21 grams; sat fat 3 grams; cholesterol 95 milligrams; sodium 430 milligrams; total carbohydrates 13 grams; fiber 5 grams; sugars 3 grams; protein 36 grams; vitamin A IUs 10%; vitamin C 60%; calcium 10%; iron 15%.

fiddlehead fern,
also ostrich fern

THESE YOUNG, UNFURLED FERN SHOOTS are a welcome sign of spring. Gathered when still curled and only about 4–6 inches high, these bright-green spirals are available only for a short time each year. Their name is derived from their resemblance to the spiral end of violins. They grow on the East Coast of North America, from Canada to Virginia.

Once they mature and uncoil, they are inedible. Although there are thousands of fern varieties, only a handful produce edible shoots. Briefly cooked, fiddlehead ferns have an appealing crunch similar to undercooked French green beans (*haricot vert*) or asparagus. The flavor is a cross between asparagus, green bean, and mushroom.

BUYING AND STORING

Look for bright green coils that are tightly closed with only 1–2 inches of stem beyond the unfurled portion. Avoid those with blackened scales.

To store, wrap, unwashed, in plastic and refrigerate. Best used within 3 days.

Domestic: *March–June*
Global: *none*

PREP

Just before using, rub between palms to remove any brown scales. Wash in several changes of cold water. Drain. If more than 2 inches of stem (beyond coil) remains, trim.

USE

Eat cooked. Cook briefly, either by blanching 3–4 minutes (drain and refresh with cold water) or steam, stir-fry, or sauté until just barely tender-crisp. Quick cooking produces crisp, bright green coils.

NUTRITIONAL INFO

1 cup is a good source of vitamin C and an excellent source of vitamin A.

SERVING SUGGESTIONS

Soup splendor: Use cooked as garnish for puréed soups, such as asparagus, fennel (see Cream o' Fennel, page 184), pea (English or sugar snap), or spinach.

Composed salad: Arrange cooked fiddleheads with assortment of cooked vegetables on salad plates (warm or room temperature), such as asparagus, artichoke hearts, and green beans. Top with vinaigrette augmented with chopped fresh tarragon (see Simple Vinaigrette, page 310). Garnish with a little finely diced sweet or red onion.

Ferns 'n' pasta: Toss warm pasta with cooked fiddlehead ferns. Add extra-virgin olive oil, a little balsamic vinegar, lemon juice, salt, and pepper; toss. Top with freshly grated Parmigiano-Reggiano cheese.

Mixed sauté: In large, deep skillet, cook 1 onion (chopped) in 2 tablespoons butter and 2 tablespoons olive oil on medium-high heat until softened. Add 2 tablespoons chopped fresh thyme, 8 ounces sliced cremini mushrooms, and 2 garlic cloves (minced); cook until mushrooms soften. Add 1 pound cooked (tender-crisp) fiddlehead ferns and 1 tablespoon minced parsley. Season to taste with salt and pepper. If desired, garnish with shavings of Parmigiano-Reggiano cheese.

Fiddlehead Fern

gai lan, also chinese broccoli

DENSE CRISP STALKS ARE REMINISCENT OF BROCCOLI but are longer, and more cylindrical. The leafy greens at the top surround clusters of tightly packed buds that can bloom into white flowers.

Gai lan's flavor profile is bolder and more complex than that of broccoli. The flavor borders on the pungent taste of rapini with a pleasant bitter edge that is balanced with sweetness. The delectably crunchy texture is best suited for quick cooking.

BUYING AND STORING

Look for those that are bright green with tightly closed buds. Stalks and leaves should be crisp. Refrigerate, unwashed, wrapped loosely in paper towels, up to 7 days.

Domestic: *year-round*
Global: *none*

PREP

Rinse with cold running water and pat dry. Leave whole, or cut stalk into 1- to 2-inch pieces, leaving florets with attached leaves whole.

USE

Cook just enough so it remains tender-crisp; blanch, steam, or stir-fry. If blanching, drain and refresh with cold water for best color. Team with spicy ingredients, either Asian elements (such as oyster sauce, chile, or soy sauce) or Italian elements (such as garlic, chile, and balsamic vinegar).

NUTRITIONAL INFO

1 cup is an excellent source of vitamins C and A.

Gai Lan

SERVING SUGGESTIONS

Oyster sauce finale: Blanch gai lan in boiling water (augmented with 1 teaspoon Asian sesame oil or peanut oil if desired) until tender-crisp. Drain and refresh with cold water; drain. Toss with enough oyster sauce or spicy oyster sauce to lightly coat.

Pasta or rice: Cut into pieces (see Prep) and blanch until tender-crisp. Drain and add to pasta or rice dishes.

Balsamic butter: Melt 5 tablespoons of butter in small saucepan on medium-high heat. Add 2 tablespoons balsamic vinegar; simmer 1 minute. Blanch gai lan whole until tender-crisp; drain. Place on serving plate and drizzle with balsamic butter. Taste and add salt or garlic salt, if needed.

Broccoli buddy: Substitute gai lan for cooked broccoli in soups, salads, or stir-fries, balancing bolder flavor by including sweet vegetables such as carrots and sugar snap peas.

galangal, ginger, turmeric

USED PRIMARILY IN SOUTHEAST ASIAN CUISINE (primarily Thai), where it is commonly teamed with lemon grass in cooked dishes, this knobby rhizome looks something like ginger. But the skin is more whitish-yellow than mature ginger's coffee-with-cream tan color. Well-defined, dark-brown ridged bands (generally spaced about ¼-inch apart) form parallel rings around thick stems. Random pink shoots may also be present. Inside, the flesh is dense and creamy white, like a red potato's interior.

Unlike ginger's versatility, its use is more limited. Used to flavor soups, curries, and stewlike dishes, galangal has a peppery, medicinal taste when cooked that is similar to eucalyptus. A dry powered form called Laos powder is also sold (a ½-inch piece of fresh galangal equals 1 teaspoon Laos powder).

Galangal

BUYING AND STORING

Should be firm without soft spots, mold, or shriveling. It has shorter storage potential than ginger. Wrap in dry paper towel and refrigerate inside unsealed plastic bag up to 7 days. For longer storage, slice and freeze in airtight container up to 3 months.

Domestic: *year-round*
Global: *year-round*

PREP

Wash thoroughly in cold running water and pat dry. Peel with paring knife; discard peel. Cut into slices or finely grate or grind into paste. For recipes that call for galangal juice, cut into thin slices and pound in mortar until mushy, then squeeze out juice using fingers.

USE

Generally cooked in chicken- or seafood-based soups and stews. When sliced and used in soups or stews, it maintains a woody texture and is often removed by diners and not consumed. It can be ground with fresh herbs, spices, and chiles to make paste to season curries.

NUTRITIONAL INFO

1 cup is a significant source of vitamin C.

ginger, mature ginger, young ginger (spring ginger)

When mature, these knobby rhizomes have a deep tan skin that is banded with subtle, same-colored rings. Inside the thin skin, the fibrous interior is light yellow and moderately juicy. The taste is pleasingly peppery with a subtle, sweet aftertaste and a spicy aroma.

Young ginger, sometimes called spring ginger, has ivory or pale yellow skin with sporadic pink shoots. The flesh is a very pale yellow, tender, and very juicy. Because it is milder than mature ginger, increase amount used when substituting for mature ginger.

Ginger

BUYING AND STORING

Skin should be smooth and free of wrinkles. Should feel firm. Leave at room temperature in cool location for up to 5 days, or wrap in paper towel and refrigerate in unsealed plastic bag up to 3–4 weeks. For longer storage, place sliced ginger in airtight jar covered with dry sherry or rice wine. Or slice and freeze in airtight container up to 3 months.

Domestic: *November–June*
Global: *year-round*

PREP

Because skin is very thin, ginger is often used unpeeled. If peeling, scrape off skin with back of small paring knife or bowl of small spoon. Cut into matchsticks, mince, or grate across the grain. If grating, a ginger grater or Microplane works well.

USE

Eat raw in cold sauces, salad dressings, marinades, and beverages. Or cook in soups, casseroles, and stir-fries, or barbecue sauces, jams, and baked goods.

NUTRITIONAL INFO

1 cup is a significant source of potassium.

turmeric, also curcuma

Think of the color of ballpark mustard or curry powder. The bright yellow color comes from turmeric in its dry powdered form. Fresh, this 2- to 3-inch rhizome is covered with brown skin tinged with orange. Dark brown bands, spaced at about ⅛-inch intervals, ring its surface. A gentle fingernail scrape reveals carrot-orange flesh that is dense and crisp.

Turmeric has a warm, mild flavor with a slight bitter aftertaste. Whether used fresh or powdered, it is primarily used to add bright color to dishes.

Turmeric

BUYING AND STORING

Should be firm without soft spots, mold, or shriveling. Wrap in dry paper towel and refrigerate inside unsealed plastic bag up to 2 weeks. For longer storage, slice and freeze in airtight container up to 3 months.

Domestic: *year-round*
Global: *year-round*

PREP

Peel with paring knife; discard peel. Finely mince or grate.

USE

Add sparingly to dishes before cooking to add vivid color. Use in rice dishes or casseroles, curries, or chutneys. Include in pickling brines.

NUTRITIONAL INFO

1 cup is a significant source of iron.

SERVING SUGGESTIONS

Chicken noodle hot and sour soup with galangal:
In Dutch oven add 2 or 3 galangal slices to 5 cups
chicken broth. Add 1 bruised stalk lemon grass
(strike once with mallet or back of wide-bladed
knife), 2 teaspoons minced garlic, 2 tablespoons
fish sauce, and 1 teaspoon sugar. Bring to boil on
high heat; reduce heat and simmer partially
covered for 20 minutes. Remove lemon grass and
galangal. Stir in 1/4 cup fresh lime juice and about
1/8 teaspoon Asian hot sauce. Fill soup bowls half
full with cooked thin rice noodles. Top with broth.
Garnish with chopped cilantro and thinly sliced
green onion.

Ginger dipping sauce: Combine 1/3 cup soy sauce,
3 1/2 tablespoons rice vinegar, 2 tablespoons water,
1 tablespoon sugar, and 1 1/2 tablespoons minced
fresh ginger. Use for dipping pot stickers
(dumplings), cooked shrimp, or sautéed scallops.
Or pour it over cooked rice or warm Asian
noodles, and garnish it all with chopped cilantro.
Or pour it over tender-crisp cooked cabbage or
grilled eggplant.

Ginger-turmeric butter: Keep this tasty
compound butter in your freezer and cut off a
nub as needed. Place a small amount on top of
broiled or grilled fish, steak, chicken, or cooked
vegetables; the heat of the food will melt butter.
Melt 2 tablespoons of butter in small saucepan
on low heat; add 2 tablespoons minced garlic and
cook it for 1 minute; add 1/8 teaspoon minced

fresh turmeric; stir and cool. Place 1/2 cup (1 stick)
butter in food processor fitted with metal blade;
process until smooth. With motor running, add
the garlic mixture, 1 tablespoon minced fresh
ginger, 1 teaspoon lemon juice, and ground black
pepper to taste. Place mixture on wax paper and
roll it into a log; seal it in plastic wrap and freeze.

Sweet ginger dreams: Add a little minced fresh
ginger to your favorite vanilla ice cream, crème
brûlée, or custard recipe. Garnish each serving with
a little minced crystallized ginger (crystallized or
candied ginger are slices of fresh ginger that have
been candied and coated with sugar).

gingered sweet potatoes

Fresh ginger livens up root vegetables in such
a delicious way. When roasting peeled root
vegetables, combine maple syrup with minced
ginger, then drizzle over veggies before they go
into the oven. In this irresistible dish, syrup and
ginger are mashed with cooked sweet potatoes,
producing a dish that can be made ahead and
easily reheated in a 250-degree oven. It's
delicious teamed with roast turkey or ham.

2 1/2 pounds sweet potatoes

3 tablespoons maple syrup

3 tablespoons butter

2 teaspoons grated fresh ginger

1 tablespoon plain yogurt, or more if needed

Salt and pepper to taste

1. Wash potatoes with cold water and dry thoroughly. Prick in several places using fork tines. Place on rimmed baking sheet and roast in 375-degree oven for about 40–50 minutes, or until fork-tender (time varies depending on size of sweet potatoes).

2. When cool enough to handle, slip off potatoes' skin using paring knife. Place in large bowl with syrup, butter, ginger, and yogurt. Use potato masher to mash, adding more yogurt if needed to acquire desired consistency. Season to taste with salt and pepper.

YIELD: 6 SERVINGS

NUTRITIONAL INFORMATION (PER SERVING): Calories 180; fat calories 54; total fat 6 grams; sat fat 3.5 grams; cholesterol 15 milligrams; sodium 240 milligrams; total carbohydrates 31 grams; fiber 4 grams; sugars 16 grams; protein 3 grams; vitamin A IUs 450%; vitamin C 40%; calcium 6%; iron 6%.

garlic

COMMON (PURPLE OR WHITE)

ELEPHANT

GREEN, SPRING

ROCAMBOLE

TO FANS, FEW AROMAS ARE MORE TANTALIZING than the scent of garlic cooking its way to creamy delectability. It's been credited with curing everything from aching teeth to open wounds. But more than likely it is garlic's culinary contributions that lure us.

Different varieties offer varying degrees of pungency. Elephant garlic's enormous cloves are gentle giants. They impart a milder, less pungent flavor profile. Midsize white or purple garlic has a sharper, more assertive taste, but it is milder than the smaller, purple-hued Rocambole.

Spring garlic is young garlic before it has formed cloves. It looks a little like immature leeks, with a small white bulb tinged in pink at one end and long, gangly green stalks at the other.

BUYING AND STORING ELEPHANT, PURPLE OR WHITE, AND ROCAMBOLE GARLIC

Avoid heads with shriveled or soft cloves. Purchase plump, firm bulbs with dry skins that have been stored at room temperature rather than refrigerated. Moisture destroys garlic. Store whole heads in cool, dark location (with plenty of breathing room) up to 6 weeks (breaking into cloves shortens their shelf life).

BUYING AND STORING FRESH, SPRING GARLIC

Refrigerate in open container away from other foods if possible. Use within 3 days.

COMMON (PURPLE OR WHITE) GARLIC
Domestic: *year-round*
Global: *year-round*

ELEPHANT GARLIC
Domestic: *year-round*
Global: *none*

GREEN, SPRING GARLIC
Domestic: *February–June*
Global: *none*

ROCAMBOLE GARLIC
Domestic: *September–March*
Global: *none*

PREP FOR ELEPHANT, PURPLE OR WHITE, AND ROCAMBOLE GARLIC

Garlic's papery covering is generally peeled before cooking, but there are exceptions. It is roasted unpeeled, and used unpeeled in dishes that use large quantities and where a subtle flavor is desired. To peel, place cloves on cutting board; using a broad-bladed knife (such as a chef's knife), press down firmly with palm of hand or strike gently. Or, when using several cloves, strike with bottom of skillet. Either way, skin separates easily. For pristine cloves, use a garlic peeler, a gizmo that looks like rubber

COMMON
(purple or white)
White and purple are the same variety, but growing conditions make one's exterior bed-sheet white, the other striated purple. ■ *Pleasingly pungent with medium burn.*

ELEPHANT
Huge, baseball-sized heads with cloves about 1 1/2 inches wide. Can weigh as much as 1 pound. ■ *Mellow, mild no-burn flavor. If desired, can roast single clove.*

GREEN, SPRING
Looks like baby leeks, with long green stalks and immature pink-tinged bulbs that haven't formed cloves. ■ *Sweet garlic flavor with texture similar to green onion. Flavor faintly similar to garlic chive (yellow nira grass).*

ROCAMBOLE
Heirloom, hard-necked, generally smaller with purple streaks on exterior. Peels easily. It's not unusual to see thin outer skin flaking and allowing cloves to separate. Small, usually about 1 1/2–2 1/2 inches across. ■ *More pungent, hotter profile. Generally less moist than other varieties.*

Green

Rocambole

Common

Elephant

tubing. For chopping or mincing, use a sharp knife. Or use the "salt method": Sprinkle a little salt on cutting board. Smash cloves on salt, using broad side of knife; then chop or mince, working salt into garlic. If using this method, reduce amount of salt in recipe.

PREP FOR SPRING GARLIC

Just before using, rinse well with cold water; trim, just barely cutting off root end.

USE

For all varieties except spring garlic, sauté, simmer, roast, or use raw. Garlic is a welcome addition in savory dishes such as soups, stews, and salads, or vegetable dishes, omelets, and stir-fries (just to name a few). Fresh spring garlic can be lightly brushed with olive oil and grilled. Or chop and sauté; use in omelets or spinach dishes.

NUTRITIONAL INFO

1 cup is an excellent source of vitamins C and B_6; good source of calcium; significant source of thiamin, phosphorus, potassium, zinc, and copper.

SERVING SUGGESTIONS

Mellow-out roasting: Roasting garlic makes the natural sugars caramelize. The flesh becomes mild and creamy. Add to savory dishes or serve as an appetizer spread on rustic bread. To roast, preheat oven to 450 degrees. Using sharp knife, cut off $1/3$ at pointed end of unpeeled garlic head, exposing cloves. Enclose in aluminum foil, cut side up; open slightly and drizzle with olive oil. If you want creamy white roasted garlic, seal foil. Or, if you want caramelization on tops of cloves, leave foil open slightly at top. Roast in preheated oven for about 30 minutes or until cloves are soft. When cool enough to handle, invert and squeeze cloves from papery covering. When roasting elephant garlic, 1 clove can be roasted at a time, if desired. They are generally so large that once they are roasted, they can be peeled with a paring knife, rather than squeezed out.

Garlic mashed spuds: Roasted garlic is a luscious addition to mashed potatoes. After draining 1 pound of cooked potatoes, add peeled cloves from head of roasted garlic, then mash (see roasting), adding milk or cream as needed for desired consistency. Season to taste with salt and pepper.

Roast pork, lamb, or beef: Insert slivers of peeled, raw garlic in meat before roasting, first poking small openings with tip of small, pointed knife.

Quick garlic butter: Combine ¼ pound (1 stick) softened butter with 2 tablespoons minced garlic. On waxed paper or plastic wrap, shape into log about ¾ inch in diameter. Chill or freeze, well-sealed. Cut off "coins" of flavored butter to top hot grilled meat, poultry, or vegetables.

creamy elephant garlic dressing

Roasted elephant garlic gives this vinaigrette an appealing savory sweetness. It can be prepared 2 days in advance and refrigerated in an airtight container.

2 large elephant garlic cloves, roasted (see Serving Suggestions), peeled

3 tablespoons sherry vinegar

OPTIONAL: *1 tablespoon sugar*

1 teaspoon Dijon-style mustard

½ teaspoon salt

Freshly ground black pepper to taste

¼ cup olive oil, extra-virgin preferred

1. Place all ingredients except oil in blender; whirl until pureed. With motor running, add oil in thin stream. Blend until smooth. Use to top mixed green salad (add just enough dressing to lightly coat leaves). Or drizzle on roasted vegetables, such as roasted root vegetables (see Root roast, page 242).

YIELD: ¾ CUP

NUTRITIONAL INFORMATION (PER TEASPOON): Calories 15; fat calories 13.5 total fat grams 1.5; sat fat 0 grams; cholesterol 0 milligrams; sodium 35 milligrams; total carbohydrates 0 grams; fiber 0 grams; sugars 0 grams; protein 0 grams; vitamin A IUs 0%; vitamin C 0%; calcium 0%; iron 0%.

gobo root, also burdock

MOST OFTEN, WE SAMPLE GOBO ROOT IN JAPANESE RESTAURANTS, a carrot-orange pickled tidbit included with sushi or grilled crisp wrapped in thin bacon. But fresh gobo root looks entirely different. These slender roots look like long, brown carrots, 12 to 30 inches long. They have a woody appearance with rough brown skin covering the white, fibrous flesh.

Both the thin skin and the flesh are edible, but it is most often peeled. Generally cooked or pickled, they are crunchy in texture and have an earthy-sweet taste similar to salsify or artichoke. The flesh turns from creamy white to grayish brown when cooked.

BUYING AND STORING

Best when about 18 inches long and no more than 1 inch in diameter. Look for roots that are soil-covered (sometimes covered with sawdust) and rigid. To store, wrap (unwashed) in moist paper towels and enclose in plastic bag. Refrigerate in crisper drawer up to 1 week, making sure towels stay damp.

Domestic: *June–October*
Global: *November–May*

PREP

Scrub under cold water. Peel with vegetable peeler, cut into manageable lengths and soak in salted water for 10 minutes (to remove bitter aftertaste). Drain and refresh with cold water. Place in acidulated water (water with a little lemon juice) to prevent discoloration. Slice, shred, dice, or cut into matchsticks.

USE

Broil, roast, or stew. Combine with other vegetables and sauté in combination of oil and butter.

Gobo Root

NUTRITIONAL INFO

1 cup is a significant source of vitamin B_6 and potassium.

SERVING SUGGESTIONS

Gobo stir-fry: Peel gobo; cut into matchsticks or 1/4-inch-thick slices. Stir-fry with other vegetables, such as asparagus, broccolini, celery, and celery root.

Gobo and mushroom soup: Cut peeled and salt water–soaked gobo (see Prep) into 1/2-inch-wide slices (about 2 cups). On medium-low heat, cover and cook with 2 chopped onions in 3 tablespoons vegetable oil until softened, about 12 minutes, stirring occasionally. In separate pan, cook 2 cups sliced button mushrooms in 1 tablespoon vegetable oil on medium-high heat until liquid evaporates and mushrooms start to brown. Add mushrooms to gobo-onion mixture; add 2 cups water and simmer 20 minutes. In large saucepan, melt 2 tablespoons butter on medium heat; stir in 2 tablespoons all-purpose flour and stir 1 minute to cook flour (do not brown). Add 1/4 cup milk in thin stream, stirring constantly. When thickened, stir in liquid from vegetable mixture in thin steam, stirring constantly. Add vegetables and stir. If too thick, add vegetable broth or milk until correct consistency is reached. Season to taste with salt and pepper.

Gobo mash: Cut peeled and salt water–soaked gobo (see Prep) into 1/2-inch-wide slices. Cook in lightly salted water with (peeled and quartered) Yukon gold potatoes until fork tender (use twice as much potato as gobo). Drain and return to pot; place on medium heat to dry vegetables, about 1 minute. Remove from heat and mash with enough milk or cream and butter to reach creamy consistency. Season to taste with salt and pepper.

greens

BEET

CHARD (SEE CHARD, PAGE 155)

COLLARD

DANDELION

KALE (COMMON GREEN, PURPLE, FLOWERING, WHITE)

MUSTARD (GREEN, RED)

SPINACH

TURNIP

GREENS, A GENERIC TERM that describes leafy vegetables with assertive flavor profiles, have a long history in Southern-style cooking. But in recent years they have gained nationwide popularity, due in part to the recognition of their nutritional merits.

The general rule is that the younger the green, the milder it will taste. Many greens need to be cooked to tame their bold flavor profiles and to tenderize their shoe-leather toughness. Long simmering or steaming works, but a few-minute parboil followed with a quick sauté is a great approach. Or, in the case of dandelion greens and spinach, a quick toss with hot bacon dressing wilts their tender leaves, coating them with rich sweetness. Baby spinach leaves, mild and sweet, are often eaten raw.

Purple Kale

Common Kale

White Kale

BUYING AND STORING

Leaves should be brightly colored with no sign of wilting or discoloration. They should smell fresh. Except with spinach, before storing, rinse in tub of cold water; repeat if necessary, until water is clear and free of grit. Shake off excess water or drain, wrap in clean kitchen cloth or paper towels, and place in plastic bag. Refrigerate up to 3 days. If buying clean spinach in cellophane bag, refrigerate in sealed package. If buying loose spinach (not sealed in plastic bags), store unwashed in plastic bag up to 2 days.

BEET
Green tops of beet plant. Long stems with large green or greenish-red leaves. Sold attached to beets or detached and sold in bundles. ▪ *Leaves on baby beets are fairly mild and tender; larger leaves are more pungent and tougher. If leaves are very young, they can be used raw in salad, mixed with milder lettuces.*

COLLARD
Large, paddlelike oval leaves that feel velvety to the touch. Attached to very large, inedible stalks that are solid and need to be removed before cooking. Sold in bundles. ▪ *Leaves are chewy unless cooked for a long time at gentle heat. Mild flavor, a little stronger than cabbage but milder than kale. Light broccoli-like aroma.*

DANDELION
Long, slender green leaves with sawtoothed edges. Sold in bundles. ▪ *Tender, with subtle bitterness. Can be stir-fried, wilted with hot bacon dressing, or when young, included in mixed green salads, napped with a sweet dressing.*

FLOWERING KALE
(a subvariety of purple kale)
Ruffled and frilly at the edges, leaves range in color from pink to magenta to white to creamy yellow. Some leaves have multiple colors. Outer leaves are sometimes shades of grayish blue-green. ▪ *Although they are edible, most often used as garnish. Will hold up under damp mixtures on buffet table for hours without wilting.*

PURPLE KALE
Long purple leaves with ruffled edges. Salad Savoy is a subvariety of purple kale. ▪ *Often used as garnish, but edible. Peppery flavor.*

COMMON KALE
(green)
Green has green leaves with frilly white edges and white midribs. ▪ *Tastes like peppery cabbage.*

WHITE KALE
White kale has more white areas than green. It has ruffled edges. ▪ *Same flavor profile as purple kale.*

MUSTARD
(green)
Medium-green leaves with subtly scalloped edge. ▪ *Distinct mustard aroma with assertive peppery bite. Cook to mellow pungent flavors.*

MUSTARD
(red)
Leaves have subtly scalloped edge and are green and red or green and burgundy. ▪ *Distinct mustard aroma with assertive peppery bite. Cook to mellow pungent flavor.*

SPINACH
Available in flat-leaf or crinkle-leaf varieties. Most markets carry both immature baby leaves and larger, more mature leaves. ▪ *For mildest, sweeter taste, buy baby spinach. Eat raw or cooked.*

TURNIP
Medium-green leaves with a scalloped, subtly ruffled edge and curved stems. ▪ *Assertively peppery bite with mustardy aroma. Cook to mellow pungent flavors.*

Domestic: *year-round*
Global: *none*

PREP

All greens except spinach should be thoroughly washed before storage (see Buying and Storing). Generally stems are removed from collards, kale, mustard, and turnip greens before cooking. Cup thumb and fingers around stem below leaf and move cupped hand toward tip of leaf, while holding leaf steady with other hand; discard stem and stack several leaves together, then roughly chop. Stems on more tender greens, such as spinach, dandelion, or young beet greens, can be pinched off at base of leaves.

USE

Most often cooked, but spinach, dandelion, and very young beet greens are eaten raw or cooked. To cook, boil, simmer, sauté, or steam. Team with salty, rich meats, such as bacon, prosciutto, or smoked turkey. Add a spark of acidity, either vinegar or lemon juice, as a final touch.

Dandelion

Beet

NUTRITIONAL INFO

Nutritional profiles vary from green to green.

BEET GREENS: 1 cup is an excellent source of vitamins A and K; significant source of vitamin C.

COLLARD GREENS: 1 cup is an excellent source of vitamins C and K.

DANDELION GREENS: 1 cup is an excellent source of vitamins C and K.

KALE AND MUSTARD GREENS, RED OR GREEN: 1 cup is an excellent source of vitamins A, C, and K.

SPINACH: 1 cup is an excellent source of vitamins A and C and folate; good source of calcium; and significant source of vitamin B_6 and potassium.

TURNIP GREENS: 1 cup is an excellent source of vitamins C and K; good source of folate; significant source of calcium.

SERVING SUGGESTIONS

Blanch the bold: Collards, kale, mustard, and mature turnip greens are best boiled, then sautéed with other flavor elements. Bring 2 quarts lightly salted water to rapid boil in large pot on high heat. Add 2 pounds cleaned,

urnip

Mustard

Collard

stemmed, and roughly chopped greens, and boil 7–9 minutes or until tender. Drain and refresh with cold water. Drain or squeeze out excess water with hands. Cook 3 slices chopped bacon in large, deep skillet on medium heat. Remove bacon with slotted spoon and drain on paper towel. In pan drippings, cook 1 medium chopped onion and 1 large clove minced garlic 2–3 minutes; do not brown. Add greens and toss. Add 3 tablespoons water and cover; cook 1–2 minutes or until heated through. Sprinkle with 1 teaspoon lemon juice or cider vinegar and salt to taste; crumble bacon and add. Toss and serve.

Blanched greens with spaghetti: Use previous Blanch the Bold technique to cook 1 pound clean collards, kale, mustard, or mature mustard greens, omitting lemon juice or vinegar. Toss with 1 pound cooked spaghetti, 1 tablespoon extra-virgin olive oil, pinch of dried red pepper flakes, 1½ tablespoons balsamic vinegar, salt, and pepper. Divide among 4 shallow bowls. Top with generous amounts of freshly grated Parmesan cheese or pecorino.

Sauté the softies—spinach, dandelion, or young beet greens: In large deep skillet or Dutch oven, heat 2–3 tablespoons olive oil or vegetable oil on medium-high heat. Add 1½–2 pounds moist clean greens; cover and cook until wilted and thoroughly warmed through, 1–2 minutes. Remove lid and cook just until any excess liquid evaporates, or place in colander and shake to remove excess liquid. Season to taste with fresh lemon juice, salt, and pepper.

Microwaving smaller amounts produces similar results with moist, tender greens (not dripping wet, but with droplets of water on majority of leaves). Place moist greens in microwave-safe bowl and cover. Microwave 30 seconds and toss; repeat in 20-second intervals until greens are hot and thoroughly wilted. Use caution when removing plastic to prevent steam burns. If desired, season with balsamic vinegar and a little butter.

Dandelion and bacon salad: Fry 2 slices of thick bacon (cut into ¼-inch-wide crosswise slices) in 2 teaspoons olive oil in large, deep skillet; fry until crisp. Meanwhile, place 14 ounces clean, drained, and dried dandelion leaves in heatproof bowl. Pour drippings and bacon over greens and toss. Return pan to heat and add ¼ cup cider vinegar and pinch of sugar. Bring to boil and pour over leaves; toss. Add salt and pepper to taste.

collard greens and carrots with balsamic glaze

The sweetness of balsamic vinegar combined with the fiery edge of dried red pepper flakes adds a perky edge to this greens-based dish. If you want to increase the sweetness, either add more sugar or increase the amount of carrots. If desired, serve with cooked rice.

1 quart water plus pinch salt

1 large bunch collard greens, about 8–10 ounces, washed, stemmed, and roughly chopped

5 medium carrots, peeled, trimmed, and cut into ½-inch crosswise slices

2 tablespoons olive oil or vegetable oil

1 tablespoon soy sauce

Pinch sugar

Pinch dried red pepper flakes

2 tablespoons balsamic vinegar

2 tablespoons chicken broth, vegetable broth, or water

1. Bring 1 quart lightly salted water in large pot to rapid boil on high heat. Add collard greens and carrots. Boil 7–9 minutes or until tender. Drain and refresh with cold water. Drain or squeeze out excess water with hands.

2. Heat oil in large deep skillet on medium-high heat. Add soy, sugar, pepper flakes, and vinegar; stir to combine. Add vegetables, broth, and cover. Reduce heat to medium and cook 1–2 minutes or until heated through. Taste and adjust seasoning as needed. If mixture is watery, place on high heat and cook until liquid evaporates.

YIELD: 4 SERVINGS

NUTRITIONAL INFORMATION (PER SERVING):
Calories 120; fat calories 63; total fat 7 grams; sat fat 1 grams; cholesterol 0 milligrams; sodium 330 milligrams; total carbohydrates 13 grams; fiber 5 grams; sugars 5 grams; protein 3 grams; vitamin A IUs 280%; vitamin C 50%; calcium 15%; iron 4%.

hearts of palm

THIS SMOOTH-BUT-FIRM VEGETABLE looks like a cylinder of glimmering white asparagus that has been sanded to perfection. Round layer upon round layer pack into tidy rolls, similar structurally to leeks.

Hearts of palm come from the core of small Sabal palmetto trees. Most often they are sold cut into pieces about 4 inches long with 1- to 1½-inch diameters. Left whole, they weigh 2–3 pounds. Available fresh wrapped in plastic packaging, they are most often available in cans or jars. The taste is a pleasing blend of artichoke and bamboo shoot.

Hearts of Palm

BUYING AND STORING

Fresh hearts of palm are sold packed in plastic trays that are sealed in plastic wrap, then refrigerated. They should look and smell fresh, without discoloration or soft spots. Refrigerate and use as soon as possible after purchase, within 3 days to avoid product contamination and food safety risks associated with low acidity. Canned or jarred product should be refrigerated once opened and used within 1 week.

FRESH HEARTS OF PALM
Domestic: *year-round*
Global: *year-round*

PREP

Fresh hearts of palm occasionally have a fibrous outer layer. To remove, make a shallow lengthwise cut and peel off and discard outer layer. Fresh or canned, they can be sliced, diced, or cut into matchsticks.

USE

Either fresh or jarred, use in salads, pasta, or entrees. Steam, sauté, or deep-fry.

NUTRITIONAL INFO

1 cup is a good source of vitamin C and iron.

SERVING SUGGESTIONS

Sweet sauté: Slice and cook in butter along with minced shallots and garlic on medium-high heat until shallots soften. Add baby spinach and cook until wilted.

Marinated for salad: Cut into matchsticks and place in nonreactive bowl. Top with Simple Vinaigrette (page 310), chopped Italian parsley, and finely diced red (or orange or yellow) bell pepper. Refrigerate several hours. Spoon over (grilled or blanched) asparagus or toss with baby lettuces.

Rice with heart: Dice hearts of palm, celery, and carrots. Heat mixture of butter and oil in deep skillet on medium-high heat. Add celery and carrots; cook until almost tender. Add hearts of palm and shelled English peas; cook until heated through. Add cooked brown rice, white rice, or orzo. Gently toss and cook until piping hot. Garnish with minced Italian parsley.

Mashed potato garnish: Finely dice hearts of palm. Sauté in olive oil until heated through; spoon over hot mashed potatoes.

horseradish, wasabi

horseradish

WHO COULD GUESS THAT THIS
GNARLED, EARTH-COLORED ROOT could
taste and smell so intriguing? Horseradish
may look like a caveman's club, but
underneath its brown peel, the flesh is firm
and creamy white and has a sharp, biting-
hot flavor. There's a very subtle sweetness,
but it's the sinus-clearing scent that may
hog the show. When it is cut, essential oils
are released; they are similar to (but
stronger than) mustard.

Generally it is peeled, grated, and
augmented with distilled white vinegar,
then used as a condiment
with red meat,
oysters, or fish.

Horseradish

Wasabi

BUYING AND STORING

Horseradish should be firm, without soft spots or
mold. Wrap in slightly moist paper towels and
place in plastic bag, then refrigerate in crisper
for up to 10 days. During long storage mold may
develop; cut away and discard moldy spots as
needed.

Domestic: *year-round*
Global: *none*

PREP

Wash and cut into 3- to 4-inch lengths. Remove
peel with paring knife; discard peel. If there are
green patches under skin, peel and discard.
Sometimes, there is a woody core inside a large
horseradish; to check, cut in half horizontally and
cut away pulpy area and discard. Grate using
stainless-steel grater. Or cut into 1/2-inch cubes
and pulse in food processor fitted with metal
blade until finely minced. To prevent
discoloration, sprinkle with distilled white
vinegar, white wine vinegar, or lemon juice.

USE

Generally eaten raw, finely grated, and tossed with vinegar or lemon juice. Use as condiment to accompany beef, fish, or oysters. Add to tomato-based cocktail sauce or Bloody Marys.

NUTRITIONAL INFO

1 cup is an excellent source of vitamin C and significant source of folate and potassium.

SERVING SUGGESTIONS

Sharp sandwiches: Add grated horseradish to taste to mayonnaise. Use on sandwiches with beef, corned beef, turkey, cheese, or ahi tuna.

Salads with attitude: Add a small dollop of grated horseradish to prepared coleslaw or potato salad.

Horseradish butter: To season butter with horseradish, place ½ cup (1 stick) cold butter in food processor fitted with metal blade. Add 2 teaspoons grated horseradish; process until blended. Place on sheet of waxed paper and roll into a cylinder; chill or freeze. Cut into thin "coins" and place on hot, grilled fish.

Prime rib team: Cut 1 (3-inch) peeled horseradish piece into ½-inch cubes. Place in food processor fitted with metal blade. Pulse until finely minced. Add 2 tablespoons white-wine vinegar, 2 tablespoons water, pinch salt, and pinch sugar. Pulse to combine. Use as is, or combine 3 tablespoons horseradish mixture with 1 cup sour cream or unsweetened whipped cream. Serve with prime rib or other beef roasts.

wasabi, also japanese horseradish, green horseradish

WASABI IS A FIERY, BRIGHT GREEN ACCOMPANIMENT to sushi and sashimi, often referred to as "Japanese horseradish." But it isn't related to horseradish. It's from the root of a perennial herb that grows wild in or on the banks of mountain streams or is cultivated in flooded mountain terraces of Japan and eastern Siberia. The plants take years to reach maturity. Fresh wasabi isn't easy to find outside Japan. Some is grown in the United States, but it is very rare. It's sold ground and dried in the U.S., both in Asian markets and many supermarkets, either in a paste (usually in tubes) or powdered (in small tins). Mix powdered wasabi with water to reconstitute.

BUYING AND STORING

Roots should be firm. If there are leaves, they should be bright green. Wrap in slightly moist paper towels and place in plastic bag, then refrigerate in crisper for up to 10 days.

Domestic: *year-round, but very rare*
Global: *year-round, but very rare*

PREP

Wash and remove peel with paring knife; discard peel. Trim and discard any discolored, dark edges. Mince very finely. Japanese sushi chefs use a sharkskin grater to get smooth, finely grated wasabi. A Microplane can also be used for grating.

USE

Generally used raw and very finely grated. Add a small amount to barbecue sauce or ketchup. Use in sushi or as a garnish with spicy fish dishes or grilled beef.

NUTRITIONAL INFO

1 cup is an excellent source of vitamin C and a significant source of calcium, potassium, and vitamin B$_6$.

SERVING SUGGESTIONS

Wasabi Mary: Add finely grated wasabi to taste to Bloody Marys.

Wakeup guacamole: Add a smidgen of finely grated wasabi to guacamole (see Guacamole reigns, page 130).

Flavored butter: Add finely grated wasabi to butter and use atop grilled fish or steak (see Horseradish butter, at left).

Wasabi mashed potatoes: Stir a small amount of finely grated wasabi into creamy hot mashed potatoes. Serve with grilled beef, pork, or chicken.

jicama, also
mexican potato, yam bean

SHAPED LIKE AN ENORMOUS TURNIP that has been flattened on top and bottom, this white-fleshed tuber is covered in thin, tan skin. Varying in size, jicamas can weigh anywhere from 8 ounces to 6 pounds.

The flesh is juicy and has an apple-like texture. It's mildly sweet with a subtle nuttiness. Although it can be cooked, it is almost always eaten raw. Native to Latin America, raw jicama is a tasty substitute for water chestnuts in Asian dishes.

BUYING AND STORING

Small or medium-size jicamas are often the best (large, thick-skinned jicamas can be dry and fibrous). Avoid those with cracks or shriveling. Store whole in cool location for several days, or refrigerate up to 3 weeks. Once cut, cover tightly with plastic wrap and refrigerate; use within 1 week.

Domestic: *none*
Global: *year-round*

PREP

Remove skin. Cut off top and bottom. Place cut side down on cutting board. Working from top to bottom and following contour of vegetable, cut off skin in strips. Cut into desired shape: cubes, slices, or sticks. Seal tightly in plastic to prevent drying and refrigerate.

USE

Generally eaten raw, but it can be cooked. Use raw in salads, or as a snack, or use as dippers with creamy dips. Substitute for water chestnuts in Asian salads and stir-fries. Jicama retains crunchiness even when cooked for several minutes.

NUTRITIONAL INFO

1 cup is an excellent source of vitamin C.

SERVING SUGGESTIONS

Mexican snack: Cut peeled jicama into sticks. Top with freshly squeezed lime juice and sprinkle with chile powder and salt. When serving children, chile powder may be omitted.

Salad crunch: Stir peeled, diced jicama into tuna or chicken salad, coleslaw, or Chinese chicken salad.

Colorful appetizers: Cut peeled jicama into thin slices; if large, cut into quarters. Top each with small spoonful of fruit salsa, such as mango salsa (see page 62) or papaya salsa. Or top each jicama slice with a dollop of shrimp salad or crab salad.

Taco or tostada garnish: Toss peeled, diced jicama with lime juice, chopped cilantro, chile powder, salt, and pepper. Add diced cooked carrots or finely shredded red cabbage, if desired. Use as part of filling for tacos and tostadas.

jicama and papaya salad

This colorful salad is a delectable accompaniment to grilled poultry, fish, or meat. If you prefer, mango can be substituted for the papaya. Salad can be prepared 2 hours in advance and refrigerated in an airtight container. Place on lettuce just before serving.

3 tablespoons fresh orange juice

1/4 teaspoon minced orange zest (colored part only)

OPTIONAL: *1 1/2 teaspoons sugar*

1/2 teaspoon salt, or more to taste

2 tablespoons cider vinegar

3 tablespoons vegetable oil

12 ounces jicama, peeled, cut into sticks about 1 1/2 by 3/8 by 3/8 inches (about 2 cups)

1 large, ripe papaya (about 1 to 1½ pounds)

¼ cup chopped cilantro

2 heads Bibb lettuce, washed, drained

OPTIONAL GARNISH: orange slices (cut in half) or orange wedges

1. In small bowl, whisk juice, zest, sugar (if using), salt, and vinegar. Add oil in steady stream, whisking constantly. Set aside.

2. Place jicama in medium-large bowl. Peel papaya and cut in half; scoop out and discard seeds. Cut into lengthwise 1¼-inch strips. Cut strips into ½-inch crosswise slices and add to jicama. Add dressing and cilantro; gently toss.

3. Arrange lettuce on platter. Top with jicama mixture. If desired, garnish with orange slices or wedges.

YIELD: 6 SERVINGS

NUTRITIONAL INFORMATION (PER SERVING):
Calories 130; fat calories 63; total fat 7 grams; sat fat 1 gram; cholesterol 0 milligrams; sodium 200 milligrams; total carbohydrates 17 grams; fiber 5 grams; sugars 8 grams; protein 2 grams; vitamin A IUs 60%; vitamin C 130%; calcium 6%; iron 6%.

Jicama

kohlrabi, also cabbage turnip

GREEN, BABY GREEN

PURPLE, BABY PURPLE

STEMS SPOUT SKYWARD from kohlrabi's squatty bulblike tuber. They look oddly misplaced, erupting from sides as well as cap, the weight of their leaves making those stems arch at graceful angles. There are two varieties, purple and green. Purple has bright purple skin, stems, and leaf veining. Green has apple-green skin, stems, and leaf veining. Inside the flesh is identical in both, a creamy white tinged with apple green. Both immature "baby" kohlrabi and more mature regular kohlrabi are sold. The babies have bulbs that are about the size of a golf ball (but flattened at top and bottom); they have a more delicate, sweet flavor profile. The bulbs of mature kolhrabis are about the size of a tennis ball.

The taste is a delicious surprise. It's a very pleasing blend of mild broccoli and cucumber flavors with a gentle sweetness and a very subtle hint of peppery radish. Purple-skinned kohlrabi tends to be slightly spicier. They are as crisp as a green baking apple and are delicious either raw or cooked. The leaves look and taste something like collard greens and can be washed, trimmed, and cooked in a similar manner (see Greens, page 201). Sometimes, especially with large kohlrabi, stems are removed before it's marketed.

FRONT TO BACK:
*Baby Green Kohlrabi, Green Kohlrabi,
Purple Kohlrabi,
Baby Purple Kohlrabi*

BUYING AND STORING

Bulbs should be firm and crisp, without bruises or cracks. Leaves, if intact, should be crisp. Refrigerate leaves and bulbs separately in plastic bags in crisper drawer. Before refrigerating leaves, wash in several changes of cold water, drain, then wrap in clean kitchen towel or paper towels and enclose in plastic bag. Store bulbs unwashed and wash bulbs right before use. Store bulbs up to 10 days; leaves up to 3 days.

Domestic: *year-round*
Global: *none*

PREP

Peel bulb with paring knife; discard peel. Cut into chunks, dice, or slice, depending on use. Before cooking leaves, roughly chop.

USE

Eat raw or cooked. To cook, steam, simmer, braise, boil, or roast. Use raw shredded into coleslaw, or include in a crudités platter with other raw vegetables to accompany dips. Use thinly sliced in sandwiches.

NUTRITIONAL INFO

1 cup is an excellent source of vitamin C and a significant source of vitamin B_6 and potassium.

SERVING SUGGESTIONS

Vegetable soup: Add diced kohlrabi bulb along with other firm vegetables (such as carrots) to vegetable soup.

Cheesy spuds: Include kohlrabi slices with potatoes in potatoes au gratin.

Waldorf with tangy attitude: In medium bowl, stir ²⁄₃ cup mayonnaise with ¹⁄₃ cup sour cream, 2 tablespoons sugar, and 2 teaspoons lemon juice. Add 1 mature or 2–3 baby kolhrabi bulbs (peeled, cut into 1-inch dice), 4 Fuji apples (cut into 1-inch dice), 3 stalks celery (thinly sliced), and ¹⁄₂ cup toasted walnuts or pecans. Toss and add salt to taste.

Roast: Cut 2 pounds peeled kohlrabi bulbs into 1-inch dice. Toss with 3 tablespoons olive oil or vegetable oil. Line rimmed baking sheet with parchment paper or foil. Season with coarse salt or seasoned salt. Bake in 450-degree oven for 35 minutes, tossing kohlrabi 2 or 3 times during roasting.

leek

BABY

CHINESE

LEEK

RAMP, WILD

MATURE LEEKS LOOK LIKE ENORMOUS GREEN ONIONS (scallions) with sturdy, deep green stalks forming a chevron-patterned crown atop a thick cylindrical bulb (about 1½ to 2¼ inches in diameter). The bulb is pearly-white at the bottom, but as it reaches toward the stalks, the color turns from white to celery green to butter-lettuce green. Related to both garlic and onions, leeks have a sweeter, subtler flavor than their lily-family cousins. When cooked, they have a luxurious, silky texture. Immature "baby" leeks are pencil-thin and have a sweeter taste than mature leeks. Because they are smaller than leeks, baby leeks, ramps, and Chinese leeks are more tender.

Ramps are wild leeks. Like baby leeks, their bulbs are scallion-like thin. Often they are lightly tinged with purple and are topped with flat, pointed green leaves. Native to eastern North America, ramps are available for a very short time each year, generally from March to June. The flavor is seductively pungent, like a combination of leeks and onion.

Chinese leeks are immature spring garlic. Fresh spring garlic is young garlic, before it has formed cloves. So the name reflects when it is harvested. A Chinese leek is the infant of the clan, looking like a very immature leek with a very small white bulb tinged in pink at one end and long, thin green stalks at the other.

BUYING AND STORING

Avoid leeks with yellowed or withered tops. White portion should unblemished and feel crisp, not slimy, and free of any splitting. The edible portion is white and light green, so look for leeks that have the largest usable area. Do not trim or wash before storing. Wrap loosely in plastic and refrigerate in crisper drawer (leeks and baby leeks from 5–14 days, depending on how fresh they are when purchased; ramps and Chinese leeks 3–4 days). Because ramps are available such a short time, chop and freeze in airtight container for later use.

CHINESE LEEKS
Domestic: *November–April*
Global: *none*

LEEKS, BABY LEEKS
Domestic: *year-round*
Global: *December–February*

RAMPS
Domestic: *March–June*
Global: *none*

PREP FOR LEEKS

Sometimes there is dirt lodged between layers, so washing is very important. Trim off root end and dark green stalks (stalks can be used in stock preparation). Cut remaining white and light-green portion in half lengthwise. Hold under cold running water, cut side up, pulling layers apart to wash away dirt with one hand, holding them together with the other. Shake off water. If slicing, place cut side down on cutting board.

PREP FOR BABY LEEKS, CHINESE LEEKS, AND RAMPS

Wash thoroughly with cold water. Trim and discard root ends. Strip off thin outer layer as you would a green onion (scallion). Often they are grilled or broiled with stalks intact.

USE

Leeks and baby leeks may be substituted for onion in recipes but not vice versa. Raw, they can be thinly sliced and added to salads, relishes, and salsas. They can be braised, baked, stir-fried, or microwaved. They are delicious in soups, casseroles, salads, pasta, rice dishes, and gratins.

Baby leeks, ramps, and Chinese leeks can be brushed with oil, seasoned, and grilled. They are delicious in stir-fries, soups, and sauces.

NUTRITIONAL INFO (LEEK, BABY LEEK, RAMP)

1 cup is a good source of vitamin A and a significant source of vitamin C and iron.

NUTRITIONAL INFO (CHINESE LEEK)

1 cup is a good source of vitamin C and a significant source of calcium and iron.

SERVING SUGGESTIONS

Leekie mashed potatoes: Prepare your favorite mashed potatoes, using about 3 pounds baking potatoes. While potatoes are boiling, cook 6 chopped leeks (white and light green part) in 4 tablespoons butter on medium heat until softened, about 8–10 minutes. Stir leeks into mashed potatoes when you add the milk. Add good pinch of minced fresh thyme.

Leek

Ramp

Chinese Leek

Frizzled leeks: Golden brown, deep-fried leeks make a great garnish. Cut leeks (white and light green portion) into thin, lengthwise matchsticks. Pat dry with paper towels. Heat about 4 inches of vegetable oil to 375 degrees. Working in small batches, fry until golden brown; remove with slotted spoon and drain on paper towels. Season with salt. Cool and store up to 24 hours in airtight container.

Braise: Place sliced leeks or whole baby leeks, Chinese leeks, or ramps in large skillet. Cover with vegetable broth or chicken broth. Simmer, partially covered, until very tender. Drain. Spoon lemony vinaigrette (see Simple Vinaigrette, page 310), on top and garnish with olives and chopped fresh herbs such as basil and parsley.

Grill thrill: Brush (cleaned, roots trimmed) whole ramps, Chinese leeks, or baby leeks with olive oil. Season to taste with coarse salt and freshly ground pepper. Arrange on hot grill in single layer until heated through and nicely caramelized. Serve as is or top with Simple Vinaigrette (page 310), finely chopped red bell pepper, and crumbled goat cheese.

leek and prosciutto tart

Serve this tasty quiche warm or at room temperature. If you like, instead of fresh oregano, use fresh basil or tarragon.

1 tablespoon olive oil, extra-virgin preferred

3 medium leeks, washed, thinly sliced (white and light green part)

3 ounces sliced prosciutto, diced

1 tablespoon chopped fresh oregano

Salt and pepper to taste

1½ cups whole milk

3 large eggs

1 (9-inch) unbaked pie crust

1. Adjust oven rack to middle position. Preheat oven to 350 degrees.

2. In medium skillet, heat oil over medium-high heat. Add leeks and cook, stirring frequently, until tender and starting to lightly brown, about 5 minutes. Off heat, add prosciutto, oregano, salt, and pepper. Set aside.

3. In separate bowl, beat milk and eggs together.

4. Spread leek mixture over bottom of pie crust. Place pie pan on rimmed baking sheet. Gently pour milk mixture on top of leek mixture. Bake in preheated oven about 35 minutes or until set (a knife inserted in center should come out clean).

YIELD: 8 SERVINGS

NUTRITIONAL INFORMATION (PER SERVING):
Calories 180; fat calories 90; total fat 10 grams; sat fat 2.5 grams; cholesterol 40 milligrams; sodium 490 milligrams; total carbohydrates 15 grams; fiber less than 1 gram; sugars 3 grams; protein 6 grams; vitamin A IUs 15%; vitamin C 8%; calcium 8%; iron 8%.

lemon grass, also
lemongrass, citronella

USED LIKE AN HERB TO ADD CITRUSY TARTNESS AND FRAGRANCE, lemon grass looks something like an elongated, sturdy green onion. It's fibrous and somewhat woody. Most often, it's the cream-colored bulb at the base that's used to flavor sauce, soup, and curry, or in stir-fries and marinades for grilled meats. Lemon grass is a signature flavor element in many Southeast Asian dishes.

BUYING AND STORING

Look for firm, unblemished, wrinkle-free stems. The fullest bulbs are most desirable. Store in plastic bag in vegetable drawer of refrigerator up to 4 weeks; keep dry, as moisture causes deterioration. Or freeze finely minced, peeled bulb (see Prep) in airtight container up to 3 months; scoop out portions as needed and use frozen.

Domestic: *year round*
Global: *December–May*

PREP

Trim off tiny bit of bulb's base if tough. Use bottom portion, just 2–3 inches of bulb (stalks— upper portion—can be cut into 3-inch pieces, crushed, and used to infuse broth and curry; stalk is removed before serving). Remove and discard 2 or 3 tough, outer layers of bulb. Finely mince remaining bulb or place in mini food processor and pulse to finely mince.

USE

Flavor drinks, broth, ice cream, sorbet, sweet or savory sauce, curry, and stir-fry.

NUTRITIONAL INFO

1 cup is an excellent source of vitamin C.

SERVING SUGGESTIONS

Lemony rice: Cut 1 stalk into 3-inch pieces. Add to 1 quart water and bring to boil. Remove from heat and let rest 30 minutes. Remove lemon grass and use water to cook rice.

Lemon Grass

Custard sauce, custard, crème brûlée, or pastry cream: Add lovely fragrance and lemony flavor to dessert. Place minced lemon grass (bulb, see Prep) in cream, about ½ teaspoon minced lemon grass per 1 cup cream; heat to simmer, cover and remove from heat. Let rest 15 minutes. Strain and proceed with crème anglaise (custard sauce), custard, créme brûlée, or pastry cream recipe.

Tangy mussels or shrimp: Add ½ teaspoon minced lemon grass (see Prep) to liquid used to cook mussels or shrimp.

fifteen-minute lemon-grass chicken

This quick-to-prepare entrée shows off the classic sweet, sour, and spicy flavors of Southeast Asian cuisine. If you prefer, add a little extra sugar to suit your taste. And if you want to boost the sour elements, serve each portion with a lime wedge so diners can squeeze on a little fresh juice if desired.

About 2 tablespoons canola oil or vegetable oil

2 pounds skinless, boneless chicken breast, cut into ½-inch strips; set on paper towel

1 medium onion, halved and thinly sliced lengthwise

3 cloves garlic, minced

3 tablespoons finely minced lemon grass bulb (see Prep)

2 tablespoons fish sauce (nuoc mam or nam pla); see Cook's Notes

1½ tablespoons sugar

1 teaspoon ground coriander

½ teaspoon ground turmeric

½ cup low-salt canned chicken broth

1 tablespoons spicy oyster sauce or 1 tablespoon regular oyster sauce plus pinch dried red chili flakes

FOR SERVING: cooked rice

OPTIONAL GARNISH: chopped cilantro

COOK'S NOTES: Fish sauce is sold at Asian Markets or some supermarkets with large Asian specialty sections.

1. Heat oil in wok or large, deep skillet over high heat. Add chicken, onion, and garlic; stir-fry until chicken is partially cooked, about 4 minutes. Add lemon grass, fish sauce, sugar, coriander, and turmeric; stir-fry 3 minutes.

2. Add broth and oyster sauce; reduce heat to simmer until sauce thickens and chicken is thoroughly cooked, about 4–5 minutes. Taste; season with salt and pepper, as needed. Serve with rice. Garnish with chopped cilantro, if desired.

YIELD: 4–6 SERVINGS

NUTRITIONAL INFORMATION (PER SERVING WITHOUT RICE): Calories 330; fat calories 171; total fat 19 grams; sat fat 5 grams; cholesterol 95 milligrams; sodium 590 milligrams; total carbohydrates 7 grams; fiber less than 1 gram; sugars 4 grams; protein 33 grams; vitamin A IUs 2%; vitamin C 4%; calcium 4%; iron 10%.

lotus root, also lily root

MAKE A CROSSWISE CUT THROUGH LOTUS ROOT'S CRUNCHY FLESH. The pattern of holes inside makes it look like a cream-colored piece of lace. Lotus root is the thickened stem of a water lily, and the holes inside are lengthwise air tunnels. Whole, it looks like plump, brown-skinned sausage links, each about 6–8 inches long. Often it's sold with one end sliced open to reveal the snowflakelike pattern inside.

The taste is slightly sweet and earthy with starchiness that is similar to jicama. Size doesn't affect flavor or crispy texture. The seeds, leaves, and flowers of this plant are also edible, but those are difficult to find except in Asian markets.

Lotus Root

BUYING AND STORING

Look for smooth, unblemished skin without cracks or soft spots. If cut (not cut into slices), cut area should look moist. If using slices whole, choose those with smaller diameters. Peel just before using. Refrigerate "links" that have been cut (not sliced) in plastic in crisper drawer up to 5 days. In Asian markets, whole, refrigerated, peeled lotus root is packaged in water-filled plastic bags.

Domestic: *none*
Global: *year-round*

PREP

Cut where "links" join. Trim off and discard necks about 1 inch from tips. Scrub under cold running water. Peel with vegetable peeler. Slice crosswise with knife or mandoline. Use immediately or place in bowl of cold water with a small amount of lemon juice to prevent browning.

USE

Include in soups and salads, stir-fries, and tempura. Generally it is sliced and quickly blanched, about 1 minute, then drained and refreshed with cold water. But it can also be steamed or stuffed, and then baked.

NUTRITIONAL INFO

1 cup is an excellent source of vitamin C and a significant source of vitamin B_6, riboflavin, potassium, and thiamin.

SERVING SUGGESTIONS

Sweet-edged beauty: Lacy disks of lotus root in fruit salad add both crunch and glamour. Combine 2 cups water with $1\frac{1}{2}$ cups sugar in large saucepan. Bring to boil on high heat; reduce to medium and simmer 1 minute or until sugar dissolves. Add peeled, sliced lotus root (cut in half if large). Cook in simmering sugar syrup until tender-crisp, about 2 minutes. Remove with slotted spoon. When cool, add to fruit mixture.

Pickles with holes: In large saucepan, combine 2 cups seasoned rice vinegar, 1 tablespoon sugar, 2 teaspoons coarse salt, 2 teaspoons ground turmeric, and 1 serrano chile (seeded and minced; use caution when working with fresh chiles—do not touch face or eyes. Wash hands thoroughly upon completion). Bring to boil on high heat; stir to combine and reduce heat to medium. Simmer until sugar dissolves. Peel 2 medium lotus roots; cut into $\frac{1}{4}$-inch-thick crosswise slices. Add to mixture and simmer 20 minutes. Remove from heat and cool. Place in glass jar and cover. Refrigerate. Use as snack or garnish.

Lotus stir-fry: Place 2 garlic cloves (minced) and $\frac{1}{2}$ jalapeño chile (seeded and minced) next to wok. (Use caution when working with fresh chiles—do not touch face or eyes. Wash hands thoroughly upon completion.) Next to that place 10 asparagus (diagonally cut into 1-inch pieces), $\frac{1}{2}$ cup peeled, sliced lotus root (cut in half if large), $\frac{1}{2}$ pound snow peas, and $\frac{1}{2}$ cup drained canned baby corn. In small bowl, combine $\frac{1}{2}$ cup chicken broth, 1 tablespoon spicy oyster sauce, and 1 tablespoon soy sauce. In another small bowl, combine 1 teaspoon cornstarch with 2 teaspoons water. Place wok on high heat. Add 2 tablespoons vegetable oil and swirl to coat. Add garlic and chile; cook 10 seconds. Add vegetables and stir-fry 3 minutes. Add broth mixture; bring to boil. Stir cornstarch mixture and add; boil until sauce thickens. Serve with rice.

malanga, also yautia

MORE THAN FORTY MALANGA SPECIES are indigenous to the tropical regions of the Western Hemisphere. Some of these tubers are plump blimp shapes, while some are tapered cylinders. Some have flesh that is creamy white, while others can be yellow, orange, pink, or reddish. Some look so much like taro root, it's almost impossible to tell them apart without tasting them. Malanga's strong flavor is similar to hazelnuts but with more pronounced earthiness.

All malangas are covered with tough brown, shaggy skin. All have firm, crisp-textured, starchy flesh. All should be eaten cooked.

BUYING AND STORING

Should be firm without soft spots, cracks, or mold. Store at room temperature up to 3 days, or refrigerate loose and dry for up to 7 days.

Domestic: *none*
Global: *year round*

PREP

Scrub with brush under cold running water. Peel skin with vegetable peeler or paring knife under running water (because it can feel slimy); discard peel. Rinse in cold water. Grate, dice, or cut into wedges or thin slices. If not used immediately, submerge in cold water.

USE

Only eaten cooked; steam, boil, deep-fry, or bake. Boiled in soups or stews, it acts as a thickening agent (when boiled for a lengthy period, it will disintegrate). When boiled just until tender, it can be combined with another root vegetable (such as sweet potato), then mashed with cream, butter, salt, and pepper.

NUTRITIONAL INFO

1 cup is a significant source of potassium and vitamin B_6.

SERVING SUGGESTIONS

Malanga chips: Cut peeled malanga into 1/8-inch crosswise slices. Place in cold water to remove excess starch. Heat canola oil or peanut oil in large, deep skillet or deep-fat fryer to 375 degrees. Pat slices dry with paper towels. Deep-fry until lightly browned. Drain on paper towels and season with coarse salt.

Malanga and sweet potato fritters: Peel 1/2 pound malanga and 1/2 pound sweet potatoes; place in bowl of cold water. In medium bowl, beat 1 egg with 2 tablespoons chopped cilantro, 1 teaspoon lemon juice, and 1 teaspoon salt. Using large holes on grater, grate malanga and sweet potato into mixture and toss (it will be easier to grab vegetables if you pat them dry first). Let mixture rest 10 minutes. Melt 1 tablespoon butter in large, nonstick skillet on medium-high heat. Add 1 tablespoon vegetable oil. When hot, pour 1/2 cup of malanga mixture into skillet, pressing it into rounds. Reduce heat to low and fry, browning on both sides, cooking until vegetables are tender, about 5 minutes. Repeat until all of mixture is used, making about 4 more rounds. Serve with Mango salsa (page 62).

Mashed, sugared, and gingered: Cook 2 pounds peeled and cubed malanga in boiling water until tender; drain and mash with 2 teaspoons finely minced ginger and 1–2 tablespoons light brown sugar. Add salt to taste.

microgreens

BULLS BLOOD

MIZUNA

POPCORN

RAINBOW

RED BEET

TATSOI

MICROGREENS, IMMATURE SALAD GREENS, are the new darlings of the chef set. Some are mild, some are spicy; some buttery, some peppery. Often they're tossed together to make a crisp, colorful garnish, then used atop or beneath appetizers or entrées. They can also be added to lettuces to make a stunning salad potpourri—a balance of color, texture, and flavor that can be napped with a wide variety of dressings.

Most of these infant greens are harvested when they are only 14–20 days old. Baby greens are more mature 35-day-old toddlers.

BUYING AND STORING

Look for greens that look crisp and fresh; avoid any that look damp or wilted. Refrigerate unwashed 2–3 days wrapped loosely in plastic bag.

Domestic: *year-round*
Global: *none*

PREP

Wash in cold water; pat dry.

USE

Combine with baby greens (such as baby spinach, baby oak-leaf lettuce and small pea shoots and leaves) to make a tasty mesclun mix for salads. Use as garnish, with one type of microgreen, or combine with others to make a colorful mixture.

NUTRITIONAL INFO

1 cup is generally a significant source of vitamins C and A, but varieties vary in nutritional content.

CLOCKWISE FROM BOTTOM LEFT:
Tatsoi, Popcorn, Red Beet, Mizuna, Rainbow, Bull's Blood

BULLS BLOOD
Bright magenta and teal leaves
■ *Perky, peppery taste.*

MIZUNA
Elongated feathery green leaves
that are notched on both sides
(similar appearance to
chrysanthemum leaves).
■ *Pleasant, earthy cabbage,
mustard-like taste; crisp texture.*

POPCORN
Long slender greenish-yellow
shoots. Leaf portion is elongated
and gently cups. ■ *Subtle
popcorn flavor; crisp texture.*

RAINBOW
Mixture of most popular
varieties of microgreens for the
season. ■ *Combination of
flavors, often a blend that includes
mizuna, tatsoi, and red beet.*

RED BEET
Elongated feathery green leaves
with red stem. ■ *A pleasant
earthy flavor with a mustard-like
edge.*

TATSOI
Infant cabbage leaf looks like a
little green spoon. ■ *Sweet with
mild pepper edge.*

SERVING SUGGESTIONS

Crab cake balance: Often warm crab cakes are
accompanied by a rich sauce, such as a creamy
aioli. Use microgreens to add texture and flavor
balance to the dish, either on top of the crab
cakes or next to them. If desired, microgreens
can be tossed with just enough extra-virgin
olive oil to lightly coat leaves.

Salad heaven: Make mixed green salad using
baby greens and microgreens. Add thin apple
wedges or seedless red grapes (halved). Toss with
Simple Vinaigrette (page 310) and some minced
fresh tarragon. Top servings with crumbled blue
cheese and a small bundle of microgreens.

Grilled chicken with green babies: Brush boned
chicken breasts with mixture of 3 tablespoons
olive oil, 2 tablespoons lemon juice, and 1
tablespoon chopped fresh rosemary leaves, plus
salt and pepper to taste. Grill until completely
cooked. Let cool 5 minutes; cut into 1/2-inch-thick
crosswise slices. Fan chicken breasts on plates
and top with microgreens. Drizzle with smidgen
of extra-virgin olive oil.

Common White

Chanterelle

mushroom

CHANTERELLE, GIROLLE	OYSTER
COMMON WHITE, BUTTON	PORCINI, CÈPES
CREMINI, CRIMINI, ITALIAN BROWN	PORTOBELLINI
	PORTOBELLO, PORTOBELLA
ENOKI	SHIITAKE, CHINESE, GOLDEN OAK
LOBSTER	
MOREL	WOOD EAR

WITH THOUSANDS OF VARIETIES, mushrooms range in color, size, shape, texture, and flavor. Caps can be smooth, pitted, honeycombed, or ruffled. Flavors can be rich to bland, earthy to nutty, mild to intense. They can look like undersea vegetation or bouquets of lilies.

BUYING AND STORING

Look for mushrooms that are free of soft spots or mold. All varieties—except enoki, oyster, and wood ear—should be firm. They should be stored with cool air circulating around them; do not store in plastic bag or packaging. Instead, place unwashed in pan or sheet in single layer with barely damp paper towel on top and refrigerate up to 1 week. Sautéed mushrooms can be frozen up to 3 months (see Freezing, page 310).

Oyster

Wood Ear

Oyster

Morel

CHANTERELLE

Trumpet-shaped with tiny vertical creases in stem and under cap. Yellow-orange caps and cream-colored stems. ■ *Rich and complex flavors, earthy with hints of pepper. Trim as little as possible at stem end. Cook completely before eating.*

COMMON WHITE

Rounded, smooth cap with closed veils (fit closely at stem). Creamy white to light brown, sizes range from small 1/2-inch buttons to 4-inch jumbos. ■ *Delicate, mild woodsy flavor. Trim small portion at stem end. Can be eaten raw or cooked.*

CREMINI, PORTOBELLINI, PORTOBELLO

When small, called cremini (look like common mushrooms with dark-brown caps). Portobellini are medium-size cremini. Mature cremini are called portobello (deep, dark gills under cap). ■ *Meaty, rich, earthy flavors increase as these mature and increase in size. Trim portion at stem end. With portobello, remove dark gills on underside of cap with spoon to prevent dish from discoloring. Cook or eat raw like common white mushrooms. Portobellini and portobello are great for stuffing or broiling.*

ENOKI

Long, slender white stems join above roots and are topped with small rounded caps. ■ *Mild flavor with almost undetectable acidity. Raw, it has a lettuce-like crunchiness and makes a beguiling garnish. Trim right above roots where joined together and separate. Quickly sautéed in oil and drained on paper towels, it can be a pasta substitute.*

LOBSTER

Name derived from color resemblance to cooked lobster. Appearance varies; looks like distorted, somewhat beat-up trumpet. ■ *Pleasant, mild taste with crunchy texture. Trim off any brown ends, cut into small pieces and cook completely.*

MOREL

Conical shapes with deep honeycomb surface and hollow interiors. Tan to deep brown, about 2–4 inches high. Note that morels should never be eaten raw and that some people are allergic to the black morel, even when cooked. ■ *Nutty, earthy flavor. Trim ends and wash thoroughly; sand sometimes gets trapped in honeycomb surface. Cook completely before eating.*

OYSTER

Trumpet-shaped, grow in clumps joined at base in varying sizes. Creamy gray to soft brown, ■ *Mild flavor and velvety texture. Can be used raw in salads, but best flavor when sautéed briefly in oil or butter. To separate, gently break off each stem at base.*

PORCINI

Shape looks like plump white mushrooms with swollen stems. Caps are reddish-brown or orange-brown. ■ *Woodsy, earthy flavor. Delectable in pasta sauces and risotto, or grilled. Cut at base of stem to remove tough portion.*

SHIITAKE

Broad, umbrella-like brown caps with open veils (not closed around stem) and shallow, tan gills. ■ *Steak-like, meaty flavor when cooked. Woody stems must be removed (some use them to flavor stocks; some discard them). Break stems off next to cap; discard stems.*

WOOD EAR

Dark brown seaweedlike or crinkled cabbage leaf appearance. Leathery and suedelike underneath, tops are shiny and moist. ■ *Crunchy, chewy, and slightly gelatinous; strips are used in classic Asian dishes such as hot-and-sour soup or mu shu pork. There texture holds up to long cooking, but they can be used in quick stir-fries as well.*

CHANTERELLE
Domestic: *July–January*
Global: *February–June*

**CREMINI (CRIMINI), COMMON WHITE (BUTTON),
ENOKI, OYSTER, PORTOBELLO, PORTOBELLA,
PORTOBELLINI, SHIITAKE, WOOD EAR**
Domestic: *year-round*
Global: *none*

LOBSTER
Domestic: *July–October*
Global: *none*

MOREL
Domestic: *April–June*
Global: *sporadic July–December*

PORCINI
Domestic: *June, September–October*
Global: *sporadic November–April*

PREP

Except the morel, never submerge in water to wash because they absorb like a sponge and become mushy. Instead, most varieties can be wiped down with moist paper towels. If extremely dirty, they can be briefly rinsed with water and thoroughly dried. Some varieties, such as lobster and chanterelle, can have grit in tiny crevises, making them trickier to clean. Try rinsing in a good stream of water. If that doesn't work, use a wet toothbrush. Dry with cloth or paper towel.

If using dried mushrooms, reconstitute by soaking in warm water until pliable, usually about 20 minutes. The soaking liquid (with the exception of the gritty bits that drop to the bottom of the bowl) is often used as an ingredient in recipes calling for dried mushrooms.

USE

Can be marinated, sautéed, simmered, broiled, roasted, or grilled. Mushrooms with hollow caps are delicious stuffed with hot or cold fillings. Portobello caps can be grilled and substituted for meat in sandwiches or used as a pizza "crust." Dried mushrooms can be ground and used to flavor bread crumbs, soups and sauces, or used as a dry rub for meat.

NUTRITIONAL INFO

1 cup sliced is a good source of vitamin D, riboflavin, and niacin; good source of pantothenic acid and copper.

SERVING SUGGESTIONS

Sautéed mushroom melange: Heat mixture of vegetable or olive oil and butter in large, deep skillet on medium-high heat. Add mixture of clean mushrooms that are all about the same size (cut larger mushrooms in halves or quarters as needed). Sauté until all liquid evaporates and mushrooms are thoroughly cooked, stirring occasionally. Add chopped fresh basil or tarragon or a little blue cheese. Use as a topper on grilled steak, warm pasta, cooked squash, or toasted slices of French bread. Or use as a vegetable side dish.

Easy mushroom soup: Sauté 1 onion (chopped) and 1 clove garlic (minced) in small amount of vegetable oil in Dutch oven or pot on medium-high heat; do not brown. Add 6 cups chicken broth; bring to simmer. Add 1 pound oyster mushrooms (they grow in clumps, break into individual mushrooms); reduce heat and simmer until mushrooms soften. Add 4-ounce can mild diced green chiles and lemon juice to taste. Season with salt and pepper.

Marinated magic: In glass or ceramic bowl, combine 1 pound clean button or cremini mushrooms, ¾ cup vegetable or extra-virgin olive oil, ½ cup red-wine vinegar, 2 tablespoons lemon juice, 2 tablespoons sugar, 3 cloves garlic (minced), and ½ teaspoon salt. Cover and marinate 24 hours in refrigerator. Stir in ½ cup chopped fresh basil.

Spanish simmer: Chop stems of 2 pounds button or cremini mushrooms, leaving caps whole. In large, deep skillet or pot, sauté on medium-high heat in 2 tablespoons olive oil until browned, about 3 minutes, tossing occasionally. Add juice of 2 lemons and 2 cloves garlic (minced). Cover, reduce heat to low, and simmer until tender, about 10–15 minutes. Serve in 6 individual ramekins.

Portobello

Enoki

Cremini

Portobellini

grilled stuffed portobello mushrooms

Warm portobello mushroom caps oozing with herbed goat cheese and sun-dried tomatoes is delectable paired with a simple green salad. Or cut into wedges and serve as an appetizer.

²/₃ cup marinated sun-dried tomatoes, drained, chopped

¼ cup soft goat cheese

1 teaspoon olive oil, divided use

½ teaspoon chopped rosemary

⅛ teaspoon ground black pepper

1 garlic clove, minced

4 portobello mushroom caps, 5–6 inches in diameter

2 tablespoons fresh lemon juice

2 teaspoons low-sodium soy sauce

GARNISH: 2 teaspoons chopped fresh cilantro or Italian parsley

1. Prepare grill.

2. In small bowl, combine tomatoes, goat cheese, ½ teaspoon olive oil, rosemary, pepper, and garlic. Stir to combine well.

3. Remove mushroom stems. Using spoon, scoop out dark gills and discard.

4. In small bowl, mix remaining ½ teaspoon olive oil, lemon juice, and soy sauce. Using pastry brush, brush soy sauce mixture on both sides of mushroom caps.

5. Grill caps: Grill stem-side down about 5 minutes. Turn and grill until soft, about 5 more minutes. Spoon ¼ cup cheese mixture into each cap, cover and grill about 3 minutes or until cheese melts. Garnish with cilantro or Italian parsley and serve.

YIELD: 4 ENTRÉE SERVINGS

NUTRITIONAL INFORMATION (PER SERVING): Calories 230; fat calories 72; total fat 8 grams; sat fat 2 grams; cholesterol 5 milligrams; sodium 150 milligrams; total carbohydrates 14 grams; fiber 4 grams; sugars 2 grams; protein 8 grams; vitamin A IUs 4%; vitamin C 8%; calcium 4%; iron 20%.

Shiitake

Enoki

nira grass

COMMON (GREEN), CHINESE CHIVE

YELLOW, GARLIC CHIVE

NIRA GRASS LOOKS LIKE A LONG, THICK, FLATTENED GRASS BLADE. The green variety, often called Chinese chive, is about 12–15 inches long, straight, and rather sturdy. The deep green stalk can be white at its root end. Generally sold in generous bundles, it tastes like green onion stalks scented with garlic but with added subtle sweetness.

The yellow variety, often called garlic chive, is more flimsy than the green; its blades twist and curl, making a bundle look like a cheerleader's pompom. Some contend that its flavor is slightly more intense than the green.

Most often used in cooked dishes, the two varieties taste very similar once heated.

BUYING AND STORING

Look for fresh-looking stalks without discoloration or sliminess. Use as soon as possible. Untie bundle and refrigerate, unwashed, wrapped in damp paper towel in plastic bag for up to 3 days.
Domestic: *year-round*
Global: *November–May*

PREP

Rinse in cold water and shake dry.
Drain well.

USE

Green nira grass and yellow nira grass can be eaten raw in a small amount. A blade can be added lengthwise to a Vietnamese spring roll or finely chopped and added in small amounts to vinaigrette. Or cook for short amount of time in soup or stir-fries.

Yellow

Common (Green)

NUTRITIONAL INFO

1 cup is an excellent source of vitamins A and C.

SERVING SUGGESTIONS

Chicken noodle soup: Chop small amount of green or yellow nira grass and add to chicken noodle soup 2 minutes before end of cooking time.

Vegetable stir-fry: Stir-fry spinach, watercress, or ong choy (see Stir-Fried Water Spinach, page 232). Chop small amount of green or yellow nira grass and add to stir-fry mixture during last minute of cooking.

Steamed mussels or clams: Add green or yellow nira grass (cut into 1-inch lengths) to water used to cook mussels or clams. Serve the seafood with strained nira-enriched broth.

okra, chinese okra

LOVE IT OR HATE IT, few vegetables evoke such passionate opinions. It's not the flavor, a pleasant blend of eggplant and green bean. It's the mucilaginous juices they exude when sliced and cooked. Some appreciate its ability to thicken gumbos; others write okra off. Okra pods are fuzzy and deeply ridged, usually about 2–5 inches long. They can be delectable fried, grilled, or pickled.

Chinese okra, also known as loofah, is not related to okra. It is an emerald green gourd with deeply ridged skin and an exterior that is leathery and firm. About 10–14 inches long, it gently tapers from a thin stem end to a larger bulb end. Sometimes it forms a dramatic curve at the stem end; sometimes it's perfectly straight. Inside, it has the taste and texture of a mature zucchini squash with fully developed seeds.

Chinese Okra

Okra

BUYING AND STORING

For okra, look for small pods, about 2–3 inches long; they will be more tender and flavorful than larger pods. Avoid pods that look dry or dull. They should snap when broken in half. Refrigerate unwashed and untrimmed in paper bag in crisper drawer 3–5 days. To freeze, cut raw pods into 1/2-inch-thick crosswise slices and place in airtight container.

For Chinese okra, look for smaller, less mature gourds with bright green skin. Avoid those that are shriveled or discolored. Refrigerate in plastic in crisper drawer for up to 3 days.

OKRA
Domestic: *April–September*
Global: *October–March*

CHINESE OKRA
Domestic: *May–October*
Global: *November–May*

PREP FOR OKRA

Wash with cold water. If cooking whole, trim a tiny portion at stem and tip without piercing interior (cooked whole, slimy juices won't be released). If slicing, stem can be cut next to cap (cook quickly over high heat to reduce sliminess).

PREP FOR CHINESE OKRA

Wash in cold water. Trim ends and discard. Peel with vegetable peeler to remove dark, ridged skin. A small portion of dark peel can be left in place if a firmer texture is desired, but all ridged areas should be removed.

USE

For okra, sauté, deep-fry, or simmer in stew as thickening agent. Raw okra can be pickled. For Chinese okra, use in stir-fries or soups. Can be used in place of zucchini in many recipes; stuff with vegetable or meat filling and bake (for meat filling see Stuffed Summer Squash, page 283).

NUTRITIONAL INFO FOR OKRA

1 cup is a good source of folate and vitamin C.

NUTRITIONAL INFO FOR CHINESE OKRA

1 cup is a significant source of vitamin C and folate.

SERVING SUGGESTIONS

Fried okra: Beat one egg with 1 cup milk. Place cornmeal on a plate. Heat 1–2 inches vegetable oil or peanut oil in deep skillet on high heat. Cut trimmed okra into 1/2-inch slices. Dip okra in egg mixture, then cornmeal. Deep-fry in hot oil (375 degrees) until golden brown. Drain on paper towels. Season with coarse salt.

Grilled green pods: Thread okra crosswise on bamboo skewer that has been soaked in water for at least 20 minutes. Brush generously with olive oil and season with coarse salt and pepper. Grill over medium fire until caramelized (some spots will be lightly blackened). Accompany with lime wedges.

Pickled pods: In 1 quart canning jar, combine 2 1/2 cups small raw okra (less than 3 inches long preferred), 1/3 cup olive oil (extra-virgin preferred), 1/2 cup lemon juice, 1 bay leaf, 1/2 cup pimiento-stuffed green olives, 1/2 teaspoon dried red pepper flakes, 1 teaspoon dried Italian herb blend, and 1 teaspoon kosher salt. Seal and gently shake jar. Refrigerate 2 days. Serve as appetizer.

Chinese okra butter braise: Peel and cut into ½-inch slices. Melt a little butter in deep, nonstick skillet on medium-high heat. Add Chinese okra and fry, lightly browning. Add ¼-inch chicken broth or vegetable broth to pan; reduce heat to low and braise until very tender. Season with minced fresh basil, salt, and pepper.

ong choy, also
water spinach, rau muong

SLENDER AND HOLLOW, THESE APPLE GREEN STALKS can be 20 inches long. No wider than a pencil, each spindly sprig is topped with several pointed leaves.

The leaves, deep green and up to 6 inches long, have a sweet taste that has a vague, mild spinach-like flavor. They soften to gentle creaminess when cooked, but stems maintain a contrasting crisp texture.

Ong Choy

BUYING AND STORING
Look for those with crisp leaves and stems. Avoid those with brown spots or shriveled leaves. Refrigerate, unwashed, in plastic bag in crisper drawer 2–3 days.
Domestic: *year-round*
Global: *none*

PREP
Cut off and discard bottom portion of stem, about 3 inches. Cut into 3½-inch-long pieces. Wash in several changes of cold water. Drain and shake dry.

USE

Can be chopped and eaten raw in mixed green salads. Or shave stems with vegetable peeler to make long strips, then store in ice water to make them curl up; use as salad dressed with vinaigrette. Most often, water spinach is stir-fried.

NUTRITIONAL INFO

1 cup is an excellent source of vitamins A and C.

SERVING SUGGESTIONS

Soup sub: Instead of bok choy or gai lan, add bite-size pieces of water spinach to soup during last few minutes of cooking.

Steam and dress: Steam water spinach until stems are tender-crisp. Toss with butter or olive oil and balsamic vinegar; season to taste with salt and pepper.

Pasta 'n' greens: Sauté water spinach and minced garlic; add to hot, cooked pasta; toss. Season to taste with salt and pepper.

stir-fried water spinach

This basic stir-fry technique can be used with a wide variety of Asian vegetables, such as gai choy, baby bok choy (halved), yu choy sum, and choy sum. It can be served as a side dish, as is, or in small bowls spooned over cooked rice.

1½ tablespoons vegetable oil or canola oil

2 medium garlic cloves, peeled, minced

1 pound water spinach, cut into 3½-inch pieces, washed, drained (see Prep)

Freshly ground black pepper

1 tablespoon fish sauce

OPTIONAL: 1 teaspoon ground bean sauce (see Cook's Notes) or oyster sauce.

COOK'S NOTES: Ground bean sauce is made with soy beans, sesame oil, sugar, and spices. It's sold at Asian markets.

1. Heat oil in large wok over high heat; add garlic and stir-fry until softened, but not browned.

2. Add water spinach and stir-fry until wilted, about 3–5 minutes. Season with pepper and add fish sauce and bean sauce or oyster sauce (if using). Toss over heat until evenly heated. Serve.

YIELD: 4–6 SERVINGS

NUTRITIONAL INFORMATION (PER SERVING): Calories 70; fat calories 45; total fat 5 grams; sat fat 1 gram; cholesterol 0 milligrams; sodium 480 milligrams; total carbohydrates 4 grams; fiber 2 grams; sugars 0 grams; protein 3 grams; vitamin A IUs 140%; vitamin C 100%; calcium 10%; iron 10%.

onion

BOILER (GOLD, RED, AND WHITE)

CIPOLLA, LARGE ITALIAN FLAT

CIPOLLINE, ITALIAN FLAT

GREEN, SCALLION, SPRING ONION

MAUI

MEXICAN BBQ

PEARL (GOLD, RED, AND WHITE)

RED, SPANISH

SWEET: OSO SWEET, TEXAS SWEET, VIDALIA, AND WALLA WALLA

WHITE

YELLOW (COMMON)

CONCENTRIC LAYER ON LAYER OF JUICY FLESH fills onion's paper-thin skin. Unruly roots dangle at its base, while the pungent-sweet bulb above holds endless culinary potential. It's too bad that most think of onions as only a flavoring element. Their delectable flavor profiles more than qualify them to take the starring role in vegetable dishes.

There are more than 500 onion varieties, and because onions are easily crossbred, new varieties and hybrids abound. Color, taste, shape, and size vary, but generally speaking, onions fall into three major categories. Those that can be stored for long periods at room temperature are dubbed "storage" onions.

They generally have a more pronounced pungency (sometimes described in loving terms as mouth burn or heat). Another group, spring onions, includes scallions (green onions) and Mexican BBQ onions. They have bright green stalks. They spoil more quickly and require refrigeration. Sweet onions are the third category. Aptly named, they

Sweet

Red Texas

Mexican BBQ

Maui

have a pronounced sweetness (or lack storage onion heat and have lower acidity). They leave a delicious, very slight pungent aftertaste. They have a shorter shelf life than storage onions but a longer one than green onions.

Each variety shares a common trait: cutting them releases eye-burning sulfuric compounds. Often, the older the onion, the more eye-irritating it becomes. Cooks have come up with interesting ways to eliminate onion tears, from wearing goggles to working next to flames to washing onions under cold water. But most agree that working quickly while using a very sharp knife is extremely helpful.

BUYING AND STORING

Bulb should be firm without soft spots. Storage onions and sweet onions should have tightly closed necks; avoid those with green shoulders. Spring onions should have bright green stalks. Place dry, unwashed storage or sweet onions in loose container (not in plastic bag) in cool, dark location; keep storage onions up to 2 months, sweet onions up to 2 weeks. Or refrigerate sweet onions (keeping them dry) up to 1 month. Unwashed green onions should be refrigerated, kept dry in plastic bag; refrigerate up to 7 days.

STORAGE ONIONS (BOILER, CIPOLLINE, CIPOLLA, PEARL, RED, WHITE, AND YELLOW)
Domestic: *year-round*
Global: *none*

SPRING ONIONS (GREEN ONIONS, SCALLIONS) AND MEXICAN BBQ ONIONS
Domestic: *year-round*
Global: *year-round*

Cipolla

White

Green

Cipolline

SWEET ONIONS

MAUI
Domestic: *year-round*
Global: *none*

TEXAS SWEET, OSO SWEET
Domestic: *January–September*
Global: *none*

VIDALIA (GEORGIA)
Domestic: *April–June*
Global: *none*

WALLA WALLA
Domestic: *June–August*
Global: *none*

BOILER
(gold, red, and white)
Storage onion that is golf-ball sized. ■ *Mild pungency. Red are sweetest, but whites are most popular.*

CIPOLLINE
(Italian flat)
Means "small onions" in Italian. Storage onion, generally about 2 inches in diameter, flat at top and bottom with thin yellow skin. ■ *Appealing sharpness balanced with sweet edge.*

CIPOLLA
Storage onion. More mature cipolline with diameters about 3–4 inches. ■ *Crunchier than cipolline and slightly sweeter.*

GREEN
(scallion or spring)
Spring onion with small, elongated white bulb and long, bright-green stalks. ■ *Mild taste. Green stalks have chivelike taste and are often included in recipes.*

MAUI
Sweet onion from Hawaii, grown in volcanic soil. Large with creamy white skin. ■ *Juicy and brimming with sweetness. Aftertaste leaves a gentle bite.*

MEXICAN BBQ
Look like large green onions with big green stalks and pearl onion–size bulb. There are several onion varieties that fall into this category; all are picked immature with stalks intact. ■ *Pungent flavor with underlying sweetness.*

PEARL
(gold, red, and white)
Storage onion smaller than boiler. Some growers name those with less than 1-inch diameters "picklers," those with 1-inch diameters as "pearls." ■ *Very mild pungency. Reds are sweetest, but whites are most popular.*

RED
(Spanish)
Storage onion with purplish-red skin, generally 4-inch diameter. ■ *Usually has mild, sweet taste. If using raw, onion has strong sharp taste; place sliced or chopped in colander in sink and pour boiling water on top, then refresh with cold water.*

OTHER SWEET ONIONS: OSO SWEET, TEXAS SWEET, VIDALIA, AND WALLA WALLA
Texas Sweets are generally softball-size with yellow skin. Vidalia are flat on stem end and round at root end with yellow skin. Walla Walla onions are large and almost round with yellow skin. ■ *Sweet and crisp, with very subtle aftertaste.*

WHITE
Very firm storage onions with tightly packed layers. These are mature white boiler onions. ■ *Pronounced sharpness and crisp texture.*

YELLOW
Most common storage onion, available in medium and large sizes. Brown skin. ■ *Thick, juicy layers with pronounced sharpness and crisp texture.*

PREP FOR STORAGE ONIONS AND SWEET ONIONS

For storage onions and sweet onions, trim top and bottom, leaving enough root end intact so that layers stay together. Cut in half lengthwise. Pull off and discard skin. Place cut side down on cutting board. Cut into wedges or slices. Or, to dice or mince, cut into parallel horizontal lengthwise slices, leaving root end intact (to mince, slices will be closer together); then cut parallel lengthwise vertical slices, leaving root end intact. Cut crosswise.

Peeling pearl onions can be a chore. To make it easier, make a shallow X in stem ends. Boil 5 minutes and drain. Refresh with cold water. When cool enough to handle, pinch at root ends and onions will pop out of skins.

PREP FOR SPRING ONIONS

Wash thoroughly in cold running water. Trim root end. Some recipes call for using green stalks; other do not.

USE

Include raw in salads, sandwiches, relishes, or dips. Boiler or pearl onions are generally cooked in stews and casseroles or pickled. Onions can be braised, boiled, grilled, sautéed, roasted, or pickled.

NUTRITIONAL INFO FOR SPRING ONIONS

1 cup is an excellent source of vitamins A and C; good source of vitamin K.

NUTRITIONAL INFO FOR STORAGE ONIONS AND SWEET ONIONS

1 cup is a significant source of vitamins C and B_6.

SERVING SUGGESTIONS

Roasted sweet: Cut peeled, trimmed sweet onions or red onions into 1-inch-thick crosswise slices. Place in single layer in baking pan greased with olive oil. Brush olive oil on top and sprinkle with chopped fresh thyme leaves. Bake in 375-degree oven until

Gold Pearl

White Pearl

soft, about 30 minutes. Top with vinaigrette (½ cup extra-virgin olive oil mixed with 1 tablespoon white wine vinegar or balsamic vinegar, salt to taste, and pinch of dried red chili flakes). Marinate at least 15 minutes. Serve as is as side dish, or chop and stir into sour cream for dip or baked potato topper.

Beet and baked onion salad: Place sliced cooked beets on salad plates. Top with roasted onion marinated in vinaigrette (see Roasted sweet, at left). Top with generous sprinkle of crumbled feta cheese. Serve warm or at room temperature.

Caramelize: Heat a combination of butter and vegetable oil in large, deep skillet on medium-high heat. Add sliced (storage or sweet) onion and, if desired, a pinch of sugar; toss to coat. Cook 4–5 minutes, stirring infrequently, so that onions start to soften. Reduce heat to medium or medium-low. Cook until nicely browned, stirring occasionally. Depending on amount of onion used, this can take 15–30 minutes. Season to taste with salt and ground white pepper. Use to top burgers, pasta, or eggs. Use on pizza, polenta, or bruschetta, or in soup or gravy. Delicious tossed into other cooked vegetables, especially mashed potatoes, green beans, or squash.

Grilled Mexican BBQ onions: Cut off roots and most of dark green stalks. Heat barbecue and brush grates with vegetable oil. Grill on medium heat, basting lightly with vegetable oil and seasoning to taste with spicy mixture such as Pico de Gallo seasoning or seasoned salt. Turn and relocate onions on cooler portion of grill from time to time to prevent burning. Grill until tender and nicely browned on both sides (generally about 10 minutes per side). Use as side dish with grilled steak (especially nice with grilled skirt steak).

Red Boilers (REAR)
White Boilers (CENTER)

Red Pearl

Gold Boilers

Creamed boilers or pearls: Blanch and peel about 2 pounds boilers or pearl onions (see Prep). Place onions in large saucepan and cover by 1 inch with water. Bring to boil on high heat; reduce heat and simmer about 15 minutes or until tender. Drain well. In saucepan, melt 6 tablespoons butter on medium heat. Stir in 4 tablespoons all-purpose flour; cook, stirring, 1–2 minutes. Whisk in 1½ cups milk and bring to boil on medium-high heat, stirring constantly until thickened. Season to taste with salt, white pepper, and pinch of ground cloves or nutmeg. Add onions and 1 tablespoon finely chopped Italian parsley.

sweet-glazed cipolline onions

Cipolline onions cooked with an appealing balsamic glaze is an extremely versatile dish. Serve warm, cold, or at room temperature with pork or poultry, or spoon over assorted roasted vegetables. Use as appetizer with other antipasti favorites or on toasted baguettes topped with crumbled Gorgonzola cheese. If you prefer to use it as a relish and want more of a sweet-sour taste, add more sherry vinegar or use white-wine vinegar instead.

1 pound peeled cipolline onions

1 large garlic clove, peeled, crushed

1 bay leaf

2 tablespoons olive oil

⅓ cup water

1 teaspoon salt

1 (4-inch) cinnamon stick

2 teaspoons light brown sugar

1 tablespoon sherry vinegar

2 tablespoons balsamic vinegar

2 teaspoons fresh thyme leaves

COOK'S NOTES: If you prefer, these onions can be glazed on stove top. Place all ingredients in large, deep skillet. Place on high heat and bring to boil on high heat. Reduce heat to medium and simmer, tossing frequently, until onions are tender and nicely glazed.

1. Preheat oven to 400 degrees (see Cook's Notes).

2. Toss all ingredients in shallow baking dish large enough to hold onions in single layer. Bake in middle of preheated oven until onions are tender, about 45 minutes, tossing to coat every 10–15 minutes. Remove bay leaf and cinnamon stick and serve. Or cool and refrigerate airtight up to 1 week.

YIELD: 6–8 SERVINGS

NUTRITIONAL INFORMATION (PER SERVING): Calories 80; fat calories 40.5; total fat 4.5 grams; sat fat .5 grams; cholesterol 0 milligrams; sodium 0 milligrams; total carbohydrates 9 grams; fiber 2 grams; sugars 7 grams; protein 1 grams; vitamin A IUs 0%; vitamin C 10%; calcium 0%; iron 2%.

parsley root, also hamburg parsley, rooted parsley, turnip-rooted parsley

PARSLEY ROOT LOOKS SOMETHING LIKE HOMELY, medium to small carrots. But instead of bright orange root portions, the color is as drab as dusty sneakers. The taste of these tapered roots is something between celery root and parsley, with a hint of carrot thrown in.

On top, the leaves are fernlike parsley leaves. Aromatic and pleasantly crisp, their flavor varies from the sweet taste of Italian parsley to the bitter-edged profile of watercress.

Parsley Root

BUYING AND STORING

Look for uniform roots without soft spots or cracks. Leaves should be a brilliant green and crisp. Store unwashed, wrapped in plastic, in vegetable drawer of refrigerator up to 1 week.

Domestic: *year-round*
Global: *none*

PREP

Wash just before using. Remove stems and leaves from root. Scrub root under cold running water with brush. Peel with vegetable peeler or paring knife, or use unpeeled, according to your own preference. Dice, slice, or leave whole if small. Wash stems and leaves under cold running water, or submerge in cold water if gritty. Shake dry.

USE

Root can be braised, steamed, boiled, simmered, or roasted. Use in stews, soups, or braised dishes. Taste leaves to determine flavor. If they aren't bitter, use as a garnish like parsley.

NUTRITIONAL INFO

1 cup is an excellent source of vitamins A and C; significant source of iron.

SERVING SUGGESTIONS

Yukon Gold–parsley root mashed potatoes: Cook peeled and cubed parsley root (2–3 medium) in large pot of boiling, salted water 5 minutes. Add 4 large peeled and cubed Yukon gold potatoes; boil 15–20 minutes, or until tender. Drain and return to pot; cook on medium heat until potatoes look dry, about 1–2 minutes. Remove from heat and mash with ½ stick butter (¼ cup), about 4 tablespoons milk, salt, and pepper. Add more milk if necessary to attain creamy texture.

Pot roast deluxe: Along with the usual vegetables added to pot roast, such as potatoes and carrots, add 2–3 whole, peeled parsley roots. When serving, garnish vegetables with chopped parsley root leaves (see Use).

Roasted roots: Toss 1½ pounds peeled parsley roots with 3 tablespoons olive oil on rimmed baking sheet. Sprinkle with coarse salt and pepper. Roast in 400-degree oven until tender, about 40 minutes, turning once or twice. If they brown too much before tender, add a little water to pan and cover with aluminum foil. In a small bowl combine 2 tablespoons balsamic vinegar and 1 teaspoon minced rosemary leaves. Drizzle over parsley root (drained if water added) and toss. Bake 3–4 minutes.

parsnip

AT FIRST GLANCE, parsnips may look like frumpy carrots. Instead of a cheerful orange, this root vegetable has skin that is tan or pale yellow, with flesh that is pallid beige. Their knobby heads taper into long, spindly root ends. And no feathery leaves crown the top; stalks and leaves are removed before they make their way to the marketplace.

They may not be glamorous, but when cooked, they have the combined sweetness of a carrot along with an appealing parsley-like herbaceous quality and subtle nuttiness.

BUYING AND STORING

Parsnips can be more than 15 inches long but are most tender when about 8 inches long. Select those that are firm and relatively smooth, without many wispy rootlets. Refrigerate, unwashed, in plastic bag in crisper drawer up to 3 weeks.
Domestic: *year-round*
Global: *none*

PREP

Trim ends. Peel with swivel-style vegetable peeler. If boiling, simmering, or sautéing, cut into desired shapes, either chunks, slices, or quartered lengthwise. If steaming or roasting, leave whole.

USE

Because they tend to be fibrous, parsnips are usually cooked. But they are sweetest when cooked until just barely tender. Boil, simmer, roast, or steam. Cooked parsnips are delicious seasoned with a little butter and either chopped fresh tarragon, minced orange zest (colored part of peel), or ground cinnamon.

NUTRITIONAL INFO

1 cup is a good source of vitamin C and a significant source of folate and potassium.

Parsnip

SERVING SUGGESTIONS

Root roast: In a roasting pan, toss chunks of trimmed and peeled parsnips and carrots with enough olive oil to coat. Sprinkle with coarse salt and chopped fresh rosemary leaves to taste; toss again. Roast in 400-degree oven until just tender, tossing once or twice, about 30 minutes. If vegetables brown too much before they are tender, add a smidgen of water to pan and cover.

Creamed: Cut trimmed, peeled parsnips into 1-inch-thick "coins." Cook in boiling water until just barely tender. Drain. Off heat, return to saucepan. Add a little plain whole-fat yogurt, chopped fresh parsley, orange zest, salt, and pepper. Toss and serve.

Almost carrot cake: Parsnip cake is delicious. Substitute peeled and grated parsnips for half of the carrots in your favorite carrot cake recipe.

Pot roast: Augment pot roast with parsnips (cut in half lengthwise) during the last 45 minutes of cooking.

pea

BLACK-EYED, COWPEA

ENGLISH, GREEN, GARDEN

PEA SHOOTS, SNOW PEA LEAVES

SNO, SNOW, CHINESE SNOW, MANGETOUT

SUGAR SNAP

THE SNO PEA'S FLAT, WIDE POD is sweet and tender-crisp, so delicate the subtle bumps of immature peas inside can be detected through its delicate skin. As with sugar snap peas, the outside is just as delectable as the plump little jewels inside.

With English peas, it's a different story. The thick pod that bulges around this string of peas, has a tough supportive lining. The bright green spheres inside are the treasure. The same is true with black-eyed peas, those beige beans with black eye-like marks on their curved bellies. Those fibrous pods can be used as a component in making broth.

Pea shoots, leaves, and tendrils from young sno pea or sugar snap vines are sweet and tender. Sometimes they are included in commercial baby lettuce mixtures.

BUYING AND STORING ENGLISH PEAS, SNO PEAS, AND SUGAR SNAP PEAS

Look for peas with bright green, glossy pods. English peas should be refrigerated, because their sugar content starts to turn to starch within six hours of harvest. They should feel heavy for their size, almost bursting with peas. Shake pod; if the peas rattle loosely inside, it's not a good sign. Often medium-sized pods have sweeter peas than really large ones. For snow peas and sugar snap peas, snap one in half. They should sound crisp. Avoid peas with limp or discolored pods. Use English peas as soon as possible; if not, store in perforated bag in crisper drawer up to 2 days. Store sugar snap or sno peas 4–7 days in perforated bag in crisper drawer of refrigerator.

BUYING AND STORING BLACK-EYED PEAS

Sold shelled, most black-eyed peas in the marketplace are either canned or frozen. Only within the past few years have these been available fresh. Packaged in sealed plastic bags or loose in plastic tubs, these peas are presoaked and partially cooked. Look for evenly colored peas without soft spots or discoloration. Store in refrigerator and use within 5 days.

BUYING AND STORING PEA SHOOTS

Avoid shoots with yellowing or limpness. Store, unwashed, in plastic bag in crisper drawer up to 2 days.

BLACK-EYED (SHELLED, PARTIALLY COOKED)
Domestic: *year-round*
Global: *none*

ENGLISH
Domestic: *May–July*
Global: *September–April*

PEA SHOOTS
Domestic: *year round, with occasional interruptions due to rain*
Global: *none*

SNO
Domestic: *April–November*
Global: *September–May*

SUGAR SNAP
Domestic: *April–November*
Global: *September–May*

PREP FOR BLACK-EYED PEAS

Most often sold shelled and partially cooked. Only brief cooking in simmering water is required.

PREP FOR ENGLISH PEAS

Shell just before use. Pinch off stem and pull string toward opposite end. Pod should pop open with gentle squeeze; push out peas with thumb and discard pod (or use pod for stock).

PREP FOR PEA SHOOTS

Remove and discard any large, woody stems. Rinse in cold water just before eating or cooking.

PREP FOR SNO PEAS AND SUGAR SNAP PEARS

Some have strings that need removal, others don't. Rinse in cold water. Snap off stem end and pull toward opposite end to remove string (sugar

BLACK-EYED, COWPEA Most often sold removed from pods, the shelled peas are light green to beige with dark-brown to black "eye" on underside. ■ *When cooked, they have pleasing starchiness and subtle sweetness with smooth texture. Often cooked with smoked meats.*

ENGLISH, GREEN, GARDEN
Bright green, bulging pods are tough and inedible. Inside, a row of round and tender green peas line up. ■ *Peas are very sweet, especially when shelled and eaten soon after harvest. Peas can be eaten raw or cooked. Pods are inedible.*

PEA SHOOTS, SNO PEA LEAVES
Green crisp vines, curly tendrils and tender leaves have been commonplace in Asian markets and are sometimes included in commercial blends of baby lettuces or baby greens.
Tender-crisp with delicate pea flavor. Eat raw or cooked.

SNO, SNOW, CHINESE SNOW, MANGETOUT
Wide, flat apple-green pod with small, immature sweet peas. ■ *All-edible, crunchy-crisp pods and delicate peas. Sweet flavor profile. Can be eaten raw or cooked. Avoid overcooking.*

SUGAR SNAP
Curved, plump deep green pod packed with tender, sweet peas.
■ *All-edible, crunchy-crisp pods filled with succulent peas. Very sweet flavor profile. Can be eaten raw or cooked. Avoid overcooking.*

Pea Shoots

English

Pea Shoot

Snow

Sugar Snap

snap peas have string at top and bottom). It is easier to remove string after blanching.

USE

Cook black-eyed peas in simmering water until tender; augment with smoked meat if desired. Drain and combine with lemony Simple Vinaigrette (see page 310) or add to pasta salad.

Snow peas, sugar snap peas, and pea shoots, as well as shelled English peas, can be eaten raw or cooked. Brief cooking is best. Stir-fry, blanch, or steam snow peas or sugar snap peas. Quickly blanch shelled English peas. Use pea shoots raw in salads or stir-fry until tender-crisp; or use as garnish.

NUTRITIONAL INFO (BLACK-EYED PEA)

1 cup is a good source of vitamins A and C; significant source of iron.

NUTRITIONAL INFO (ENGLISH PEA, SNOW PEA AND SUGAR SNAP PEA)

1 cup is an excellent source of vitamin C, a good source of vitamin A, and a significant source of iron.

NUTRITIONAL INFO (PEA SHOOTS)

1 cup is a significant source of vitamins A and C.

SERVING SUGGESTIONS

Dippers: Serve snow peas or sugar snap peas either raw or blanched (cook in boiling water 1–2 minutes, then drain and refresh with cold water) with creamy dip. Cooked in this manner, they are delectable added to mixed green salads, spring rolls, or coleslaw (cut into diagonal slices).

Rice and peas: Gently toss cooked, well-seasoned rice with black-eyed peas (cooked) or English peas (very briefly blanched). Add grated Parmesan cheese to taste.

Stir-fry beauty: For best color and flavor, blanch snow peas or sugar snap peas (see Dippers, at left), then add to your favorite stir-fry dish during last 1 minute of cooking.

Pea-camole: Use cooked and mashed English peas along with avocado to make guacamole using a 1:3 ratio (1 part peas to 3 parts avocado). Serve as dip with sturdy tortilla chips.

warm sugar snap and black-eyed pea mélange

Warm black-eyed peas make a pleasing creamy contrast with crunchy sugar snap peas. In this warm mixture, fresh grape tomatoes and basil add both color and flavor. If you want to add a smoky taste, cook a little chopped bacon or ham along with the shallots, then add the garlic during the last 30 seconds of cooking.

½ pound sugar snap peas

1 tablespoon olive oil

2 shallots, minced

2 garlic cloves, minced

2 cups black-eyed peas (see Cook's Notes)

2 cups grape tomatoes, cut in halves

½ cup fresh basil leaves, finely chopped

Salt and pepper to taste

COOK'S NOTES: Black-eyed peas that are sold in the fresh produce section (packaged in sealed plastic bags or loose in plastic tubs) are preferred; these peas are presoaked and partially cooked.

1. Bring large saucepan with enough water to cover sugar snap peas to boil on high heat. Add sugar snap peas and cook 1–2 minutes, or until cooked tender-crisp. Drain and refresh with cold water. Remove strings, if needed. Cut in half crosswise on diagonal. Set aside.

2. In large, deep skillet, heat oil on medium-high heat. Add shallots and cook until starting to soften, about 1 minute. Reduce heat to medium and add garlic; cook 30 seconds. Add black-eyed peas and heat thoroughly, about 3 minutes. Stir in sugar snap peas and toss; cook about 30 seconds. Remove from heat. Add tomatoes and basil; gently toss. Season to taste with salt and pepper.

YIELD: 4 SERVINGS

NUTRITIONAL INFORMATION (PER SERVING): Calories 220; fat calories 40.5; total fat 4.5 grams; sat fat 0 grams; cholesterol 0 milligrams; sodium 310 milligrams; total carbohydrates 34 grams; fiber 8 grams; sugars 5 grams; protein 11 grams; vitamin A IUs 15%; vitamin C 35%; calcium 4%; iron 30%.

potato

CREAMER PURPLE, PURPLE

CREAMER RED, RED

CREAMER RUBY GOLD

CREAMER WHITE, WHITE

CREAMER YELLOW DUTCH

FINGERLING FRENCH

FINGERLING PURPLE PERUVIAN

FINGERLING RUBY CRESCENT

FINGERLING RUSSIAN BANANA

RUSSET

YUKON GOLD

PERHAPS POTATOES ARE THE ULTIMATE COMFORT FOOD. Whether the texture of these luscious tubers is flaky or waxy, their rich, earthy flavor profile seems to be universally appealing. Eaten on their own or paired with other foods, potatoes are so popular that according to statistics from the U.S. Department of Agriculture, Americans eat 140 pounds per capita each year.

Varieties include a wide assortment of colors, shapes, and sizes. Small waxy spuds (rounded or oblong), generally called creamers, can have yellow, red, purple, or tan skins. More mature, they drop their "creamer" label and are dubbed with an abbreviated title. For example, creamer red (sometimes labeled baby red) become red when larger than a golf ball.

Fingerlings, heirloom varieties that are often elongated or digit-shaped, have light tan, red, gold, purple, or red skins. Larger, oblong potatoes, such as russets or Yukon Golds have flakier, less waxy consistencies when cooked.

There are hundreds of potato varieties. Below are some of the most popular ones.

CREAMER PURPLE, PURPLE
Creamers are smaller than 2 inches long. Somewhat round or oblong with fine-textured blue skin and deep purple flesh (some have purple rings dispersed in cream-colored flesh). Purple are larger than creamer specifications. ■ *Bold, sweet taste. Texture is waxy but flakier than red potatoes.*

CREAMER RED, RED
Rounded to oblong with smooth red skin. Creamers generally less than 2 inches long. Red are larger than creamer specifications. ■ *Low starch, firm flesh with waxy texture. Slightly sweet. Hold together well in cooking.*

CREAMER RUBY GOLD
Similar to red potato in appearance but with yellow flesh. Generally oblong, about 2 inches long. ■ *Very waxy texture. Flavor is buttery, similar to yellow Dutch.*

CREAMER WHITE, WHITE
Oblong with very pale tan skin and white flesh. Creamers are less than 2 inches long. White larger than creamer specifications. ■ *Milder flavor profile than russet with waxy texture (less waxy than red).*

CREAMER YELLOW DUTCH
Yellow skin with yellow flesh. Generally oblong, about 2 inches long. ■ *Waxy texture with buttery flavor.*

FINGERLING FRENCH
Small, elongated and almost knob-free, with light red skin and bright yellow flesh. ■ *Waxy texture and taste similar to red potato.*

FINGERLING PURPLE PERUVIAN
Small, oblong with brownish-purple skin. Flesh has purple rings dispersed in creamy white flesh. ■ *Bold, delectably sweet flavor. Texture is somewhat flaky.*

FINGERLING RUBY CRESCENT
Small, slightly crescent shape with pink skin and yellow flesh. ■ *Distinct chestnut-like flavor. Firm, waxy texture.*

FINGERLING RUSSIAN BANANA
Small, knobby, elongated but pudgy. Pale tan skin with dark yellow flesh. Most popular fingerling. ■ *Waxy but flakier than red, buttery rich flavor, with pleasing "green vegetable" taste.*

RUSSET
Long, slightly rounded. Thick, dark brown skin and low-moisture, white flesh. High starch content. ■ *Earthy aroma and flaky, fluffy texture. When grown organically, has more earthy sweetness.*

YUKON GOLD
Oblong with yellow or tan skin. Flesh is golden yellow and can give the impression that it's been augmented with butter. ■ *Sweet flavor with slight earthiness. Moderately flakey in texture.*

BUYING AND STORING

Choose potatoes that are wrinkle free, without green tinges, sprouts, or cracks. Store in dark, airy, cool location. Place in an open paper sack or basket, not a sealed plastic bag. Do not store in container with onions. Do not refrigerate for a long period of time because starch in potato will gradually convert to sugar, causing a disagreeable taste, especially in russets or Yukon Golds. Red potatoes can be stored in refrigerator.

CREAMERS AND REGULAR
Domestic: *year-round*
Global: *none*

FINGERLING
Domestic: *September—March*
Global: *none*

PREP

Wash thoroughly with cold water and dry. Solanine, green patches in skin or flesh, is a natural toxin that occurs when potatoes are exposed to bright light. Remove all green areas before cooking. Russets and Yukon Golds are generally peeled, except when baked. Use vegetable peeler or paring knife. Most often other varieties are cooked skin on.

Russet

Yukon Gold

Creamer Yellow Dutch

USE

Use waxier potatoes when you want them to retain shape when cooked. Use flakier potatoes when starchy taste is desired. For example, add waxy red potatoes to soup, and they hold their shape. Add flakier potatoes, such as russets, to soup, and they will fall apart and starch will thicken broth. Essentially, all potatoes can be baked, broiled, roasted, grilled, simmered, steamed, sautéed, or boiled. (See chart on page 247 to determine waxy or flaky characteristics.)

NUTRITIONAL INFORMATION

1 small potato is a significant source of potassium, niacin, magnesium, and vitamin B$_6$; excellent source of vitamin C.

SERVING SUGGESTIONS

Rustic caldo verde: Here's soup that's a snap. Soften 2–3 minced garlic cloves in a little olive oil on medium heat in a large pot. Add 2 pounds peeled potatoes cut into chunks, along with 8 cups vegetable or chicken broth. Boil on high heat; reduce to medium-low and simmer, covered, until fork tender, about 20 minutes; partially mash potatoes with potato masher. Remove ribs from ³/₄ pound kale (see Prep, page 201) and cut into bite-size pieces. Add to potatoes and simmer covered until barely tender. Season to taste with salt and pepper. Offer optional hot sauce on the side.

Gold

Fingerlings supreme: Steam skin-on fingerlings over simmering water until fork tender (time will vary according to size). Toss with fruity olive oil or truffle oil (enough to lightly coat). Season to taste with coarse salt, such as kosher or *fleur de sel.* If desired, crisp lightly on rimmed baking sheet in 400-degree oven.

Skin-on rustic red mash: Boil red potatoes in water to cover until fork tender; drain. Add sour cream and butter to taste and mash. Stir in thinly sliced green onions (include dark green stalks) and salt and pepper to taste.

Grill-roasted russets or Yukon Golds: Cut clean unpeeled potatoes in half lengthwise. Brush cut side with olive oil, sprinkle with seasoned salt, and top with sprig of fresh rosemary or thyme. Place cut side (herb side) down on oiled and heated grill. Grill until fork tender, about 10 minutes. Watch to prevent burning; move spuds to cooler location on grill as needed.

red, white, and blue potato salad

An assortment of creamers (baby potatoes) cooked skin-on create a colorful dish. This salad uses a patriotic mix of red, white, and blue spuds, but if you prefer, you can substitute fingerling varieties, adjusting cooking time as needed. Or for a flakier version, use russet or Yukon Gold potatoes, peeling them when cool enough to handle; cut into bite-size chunks before tossing with dressing.

White

Red

Purple

White Creamer

Red Creamer

Purple Creamer

4 sprigs fresh thyme

1 sprig fresh rosemary

1 cup dry white wine

2 medium cloves garlic

½ pound clean red creamer (baby) potatoes

½ pound clean purple creamer (baby) potatoes

½ pound clean white creamer (baby) potatoes

1 tablespoon salt, kosher preferred, plus more for dressing

¼ cup white wine vinegar

1 tablespoon whole-grain mustard

2 teaspoons salt, kosher preferred

Freshly ground black pepper, to taste

½ cup extra-virgin olive oil

2 stalks celery, trimmed, thinly sliced

2 tablespoons minced Italian parsley

2 green onions, thinly sliced, include dark green stalks

1. Place thyme, rosemary, white wine, and garlic in large saucepan or Dutch oven. Cut potatoes into 1-inch cubes, leaving skin intact. Add to pan. Add cold water to cover by 1 inch. Add salt.

2. Bring to boil on high heat. Reduce heat to medium and boil gently until potatoes are tender, about 10–12 minutes.

3. Meanwhile, prepare dressing: in large bowl, combine vinegar, mustard, salt, and pepper. Whisk in olive oil in thin stream.

4. Drain potatoes and discard herbs. Gently toss warm potatoes with enough dressing to coat. Add celery and toss. Cool. Add parsley and green onions; gently toss. Taste and correct seasoning if needed. Serve at room temperature.

YIELD: 6 SERVINGS

NUTRITIONAL INFORMATION (PER SERVING):
Calories 290; fat calories 162; total fat 18 grams; sat fat 2.5 grams; cholesterol 0 milligrams; sodium 650 milligrams; total carbohydrates 23 grams; fiber 2 grams; sugars 2 grams; protein 3 grams; vitamin A IUs 10%; vitamin C 50%; calcium 2%; iron 8%.

pumpkin

BABY (ORANGE, WHITE)

COMMON (ORANGE)

FAIRYTALE

MINI (ORANGE, WHITE)

SWEET, PIE

WHITE

AS WITH OTHER WINTER SQUASH, pumpkin's interior is hollow. The seeds become edible only when removed and roasted. The showy shell is hard enough to use as a container for several types of dishes, such as soup, stew, rice pilaf, or chili. But perhaps the pumpkin is most recognized for its potential as carved jack-o'-lanterns, the symbol of Halloween.

For pie filling, look for orange pumpkins identified as "sweet" or "pie" pumpkins. They have thicker, sweeter flesh and are intended for cooking rather than carving. Pumpkins in generally have rather bland flavor profiles and rely on spice blends, such as clove, ginger, cinnamon, and nutmeg, to add signature holiday tastes.

BUYING AND STORING

Avoid those with cracks or soft spots (look carefully at stem area). Store at room temperature for up to 1 month.

ALL VARIETIES, EXCEPT CINDERELLA
Domestic: *September–November*
Global: *none*

FAIRYTALE
Domestic: *October*
Global: *none*

PREP

To cook flesh, cut off stem end with sturdy knife. Scoop out membranes and seeds with sturdy spoon (reserve seeds for roasting, if desired). If not baking whole, cut pumpkin into wedges, then peel and cut into chunks.

USE

Can be cooked or used ornamentally, either whole or as containers. To cook flesh, boil or braise trimmed chunks in small amount of water or broth or steam trimmed chunks; purée, if desired. To use as container, scoop out seeds and membranes. Use raw or bake on sturdy rimmed baking sheet at 325 degrees until flesh is tender. Or pumpkin chunks can be brushed with vegetable oil or olive oil, then grilled (see Serving Suggestions).

NUTRITIONAL INFO

1 cup is a significant source of vitamin C and potassium; excellent source of vitamin A.

White

Fairytale

Sweet

BABY
(orange, white)
Orange skin, about softball size.
■ *Generally used for ornamental purposes or as containers. When baked, flesh has subtle sweet potato taste and is fairly dry.*

FAIRYTALE
Deeply fluted light orange, almost-tan skin. Flesh is bright orange. ■ *Primarily used for ornamental purposes. Flesh can be pulpy and stringy.*

COMMON
(orange)
Bright orange skin and flesh. Fairly thin walls make them suitable for carving. ■ *Mild, fairly bland taste.*

MINI
(orange, white)
Orange or white skin, smaller than softball size, generally baseball size. Moderately fluted.
■ *Use ornamentally or as containers. Flesh is faintly sweet and can be stringy.*

SWEET, PIE
These cooking varieties have shallower fluting and are more spherical. They have thicker walls and are generally smaller than carving pumpkins; when comparing same-sized pumpkins, cooking pumpkins feel heavier than common carving pumpkins. ■ *Deeper flavor and added sweetness.*

WHITE
Most commonly basketball size with creamy-white skin.
■ *Very mild flavor. Generally used for ornamental purposes.*

SERVING SUGGESTIONS

Pretty stew: Prepare beef stew and bake large, whole pumpkin (see Prep) on sturdy rimmed baking sheet until just barely fork tender, about 25 minutes. Spoon stew into hollowed-out pumpkin. Bake 10–15 minutes in 350-degree oven, or until pumpkin flesh is tender. When serving, scrape a small portion of pumpkin flesh into each portion.

Mini-pumpkin containers: Use them raw (seeds and membranes removed) to hold cold dishes such as spinach dip, or bake to hold individual portions of warm dishes. To bake, cut off top, and remove seeds and membranes. Brush interior with melted butter and honey. Replace top and place in roasting pan with 1 inch of water. Bake at 325 degrees for 30 minutes or until flesh is tender. Invert before filling to remove any liquid. Fill with pumpkin soup, butternut squash soup, rice pilaf, creamed scallops, stir-fried vegetables, or garlic mashed potatoes. They are also delicious filled with bread stuffing broiled just long enough to lightly brown top.

Pumpkinseeds roasted: Rinse strings from 2 cups pumpkinseeds and pat dry. Mix seeds with 2 tablespoons vegetable oil and 1 teaspoon coarse salt; stir well to coat. Spread in single layer on rimmed baking sheet and bake 12–15 minutes in 350-degree oven. Taste; add more salt if desired. For variation, use olive oil in place of vegetable oil and add 1 tablespoon each dried rosemary and basil along with salt, or add 2 teaspoons chili powder along with salt, or add 1½ tablespoons curry powder and a pinch of cayenne pepper along with salt.

Grill: Cut peeled and seeded pumpkin wedges into 1-inch-thick slices. Brush with a combination of olive oil, minced garlic, and chopped fresh rosemary. Grill, turning as needed with spatula, and basting, until just tender. Sprinkle with minced fresh basil or cilantro and a squeeze of fresh lime juice.

Common

Baby Orange

Baby White

radicchio, also
italian chicory, red chicory

COMMON

TREVISO

OVER THE PAST TWENTY YEARS OR SO, American chefs have embraced radicchio, featuring it in everything from appetizers to soups, salads, and entrées. There are several varieties of this colorful member of the chicory tribe, including the most common, Chioggia, a version that looks like a round head of wine-red cabbage. Another variety, Treviso, is elongated and has a milder, less bitter flavor profile.

The leaves have a bracing bitterness and pleasing crunch. Often we see bite-size pieces jumbled with milder greens in bagged salad mixtures. The bright red color lends a visual perkiness to the package, plus its wake-up taste adds flavor interest. Cooking radicchio gives a softer side to its bitterness, adding a hint of subtle sweetness.

Common

Treviso

BUYING AND STORING

Choose heads with bold red color, avoiding those with browning, blemishes, or holes. The base (root end) should be firm. To store whole, wrap dry radicchio in plastic and place in refrigerator vegetable drawer 1–2 weeks. For using raw, rinse in cold water, dry, wrap in clean cloth or paper towels, and place in plastic bag in crisper drawer. Generally, warm-weather growing conditions increase bitterness, as does lengthy storage.

Domestic: *May–January*
Global: *February–April*

PREP

Remove outer leaf or leaves, if they are discolored. To cook, cut off at base (root end) and trim leaves as needed. To grill, cut into lengthwise quarters leaving core intact. To use in salad, tear into bite-sized pieces.

USE

Use raw or cooked. Can be braised, grilled, roasted, or sautéed. When leaves are shaped like cupped cabbage leaves, use as edible containers for soft cheeses, dips, or fruit salad. Add a little chopped radicchio to risotto or minestrone soup.

NUTRITIONAL INFO

Significant source of vitamin C.

SERVING SUGGESTIONS

Great grilled: Preheat grill. Cut into lengthwise quarters, leaving core intact. Toss with enough extra-virgin olive oil to lightly coat leaves. Grill over medium fire, turning to caramelize and to very lightly char each side. Place on platter and season to taste with salt and pepper. If desired, sprinkle with grated Parmesan or pecorino cheese, or drizzle with a little balsamic vinegar.

Radicchio bruschetta: Cut into lengthwise quarters. Place cut side down on work surface and cut into thin, crosswise strips. Heat 2 tablespoons olive oil in large, deep skillet on medium-high heat. Add 1 onion (chopped) and lightly brown, stirring occasionally, about 6 minutes. Add 2 tablespoons balsamic vinegar, radicchio, salt, and pepper. Cook until radicchio is lightly browned and soft, about 4 minutes. Place on toasted slices of French bread spread with goat cheese and serve as appetizers.

Quick side dish: Sautéed radicchio with bacon and pecans teams beautifully with pork, game, or poultry. Cook 4 slices bacon (chopped) until crisp in large, deep skillet. Remove with slotted spoon and drain on paper towel. Pour off all but 1 tablespoon drippings. Add 1 tablespoon olive oil and heat on medium high. Add 1 head radicchio cut into crosswise strips (see Radicchio bruschetta, above). Cook until wilted, stirring occasionally, about 6 minutes. Add 3 tablespoons sherry vinegar or balsamic vinegar and cook 2 minutes, stirring frequently. Add ½ cup toasted pecans and bacon; toss. Add salt and pepper.

radicchio and pine nut salad

If you can't find both radicchio varieties, use an equal amount of either variety in this elegant salad. If you prefer, use toasted walnuts instead of pine nuts.

1 head Chioggia (round head) radicchio

1 head Treviso (elongated head) radicchio

½ medium red onion, thinly sliced

4 tablespoons olive oil

4 tablespoons balsamic vinegar

3 ounces toasted pine nuts (see Cook's Notes)

½ cup crumbled blue cheese

Salt and pepper

COOK'S NOTES: To toast pine nuts, place in small skillet on medium-high heat. Lightly brown, shaking skillet handle to redistribute nuts. Watch carefully because pine nuts burn easily. Cool.

1. Soak radicchio in ice cold water for 10 minutes. Drain, chop, and place in salad bowl. Add onion and toss.

2. In small bowl, whisk oil and vinegar together. Drizzle over salad and toss. Add pine nuts and cheese; toss. Add salt and pepper to taste; serve.

YIELD: 8 SERVINGS

NUTRITIONAL INFORMATION (PER SERVING): Calories 200; fat calories 162; total fat 18 grams; sat fat 4 grams; cholesterol 15 milligrams; sodium 350 milligrams; total carbohydrates 5 grams; fiber less than 1 gram; sugars 2 grams; protein 5 grams; vitamin A IUs 4%; vitamin C 6%; calcium 8%; iron 6%.

radish

BLACK

COMMON (RED)

DAIKON (JAPANESE)

EASTER EGG

FRENCH BREAKFAST

ICICLE

LO BOK (KOREAN)

WATERMELON

SOME RADISHES ARE PRETTY AND PETITE, covered in skin that is crimson, purple, or white. With alluring names such as Easter Egg, French Breakfast or Icicle, these small table radishes vary in shape, from plump spheres to skinny, carrot-like formations. Common red radishes are part of this group, too. Consistently crisp, these small root vegetables have flavor profiles that vary from mild to moderately peppery. The green leaves that spring from their tops are edible. They are peppery and can be cooked or used raw mixed with other milder greens in salad.

Black radishes and tricolor watermelon radishes are midsized, roughly 3–5 inches in diameter. They are shaped like turnips, and their flavor profiles range from mild turniplike tastes for the watermelon radishes to the biting assertiveness of the black variety. Greens are seldom sold attached.

Larger radishes such as daikon and lo bok, sometimes classified as Asian radishes, can be more than 15 inches long. They can be used interchangeably in recipes.

BUYING AND STORING

Look for firm radishes without cracks or soft spots. If greens are attached, they should be crisp. With table radishes, if they are large for their variety, the interior may be pithy.

If purchased with greens attached, trim leaves before storage, leaving about ½ inch of stems attached to radish. Refrigerate separately, unwashed, in plastic bags in crisper drawer. Refrigerate without leaves up to 14 days; larger radishes, such as black, watermelon, daikon, and lo bok, can often be stored longer. Greens deteriorate quickly; use within 2 days.

Domestic: *year-round*
Global: *none*

PREP

Wash thoroughly in cold running water. For small table radishes, trim and discard roots. Trim stem ends or leave a small portion of stem to use as a "handle" when serving raw as finger food. Serve whole, or slice. For black radish, daikon, lo bok, or watermelon radish, peel with vegetable peeler. Slice, dice, or shred.

USE

Table and watermelon radishes are generally served raw but can be delicious when cooked, either braised, sautéed, or simmered. Black radish is most often salted, then drained to take away some of its assertive flavor; it is then served raw as a condiment or as crudités. Or dice, blanch, and serve as vegetable side dish. Daikon and lo bok are most often used raw or pickled but can be cooked in stews, soups, and braises.

Icicle

Easter Egg

French Breakfast

BLACK

Dull black or dark brown skin. Medium-large, baseball- to softball-sized and turnip-shaped. ■ *Sharp pungent bite. Crisp but drier than other varieties.*

COMMON (RED)

Round or oval table radishes with bright red skin and white flesh. ■ *Crisp with varying degrees of peppery bite.*

DAIKON

(Japanese)

Long, tapering carrot-like shape (most often sold trimmed). Large. Can be 1–2 feet long with 3–5-inch diameter. Creamy white skin and flesh. ■ *Juicy with flavor profile that is more peppery than table radishes but milder than black radish.*

EASTER EGG

Group of small table radishes that vary in vibrant colored skin: pink, purple, red, white, and violet. Generally spherical. All have white flesh. ■ *Crisp and very moderately peppery.*

FRENCH BREAKFAST

Oblong table radishes with scarlet skin that is white at tip. ■ *Crisp and moderately peppery.*

ICICLE

Tapered, carrot-like table radishes with white skin and flesh. ■ *Crisp and very moderately peppery.*

LO BOK

(Korean)

White with green shoulders. Similar to daikon, but less elongated and plumper at the "waist." Large, generally 6–15 inches long and 4–6 inches in diameter. ■ *Crisp and peppery.*

WATERMELON

Turnip-shaped with pale green skin and interior color similar to watermelons (bright fuchsia surrounded with white). Medium size, generally 3–4 inches diameter. ■ *Crisp and mild turniplike taste.*

Lo Bok

Daikon

NUTRITIONAL INFO

1 cup is a good source of vitamin C.

SERVING SUGGESTIONS

Crudités with chic salt option: Place several varieties of table radishes in a bowl of ice water. For optional dipping, provide small bowls of different types of sea salts, such as *fleur de sel* and Danish smoked sea salt.

Watermelon radish salad: In medium bowl, mix ¼ cup seasoned rice vinegar with 3 tablespoons sugar; stir to dissolve. Add 1 teaspoon salt and 2 tablespoons water; stir to combine. Cut 2 peeled watermelon radishes in half lengthwise, then cut into very thin slices; add to bowl and toss. Chill 30–40 minutes. Serve topped with toasted sesame seeds and thinly sliced green onion.

Roast duck with radishes: Toss table radishes with olive oil and season lightly with coarse salt. Place next to duck during last 25 minutes of roasting.

Cold "steak" salad with radishes: In medium bowl, whisk ½ cup olive oil or vegetable oil into ¼ cup red-wine vinegar. Add salt and pepper to taste, plus 1 cup sliced table radishes, 1 tablespoon chopped fresh parsley, and ¼ cup crumbled feta cheese; toss. Marinate at room temperature 30 minutes. Place handfuls of mixed baby greens on 4 plates. Top with thin slices of cold, cooked steak, pork, or chicken. Toss radish mixture and spoon over salads. Garnish with olives, if desired.

pickled daikon and maui onion relish

These daikon pickles are delicious eaten out of hand on their own or spooned next to grilled or miso-marinated broiled salmon or cold roast pork. Or for a small salad, spoon 1 or 2 daikon slices along with some onion over a handful of mild baby lettuces, drizzling a little brine over top; garnish with toasted sesame seeds.

1½ cups rice vinegar

1 cup sugar

1 tablespoon soy sauce

1 (¾-inch) knob fresh ginger, peeled, cut into thin slices

1 medium-sized sweet onion such as Maui, peeled, cut in half lengthwise, cut into thin slices

1½ pounds daikon, peeled, thinly sliced crosswise

1. Place vinegar, sugar, soy, and ginger in saucepan. Bring to boil on high heat.

2. Meanwhile, place onion and daikon in large, heatproof bowl. Pour hot vinegar mixture over vegetables. Cool.

3. Place in 2 (1-quart) canning jars. Seal and refrigerate at least 24 hours, or up to 3 weeks.

YIELD: ABOUT 2 QUARTS, ABOUT 20 SERVINGS

NUTRITIONAL INFORMATION (PER SERVING): Calories 30; fat calories 0; total fat 0 grams; sat fat 0 grams; cholesterol 0 milligrams; sodium 30 milligrams; total carbohydrates 7 grams; fiber less than 1 gram; sugars 5 grams; protein 0 grams; vitamin A IUs 0%; vitamin C 20%; calcium 2%; iron 2%.

rapini, also rabe, broccoli raab, italian broccoli, american gai lan

JAGGED-EDGED DARK GREEN LEAVES top rapini's thin stalks. At first glance, you might mistake it for broccoli. Look closer. The stalks are more slender than broccoli, plus they are capped with only the occasional cluster of compact buds. Sometimes those buds open into yellow blossoms.

And the taste is very different from broccoli. The flavor is fairly assertive: bitter combined with green vegetal tones. Until just the past few years, in America it was limited to Italian and Asian cuisines, designed for taste buds that appreciate up-front bitter elements. In either cuisine, it's paired with other assertive flavors, such as chile and garlic or ginger.

Rapini

BUYING AND STORING

Avoid rapini with soggy or yellowed leaves. Leaves should be deep green and crisp. To store, place unwashed, unwrapped rapini in vegetable drawer in refrigerator for 3–5 days.

Domestic: *year-round*
Global: *none*

PREP

Just before using, rinse in cold running water; shake off excess water. If stalk base is large and tough, cut base portion off. Generally stalk base is tender. In that case, trim off a very small portion. Prepare whole or cut into bite-sized pieces.

USE

Eat cooked. Steam, boil, sauté, microwave, or bake. Rapini adds lively note to bland foods, such as tofu, pasta, or potatoes. Good in stir-fries, soups, quiches, or omelets.

NUTRITIONAL INFO

Excellent source of vitamins A and C.

SERVING SUGGESTIONS

Steam or micro: Steam or microwave in covered microwave-safe container with a little water until tender-crisp. Drain (if needed) and toss with prepared Asian garlic-chile sauce to taste. Or toss with extra-virgin olive oil, salt, and pepper.

Stir-fry quickie: Cut off leaves and set aside. Cut stems into 1½-inch pieces. Heat 1–2 tablespoons vegetable or olive oil in wok on high heat. Add minced garlic and stir-fry 20–30 seconds (do not brown). Add stems and stir-fry until cooked tender-crisp, about 3 minutes. Add leaves and stir-fry until wilted. Season with salt and pepper. Serve over steamed rice and top with Ginger Dipping Sauce, page 192.

Boiled and buttered: Cut rapini into 2-inch pieces. Bring pot of water to boil. Add rapini and boil until tender-crisp, about 6–8 minutes. Drain and toss with butter and chopped Italian parsley. Season with salt or garlic salt and pepper. Top with grated Parmesan cheese.

pasta with rapini, mushrooms, and pecorino

Teaming rapini with pasta and chile is a classic combination. In this version, cremini or portobellini mushrooms along with a generous topping of pecorino cheese delectably balance rapini's bold flavor.

8 ounces spaghetti or linguine

2 tablespoons olive oil

2 medium garlic cloves, minced

6 ounces cremini or portobellini mushrooms, sliced

½ pound rapini, cut into 1-inch pieces

¾ cup chicken broth, reduced-sodium preferred,

plus additional if needed

Salt and freshly ground black pepper to taste

Pinch of dried red pepper flakes

GARNISH: ½ cup grated pecorino cheese

1. Bring large pot of water to boil on high heat. Cook pasta al dente, according to package directions. Drain.

2. Meanwhile, heat oil in Dutch oven or large, deep skillet on medium-high heat. Add garlic and cook, stirring, about 20 seconds (do not brown). Add mushrooms and cook, stirring frequently, until browned and all liquid evaporates. Remove mushrooms from pan and set aside.

3. Return pan to heat. Add rapini and broth. Bring to boil on high heat. Reduce heat to medium-low, cover and simmer until rapini is tender, about 8 minutes (add more broth, if needed). Remove lid; add mushrooms and stir. Add salt, pepper, and red pepper flakes. Stir and taste. Adjust seasoning as needed. Add drained pasta and toss until heated through.

4. Divide among 4 plates. Top each with pecorino cheese. Serve.

YIELD: 4 SERVINGS

NUTRITIONAL INFORMATION (PER SERVING): Calories 330; fat calories 90; total fat 10 grams; sat fat 2 grams; cholesterol 5 milligrams; sodium 440 milligrams; total carbohydrates 42 grams; fiber 2 grams; sugars 3 grams; protein 19 grams; vitamin A IUs 70%; vitamin C 90%; calcium 10%; iron 20%.

rhubarb, also pieplant

FIELD-GROWN RHUBARB LOOKS TROPICAL, with its long fuchsia stalks shaded below leaves so enormous they look like deep-green elephant ears. But rhubarb doesn't grow in the steamy tropics. It prefers colder conditions. When it's grown in hothouses, the flavor is milder and the stalks are a less vibrant pink, the leaves a yellow-green. Experts argue about which is best.

Rhubarb is revered for the sour perkiness it adds to sweet or savory dishes. Only the stalks should be eaten; the poisonous leaves contain oxalic acid and should be discarded.

BUYING AND STORING

Choose stalks that are firm and crisp with glossy skin that is free of blemishes. Wrap, unwashed, in plastic and refrigerate 3–7 days. Or wash and chop, place in freezer containers, and freeze up to 3 months (see Freezing, page 310).

Domestic:
  Hothouse: *December–March*
  Field-grown: *March–October*
Global: *none*

PREP

Remove and discard leaves; trim off bottom end of stalk. Wash in cold water and if stringy, peel. Cut into 1/2-inch pieces. Because of its mouth-puckering tartness, rhubarb is generally teamed with sugar and cooked. Often it's combined with strawberries, apples, or ginger. It can be paired with game such as duck or venison in savory dishes. Or, in sweet dishes, it's used for pies, jams, sauces, cobblers, crisps, and ice cream topping.

NUTRITIONAL INFO

1 cup diced is a significant source of vitamin C, calcium, and potassium.

SERVING SUGGESTIONS

Rhubarb sauce: In medium, nonreactive saucepan, combine 1 cup water and 1 cup sugar; bring to boil on high heat. Add 4 cups rhubarb cut into 1/2-inch pieces; reduce heat to medium. Simmer, stirring frequently, for 4–6 minutes. Cool. If desired, stir in 1 cup fresh raspberries. Spoon over cheesecake, pound cake, ice cream, or rice pudding. Makes 4 cups.

Fast appetizers: Use Rhubarb sauce on savory hors d'oeuvres. Top thin slices of French baguette with thinly sliced smoked duck breast, ham, or lamb and add a dollop of sauce.

Rhubarb marmalade: Place 2 1/2 cups roughly chopped rhubarb and 1 1/2 cups orange marmalade in heavy-bottomed, medium-sized nonreactive saucepan. Simmer on medium-low until rhubarb softens, about 10 minutes. Mash with potato masher. Stir in 2 cups sliced strawberries and ¼ cup sugar; bring to boil on medium-high heat. Boil 1 minute and remove from heat. Cool and serve on pancakes, waffles, or toast. Makes 3 cups.

rhubarb crisp

Crunchy, sugar-topped crisp is one of the best ways to show off the sour cherry flavors of rhubarb. It's irresistible warm, but even at room temperature it's delicious. If preferred substitute chopped walnuts of slivered almonds for pecans.

6 cups (½-inch chunks) fresh trimmed rhubarb

⅔ cup sugar

2 tablespoons all-purpose flour

1 tablespoon butter, melted

1 teaspoon minced orange or tangerine zest, colored part of peel

1 teaspoon ground cinnamon

TOPPING

1 cup packed golden brown sugar

½ cup all-purpose flour

6 tablespoons butter, cut into 6 pieces

⅔ cup coarsely chopped pecans, toasted (see Cook's Notes)

COOK'S NOTES: To toast nuts, place on baking sheet and toast in 350-degree oven until lightly browned. Watch carefully because nuts burn easily.

1. Preheat oven to 375 degrees. In large bowl, combine rhubarb, sugar, flour, melted butter, zest, and cinnamon. Toss to combine and place in 9-inch square baking pan. Bake in preheated oven 10 minutes.

2. Prepare topping: in food processor fitted with metal blade, combine brown sugar and flour; pulse to combine. Add butter and pulse until crumbly and butter is cut into tiny pieces. Stir in nuts. Sprinkle over rhubarb mixture.

3. Bake until browned and bubbly, about 25–30 minutes. Serve warm or room temperature. Accompany with ice cream or sweetened whipped cream.

YIELD: 6 SERVINGS

NUTRITIONAL INFORMATION (PER SERVING): Calories 510; fat calories 207; total fat 23 grams; sat fat 9 grams; cholesterol 35 milligrams; sodium 20 milligrams; total carbohydrates 76 grams; fiber 4 grams; sugars 60 grams; protein 4 grams; vitamin A IUs 10%; vitamin C 15%; calcium 15%; iron 10%.

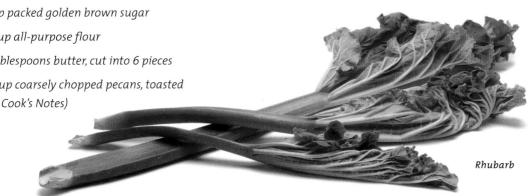

Rhubarb

rutabaga, also swede

MOST THINK OF THIS JOLLY VEGETABLE as a softball-sized turnip. True, that's how it looks, with its yellowed white skin shaded purple or reddish pink at the stem end. But in fact, it's a cross between savoy cabbage and turnip. When compared to turnips, its flavor profile is earthier, with a peppery taste that's balanced with pronounced sweetness.

Rutabagas have a dense texture similar to a red potato, and they're often coated with a thin layer of wax to prevent dehydration and extend shelf life.

BUYING AND STORING

Choose those that are heavy for their size and free of cracks, shriveling, or soft spots. They should feel firm. Refrigerate, unwashed, in plastic bag up to 3 weeks.

Domestic: *year-round*
Global: *year-round*

PREP

Scrub well under running water. Cut off top and bottom. Place cut side down on cutting board. Cut into quarters from top to bottom. Peel off skin with paring knife. Cut into chunks, wedges, slices, or cubes, as desired.

USE

Peeled and sliced rutabaga can be served raw with a dip or arranged with other vegetables on a crudités platter. To cook tender-crisp, boil, simmer, roast, or steam. Blanched for about 4 minutes and cooled, they can be covered with tempura batter and deep-fried.

NUTRITIONAL INFO

1 cup is an excellent source of vitamin C and a significant source of potassium.

SERVING SUGGESTIONS

Cheesy blues: Cut 2 pounds peeled rutabaga into $1/2$-inch dice. Cover with water and boil until tender-crisp, about 15 minutes. Meanwhile, prepare cheese sauce: in medium saucepan, melt 1 tablespoon butter on medium heat. Stir in 1 tablespoon all-purpose flour; cook, stirring, for 1 minute (do not brown). Off heat, stir in $3/4$ cup milk. Return to heat and bring to simmer, stirring constantly until mixture thickens. Remove from heat and stir in $1/2$ cup crumbled blue cheese and freshly ground black pepper to taste. Drain rutabaga and place in serving dish. Drizzle sauce on top.

Rutabaga

Rutabaga with herbs and buttered crumbs:
Brown ²/₃ cup fresh bread crumbs in skillet with 2 tablespoons butter, tossing frequently to brown on all sides; when toasted, place on plate and set aside. Cut 1¹/₂ pounds peeled rutabaga into ¹/₂-inch chunks. Cover with water and boil until tender-crisp, about 20 minutes. Drain and toss with 2 tablespoons chopped chives, 1 tablespoon chopped fresh tarragon, and 2 tablespoons chopped Italian parsley. Season with salt and pepper. Place on serving dish and top with buttered bread crumbs.

Pickled along with carrots: In a large, nonreactive saucepan, place 1 cup rice vinegar, 1¹/₂ cups distilled white vinegar, 2¹/₂ cups water, and ³/₄ cup sugar. Bring to boil on high heat. Add 3 tablespoons chopped fresh ginger, 1 tablespoon salt (kosher preferred), 10 whole black peppercorns, 2 tablespoons celery seed, and 1 teaspoon mustard seeds. Reduce heat to medium; simmer 5 minutes. Remove from heat. Place 5 medium carrots (peeled, cut into 3-by–¹/₄-inch sticks) and 1 large rutabaga (peeled, cut into similar sticks) in heatproof container. Pour vinegar mixture over vegetables, covering completely. Chill. Use within 1 week.

salicornia, also sea bean, sea asparagus

SALTY AND AS CRUNCHY AS A PICKLE, salicornia grows next to the sea along marshes or tucked into cliff-side crevices. Some might mistake its appearance for seaweed, but it can't exist for long periods submerged in salt water. Thin but bushy, deep-green branches no larger than twine spring from a central stem. Generally the stem, approximately 4 inches long, supports 4–7 branches.

Native to the coast of Brittany in France, as well as the English coast salicornia is now grown on the shores of the Sea of Cortez in Mexico.

Salicornia

BUYING AND STORING

Look for bright green color; avoid any with discoloration or soft spots. Refrigerate, unwashed, in plastic bag in crisper drawer up to 1 week.
Domestic: *none*
Global: *year-round*

PREP

Before use, wash with cold water and pat dry. Trim off wiry roots at bottom. Cut into bite-sized "twiglets," except when using as garnish on large platter.

USE

Very salty. Omit salt from dish when using. Great in dishes that need salt and crunch, such as pasta, rice, or grains. It is a glorious garnish on seafood presentations. If cooked, sauté, stir-fry, or steam briefly.

NUTRITIONAL INFO

1/2 cup is a significant source of vitamin A.

SERVING SUGGESTIONS

Couscous boost: Omit salt from couscous. For 4 cups of ready-to-serve couscous, add 1/3 cup roughly chopped salicornia. Toss and garnish with salicornia branch.

Guacamole: Omit salt from guacamole. For two cups of guacamole, add ¼ cup roughly chopped salicornia and toss. Garnish with sprig of salicornia.

Marinated vegetable salad: In small bowl, whisk ⅓ cup freshly squeezed lemon juice, 2½ teaspoons sugar, 1 teaspoon chopped fresh basil and 1 clove garlic (minced). Whisk in ⅓ cup vegetable oil. On a medium platter or large plate with lip, place 1 large red tomato (sliced), 1 large yellow tomato (sliced), 1 large red onion (sliced), 1 medium hothouse cucumber (peeled and sliced), and 4 ounces salicornia (roughly chopped). Stir dressing and pour over vegetables. Cover and chill at least 2 hours but not more than 4 before serving.

Margarita salicornia gelatin shots: Boil 2 cups margarita mix. Stir in 6-ounce package lime gelatin; stir to dissolve. Add 1 cup cold margarita mix and 1 cup tequila; stir to combine. Stir in 2 ounces finely chopped salicornia. Pour into about 30 (1-ounce) plastic soufflé cups. Chill until set.

salsify, also oyster plant, oyster vegetable

THE VARIETY OF SALSIFY distributed in the United States looks like a long, muddy carrot, about 1–2 feet long and 1 inch in diameter. Generally they've been kept in cold storage, so rather than being topped with greens that would darken, they're trimmed.

Inside the brownish-black skin, the flesh is dense and grayish-white. To some, the taste is reminiscent of oysters. To others salsify offers the subtle flavors of artichokes and asparagus. Some say it has a slight coconut aftertaste, but nutty rather than sweet.

A white variety exists, but generally isn't available in supermarkets.

BUYING AND STORING

Salsify should be free of soft spots and firm (but not as firm as a carrot). Skin should completely cover flesh; broken skin is a sign of deterioration. Refrigerate, unwashed, loose in crisper drawer up to 14 days.

Domestic: *none*
Global: *year-round but with potential gaps in September*

PREP

Remove skin with paring knife or vegetable peeler; discard skin. If not used immediately, place in acidulated water. If boiling or roasting, cut into 1-inch slices. For frying, see Serving Suggestions.

USE

Eat cooked, simmered, boiled, roasted, or fried. Pairs well with meat or game. If simmering or boiling, use a squeeze of lemon juice in cooking water to prevent discoloration.

NUTRITIONAL INFO

1 cup is a significant source of vitamins C and B_6, riboflavin, and potassium.

Salsify

SERVING SUGGESTIONS

Salsi-fried: Cut peeled salsify into $2\frac{1}{2}$-inch-long segments. Cut into planks about $\frac{1}{3}$ inch thick. Heat canola or peanut oil to 360 degrees. Deep fry until tender and lightly browned. Season with coarse salt and freshly ground black pepper.

Mashed: Cut peeled salsify into 1-inch lengths. Boil until tender in water to cover, about 20–30 minutes. Drain and return to pan. Add butter, dollop of sour cream, or plain yogurt, and salt and pepper. Mash with potato masher. Top with chopped fresh parsley.

Soup: Add chunks of peeled salsify to your favorite vegetable soup.

salisify with béchamel sauce

This creamy salsify dish is a great accompaniment to roast beef. If you like, augment it with 1–2 tablespoons minced fresh Italian parsley or minced fresh tarragon when adding the salt and pepper to the sauce in Step 2.

2 pounds salsify, peeled, cut into 1-inch pieces
$\frac{1}{2}$ teaspoon lemon juice
$2\frac{1}{2}$ tablespoons butter, plus more for greasing pan
$3\frac{1}{2}$ tablespoons all-purpose flour

2 cups hot whole milk

½ teaspoon salt

½ teaspoon ground white pepper

1. Preheat oven to 350 degrees. Bring 1 quart water to boil on high heat in large saucepan. Add salsify and lemon juice; boil until tender. Drain well. Place in shallow, greased 1½-quart ovenproof dish.

2. In medium saucepan, melt butter on medium-high heat. Stir in flour. Cook 1–2 minutes, stirring constantly (do not brown).

Off heat, whisk in milk in thin steam. Return to heat and simmer 2–3 minutes, stirring frequently. Stir in salt and pepper.

3. Pour sauce over salsify. Bake in preheated oven for 20 minutes.

YIELD: 6 SERVINGS

NUTRITIONAL INFORMATION (PER SERVING): Calories 230; fat calories 72; total fat 8 grams; sat fat 4.5 grams; cholesterol 20 milligrams; sodium 260 milligrams; total carbohydrates 35 grams; fiber 5 grams; sugars 4 grams; protein 8 grams; vitamin A IUs 4%; vitamin C 20%; calcium 20%; iron 8%.

shallot

COPPER-TINGED BROWN SKIN, parchment thin and brittle, covers the shallot's milder-than-onion flesh. A member of the Allium (onion) genus, it's formed something like garlic (and is about the same size) but generally has only 2 or occasionally 3 or 4 large cloves. Unlike garlic, it isn't enclosed in a surrounding sheath, so the cloves easily separate from one another.

The flesh is off-white and can be tinged with purple. Arranged in onionlike layers, the shallot is sweeter than onion both in taste and aroma.

BUYING AND STORING

Look for dry, firm bulbs free of sprouts, soft spots, or mold. Store in cool, well-ventilated area up to 3 weeks.

Domestic: *year-round*
Global: *year-round*

PREP

Cut off ends, making a very shallow cut at root end so layers stay intact. Cut in half lengthwise. Use paring knife to peel: catch end of papery brown skin with knife, then holding skin, pull in opposite direction. Place cut-side down on work surface; slice, dice, or mince, as desired.

Shallot

USE

Substitute for onion when a subtler, sweeter flavor is preferred. Can be eaten raw and used in salads, relishes, and salsas. To cook, braise, sauté, simmer, or roast.

NUTRITIONAL INFO

1 cup is a significant source of vitamins A and C.

SERVING SUGGESTIONS

Roasted shallots: Halve and peel 12 shallots (see Prep), or, if small, leave whole and peel. Toss with 3 tablespoons balsamic vinegar, 3 tablespoons olive oil, and 2 teaspoons chopped fresh or dried thyme. Place in covered casserole; add 1 tablespoon vegetable broth. Bake in 375-degree oven for 30 minutes; uncover, toss, and return to oven uncovered. Bake until shallots caramelize, about 25–35 minutes. Season to taste with salt and pepper. Serve with vegetables or roast meats. Toss with pasta, or refrigerate and serve cold with salads or olives.

Egg salad, tuna salad, or salmon salad: Use chopped shallots instead of onion in mayonnaise-bound salads. Be sure to include some finely chopped fresh herbs, such as tarragon, Italian parsley, or basil.

Crisp fried shallots: Crispy bits of fried shallots add color and crunch to cold noodle or vegetable dishes or mixed green salads. Fry thinly sliced shallots in 1 inch of vegetable oil or canola oil (hot but not smoking) on medium-high heat until golden brown, stirring frequently. Don't crowd the pan; fry in batches if necessary. Remove shallot slices with slotted spoon and drain on paper towels. When cool, use as garnish just before serving.

garlic mashed potatoes with shallots

Minced shallots, fried until soft in butter, make a tantalizing addition to garlic mashed Yukon Gold potatoes. Shallots add a subtle sweet edge and appealing texture.

¼ cup (½ stick) butter

6 shallots, minced

2 large cloves garlic, minced

1 cup milk or cream, plus more as needed

6–7 medium Yukon Gold potatoes

Salt and white pepper to taste

1. Melt butter in medium saucepan on medium heat. Add shallots and garlic. Cook until soft, stirring occasionally, about 5 minutes (do not brown). Add milk or cream and bring to simmer. Set aside.

2. Peel potatoes. Cut into ½-inch slices. Place in pot and cover with water by 1 inch. Bring to boil on high heat; reduce heat to medium-low and simmer until fork tender, about 15–20 minutes. Drain and return to pot. Place on medium heat for 1–2 minutes to dry potatoes.

3. Remove from heat and add milk mixture. Mash with potato masher, adding more milk or cream to attain desired consistency. Taste and add salt and white pepper. Serve.

YIELD: 6–8 SERVINGS

NUTRITIONAL INFORMATION (PER SERVING): Calories 150; fat calories 63; total fat 7 grams; sat fat 4 grams; cholesterol 20 milligrams; sodium 320 milligrams; total carbohydrates 19 grams; fiber 1 grams; sugars 1 grams; protein 3 grams; vitamin A IUs 6%; vitamin C 30%; calcium 4%; iron 4%.

summer squash,
squash blossom

FAST GROWING AND PROLIFIC, summer squash have beguiling shapes and colors: bright yellow wonders with swanlike necks; disks with ornamental scalloped edges; or bold green batons that are slightly larger at the bottom than at the top.

Summer squash are harvested when seeds and skin are still tender. All are members of the gourd family, as are an eclectic group of squashlike gourds that have tougher, inedible skin. They don't fit into the winter squash category, because their seeds are edible. Plus, although exteriors are rigid, no heavy-duty equipment is needed to break through their rinds.

edible skin

BABY CROOKNECK, CROOKNECK

BABY GOLD BAR, GOLD BAR

BABY SCALLOPINI, SCALLOPINI

BABY SUMMER GREEN (PATTYPAN), SUMMER GREEN

BABY SUMMER YELLOW (PATTYPAN), SUMMER YELLOW

BABY ZUCCHINI, ZUCCHINI

EIGHT BALL

TATUMA

nonedible skin

CHAYOTE (MIRLITON)

CUCUZZA

MO QUA

PUL QUA (OPO)

WINTER MELON

squash blossoms

The avocado-shaped chayote is an example. Its furrowed skin, often an inviting celadon color, most often is tough and needs to be removed before eating, either raw or cooked. And although they are often referred to as "melons," many Asian squash fit into this category, such as winter melon, mo qua (fuzzy melon), and pul qua (opo).

BUYING AND STORING

For summer squash with edible skin, look for exteriors that are free of soft spots, nicks, or shriveling. Smaller, less mature squash will have fewer seeds and more delicate flavor. Large, overmature specimens can be woody and bitter. Store in plastic bag in crisper drawer of refrigerator up to 4 days; baby varieties are more perishable, so use within 2 days.

For squash with inedible skin (Asian squash, cucuzza, and chayote), look for product that is heavy for its size and free of bruises or shriveling. Store chayote, cucuzza, mo qua, and pul qua in plastic bag in crisper drawer (chayote, cucuzza, mo qua up to 7 days; pul qua up to 4 days). Winter melon can be stored in cool location for several months, but once sliced should be refrigerated in plastic bag and used within 2 days.

Store squash blossoms in plastic bag in crisper drawer; use as soon as possible.

EDIBLE SKIN:

CROOKNECK, GOLD BAR, SUMMER GREEN, SUMMER YELLOW, ZUCCHINI

Domestic: *May–December*

Global: *December–May*

BABY CROOKNECK, BABY GOLD BAR, BABY SUMMER GREEN (PATTYPAN), BABY SUMMER YELLOW (PATTYPAN), BABY ZUCCHINI

Domestic: *April–July*

Global: *year-round, peak in spring and summer*

BABY SCALLOPINI, SCALLOPINI
Domestic: *March–April*
Global: *none*

EIGHT BALL
Domestic: *April–May*
Global: *January–May*

TATUMA
Domestic: *none*
Global: *year round*

NONEDIBLE SKIN:
CHAYOTE (MIRLITON)
Domestic: *May–October*
Global: *October–May*

CUCUZZA
Domestic: *June–October*
Global: *none*

MO QUA
Domestic: *May–November*

Global: *November–May*

PUL QUA (OPO)
Domestic: *May–December*
Global: *November–May*

WINTER MELON
Domestic: *May–October*
Global: *November–May*

SQUASH BLOSSOMS
Domestic: *June–July*
Global: *February–August*

PREP

For edible-skinned squash, just before using wash thoroughly and trim ends. For inedible-skinned squash, peel skin with paring knife or vegetable peeler. When peeling chayote, a liquid may ooze out that is irritating to some, so plastic gloves should be worn. Once chayote is peeled, rinse with cold water.

Eight Ball

Baby Crookneck

Crookneck

edible skin

BABY CROOKNECK, CROOKNECK

Tapers from bulbous bottom to long, curved neck with bright yellow, thin skin that is sometimes bumpy. Baby varieties about 3 inches long; regular about 7 inches long. ■ *Creamy flesh with mild squash flavor. Baby varieties more tender with fewer seeds.*

BABY GOLD BAR, GOLD BAR

Cylindrical with sunshine yellow with deep green tip. Baby variety about 3 inches long. Regular about 7 inches. ■ *Flesh is tender and delicately mild. Baby varieties contain less edible seeds.*

BABY SUMMER GREEN (PATTYPAN), SUMMER GREEN

Disks with scalloped edges and light- to dark-green exterior.

Baby varieties about 2 inches across. Regular size about 5 inches across. ■ *Both offer mild squash flavor. Baby varieties contain less edible seeds.*

BABY SUMMER YELLOW (PATTYPAN), SUMMER YELLOW

Sunny yellow disks with scalloped edges; dark green sunburst patterns appears on both blossom and stem ends. Baby varieties about 2 inches across. Regular size about 5 inches across. ■ *Mild and buttery flavor profile. Baby varieties contain less edible seeds.*

BABY SCALLOPINI, SCALLOPINI

Disks with scalloped edges. Thin, yellow-green skin. Baby varieties about 2 inches across. Regular size about 5 inches across. ■ *Deliciously creamy and mildly nutty.*

BABY ZUCCHINI, ZUCCHINI

Cylindrical with glossy green exterior often dotted with lighter green speckles. Baby variety about 3 inches long. Regular zucchini about 7–14 inches, depending on maturity at harvest. ■ *Creamy-white flesh with mild squash flavor. Baby varieties more tender with fewer seeds. Edible zucchini flowers are sometimes attached to baby variety.*

EIGHT BALL

Shaped like tennis balls, these round, deep green zucchini-like squash are great for stuffing. ■ *Zucchini-like flavor.*

TATUMA

Cylindrical zucchini shape with light, grayish-green exterior. About 6 inches long, but when more mature, can be about 11 inches long. ■ *Milder flavor than zucchini, with more tender skin.*

USE

Tender-skinned or peeled inedible-skinned summer squashes can be grilled, boiled, microwaved, or sautéed, or eaten raw tossed into salads. Use in soups, stews, or casseroles. Stuff and bake, or dredge in bread crumbs and fry. Blossoms can be stuffed and fried or used in soup.

NUTRITIONAL INFO (FOR EDIBLE-SKINNED SQUASH)

1 cup is generally a significant source of vitamin C.

NUTRITIONAL INFO (FOR INEDIBLE-SKINNED SQUASH)

1 cup is generally a significant source of vitamin C.

NUTRITIONAL INFO (FOR BLOSSOMS)

1 cup is a significant source of vitamins C and A.

nonedible skin

CUCUZZA

Shaped like a baseball bat, this firm Italian squash has light-green skin and pure white flesh. It can grow anywhere from 15 inches to 3 feet long and to 3 inches in diameter. Stem remains attached to nourish the squash up to 1 month after picking. ■ *Offers a slightly sweet, mild cucumber flavor and a fairly firm inviting texture.*

WINTER MELON

Large and round with light-green rind tinged with white. Rind has waxy feel. Can measure 15 inches in diameter, about 12 pounds. Often sold by the slice. ■ *Mildly flavored white flesh with watermelon-like texture. Because winter melon has a subtle and rather bland taste, it loves powerful seasonings.*

PUL QUA

(opo)

Cylindrical-shaped, smooth skin can range from chartreuse to light green. Usually harvested at 10–12 inches long. ■ *Flavor is refreshing blend of summer squash and cucumber.*

MO QUA

(fuzzy melon)

Resembles an extra-large cucumber with a subtle waistline with splotchy green rind. Young mo qua have rinds with soft downy hairs that disappear when it matures. Usually 6–10 inches long and about 2 inches in diameter. ■ *Firm-textured flesh has subtle cucumber-like flavor.*

CHAYOTE

(mirliton)

Somewhat pear-shaped with ridged pale green to celadon skin. Large central seed is edible. About 3–5 inches long, but can be 7 inches when mature. ■ *Offering a very sweet and mild flavor sometimes described as a blend of a cucumber and zucchini with a slight hint of a tart apple. The seed inside is edible.*

squash blossoms

Varying shades of yellow and orange, they are best when freshly picked. ■ *Similar but milder flavor than the squash it produces, they have meaty petals. Summer and winter squash produce edible blossoms.*

SERVING SUGGESTIONS

Zucchini fettucine: Cut zucchini (or any edible-skinned squash) into matchsticks. In large, nonstick skillet, heat olive oil on high heat. Add squash and stir-fry until golden. Add 1 large clove garlic (minced) and salt to taste; cook 20 seconds and remove from heat. Add cooked fettucine and minced fresh herb (such as basil or Italian parsley); toss. Top with grated Parmesan or pecorino cheese and freshly ground black pepper.

Soup or slaw: Cook peeled, seeded, and diced chayote in vegetable soup (spiked, if you prefer, with a little minced lemon grass and Asian chili sauce). Or add raw, peeled and shredded chayote to your favorite coleslaw recipe.

Easy Asian rice: Stir-fry mixed assortment of diced edible-skinned squash in a little hot olive oil in large, nonstick skillet; cook until lightly browned and softened. Add handful of sliced green onion and sauté 1 minute. Add cooked brown or white rice; stir-fry about 3 minutes, adding soy sauce and pepper to taste.

Summer Green

Tatuma

Baby Yellow Scallopini

Baby Summer Green

Blossom bundles: Stuff blossoms with small amount of store-bought garlic-and-herb soft cheese. Both male flowers (the ones with long straight stems) or female flowers (those attached to small 2–3-inch zucchini) can be used. If using male flowers, remove and discard stamens. Combine ⅔ cup all-purpose flour and ¾ cup beer; stir until thoroughly mixed. Wash flowers with cold water and pat dry. Heat 1 inch vegetable or peanut oil in deep skillet on high heat (375 degrees). Dip in batter and carefully place in hot oil. Fry 3–5 minutes or until nicely browned, turning once. Drain on paper towels and season with coarse salt.

stuffed eight balls

Any variety of summer squash (with edible skin) can be stuffed and baked. But because the Eight Ball squash has such an intriguing spherical shape, it is a visual knockout when stuffed. This filling is flavor-spiked with Italian sausage, but if you prefer a vegetarian version, omit the meat and season the mixture with a pinch of dried red chile flakes, salt, and dried Italian herb seasoning (usually a mixture of dried thyme, basil, rosemary, and oregano).

6 medium Eight Ball squash, rinsed

1 tablespoon olive oil

1 small onion, diced

2 large cloves garlic, minced

¼ cup finely chopped mushrooms

¼ cup finely chopped celery

1 pound hot or sweet bulk Italian sausage (or a combination of both)

2 tablespoons dry white wine

3 tablespoons chopped fresh basil

¾ cup grated Parmesan cheese

1 egg, lightly beaten

¾ cup fresh bread crumbs

Salt and pepper to taste

Zucchini

Baby Green Zucchini

Gold Bar

*Baby Green Zucchini
with Flower*

1. Preheat oven to 375 degrees.

2. Cut tops of squash off ¾ inch below stem end (reserve). Cut off small slice at bottom so that squash will "stand up." Scoop out inside with small spoon to make room for filling, leaving sides and bottom portion about ¼–¾ inch thick; reserve half of cored portion and chop.

3. Heat oil on medium-high heat in large, deep skillet. Add onion, garlic, mushrooms, and celery; cook until celery starts to soften, 7–9 minutes, stirring occasionally. Add sausage and break into small pieces with spatula or wooden spoon. Sauté until sausage is cooked, about 4–6 minutes. Add white wine and reserved chopped squash spooned from inside; increase to high heat and bring to boil. Boil until wine evaporates.

4. Remove from heat. Stir in basil and cheese. Stir in egg and bread crumbs. Taste and adjust seasoning as needed.

5. Season squash interior with salt and pepper. When sausage mixture is cool enough to handle, stuff loosely in squash, mounding so filling is a little above cut edge. Place filling-side up in 9-by-13-inch baking pan. Cover each with reserved tops, if desired. Place ¼ inch of water in bottom of pan (you may need to remove one squash to add water, then replace it).

6. Bake in preheated oven, 30–40 minutes, or until squash is tender-crisp and filling is thoroughly cooked. Carefully remove with wide spatula and serve.

**YIELD: 6 MAIN COURSE SERVINGS OR
12 HALVED FIRST COURSE SERVINGS**

NUTRITIONAL INFORMATION (PER FIRST COURSE SERVING): Calories 190; fat calories 70; total fat 8 grams; sat fat 2.5 grams, cholesterol 45 milligrams; sodium 580 milligrams; total carbohydrates 18 grams; fiber 2 grams; sugars 2 grams; protein 12 grams; vitamin A IUs 6%; vitamin C 30%; calcium 10%; iron 10%.

sunflower choke,
also jerusalem artichoke, sunchoke, girsole

AT FIRST GLANCE, sunflower's plump knobby root might be mistaken for ginger root. The thin, edible skin is generally ginger-like light brown but can have tinges of red or purple. Inside, the creamy white flesh has a crisp, crunchy texture. The taste is nutty and subtly sweet, something like a blend of jicama and potato. Unpeeled, it has an earthy aroma.

Native to North America, sunflower chokes became a popular French ingredient in the seventeenth century.

BUYING AND STORING

Avoid sunflower chokes that are moist or softened. Look for firm product without sprouts or blotches. Store, unwashed, in plastic in vegetable drawer of refrigerator up to 1 week.
Domestic: *October–July*
Global: *none*

PREP

Scrub with brush and dry. The peel is edible, but it doesn't look appealing, especially if dish is puréed. If cooked whole, skin can be removed before or after cooking with paring knife. To prevent discoloration of raw (peeled or cut) sunflower choke, store in acidulated water (2 cups cold water mixed with 1 tablespoon lemon juice).

USE

Eat raw or cooked. Use raw in salads, thinly sliced, grated, or cut in matchsticks; or use with crudités (raw vegetables, generally for serving with dip). To cook, blanch, bake, sauté, or roast. Be careful not to overcook. When cooked too long, they turn to mush.

NUTRITIONAL INFO

1 cup is a significant source of vitamin C; very good source of iron; good source of thiamin, phosphorus, and potassium.

SERVING SUGGESTIONS

Dip dippers: Cut into sticks and, to prevent discoloration, dunk in acidulated water (see Prep). Serve along with other raw vegetables with dip.

Sunflower Choke

Roasted with meat: Toss whole sunflower chokes in combination of melted butter and vegetable oil and place in roasting pan around roast beef or pork for last 30 minutes of cooking. If desired, top with fresh bread crumbs and grated Parmesan cheese for the last 10 minutes.

Steamed or boiled: To steam, place whole in steamer rack over boiling water. Steam until just barely tender, about 8–15 minutes, depending on size. Or to boil, place whole in water to cover in large saucepan. Cover and boil on high heat until just barely tender, about 6–10 minutes, depending on size. Drain and season with salt and pepper. If desired, squeeze fresh lemon juice on top. Serve hot.

Asian Salad substitute: Sliced raw sunflowers chokes can be added to salad in place of water chestnuts.

cream of sunflower choke soup

Creamy soup is an irresistible way to show off the nutty flavor of sunflower chokes. If you like, top this soup with a rustic crouton. Cut slices of peasant-style bread (ciabatta or whole wheat baguette) into ¼-inch-thick slices. Brush with butter on both sides and bake on baking sheet in 350-degree oven until crisp and lightly browned.

1½ pounds sunflower chokes, peeled, cut in 1-inch-thick slices

1 cup milk

1½ cups chicken broth, sodium-reduced preferred, or vegetable broth

Salt and white pepper to taste

3 tablespoons minced Italian parsley

OPTIONAL: croutons

1. Place sunflower chokes, milk, and broth in nonreactive, large saucepan. Bring to simmer on medium-high heat; reduce to medium-low heat and simmer partially covered, about 12–14 minutes. Remove ½ cup liquid.

2. Purée in batches in food processor fitted with metal blade or blender, using caution because ingredients are hot. Add reserved liquid if soup is too thick. Taste and add salt and generous amount of pepper. Ladle into 4 soup bowls. Top with parsley, and croutons, if desired.

YIELD: 4 SERVINGS

NUTRITIONAL INFORMATION (PER SERVING WITHOUT CROUTONS): Calories 170; fat calories 13.5; total fat 1.5 grams; sat fat 1 gram; cholesterol 5 milligrams; sodium 380 milligrams; total carbohydrates 33 grams; fiber 3 grams; sugars 20 grams; protein 7 grams; vitamin A IUs 8%; vitamin C 20%; calcium 10%; iron 35%.

sweet potato

ASIAN (JAPANESE, OKINAWA)

BONIATO, CUBAN, BATATA, WHITE

ORANGE FLESH (BEAUREGARD, JEWEL, AND GARNET)

YELLOW FLESH (JERSEY)

THESE BRIGHT-COLORED EDIBLE ROOTS are generally labeled either sweet potatoes or yams and, unlike potatoes, are members of the morning glory family. Those with lighter tan skin and flakier, drier flesh (when cooked) are thought of as sweet potatoes. Those with darker, red-brown skin and moister interiors (when cooked) are commonly labeled yams. But in fact, true yams are from a different botanical group.

Often, sweet potatoes have a long cylindrical shape that is tapered at each end. Others are shaped more like a teardrop, tapered at one end but large and rounded at the opposite end. All have a natural sweetness that increases during storage and cooking.

(True yams, sometimes labeled *ñame* or *igname,* have hairy, off-white or brown skin and are sold in cylindrical chunks that can weigh several pounds.)

BUYING AND STORING

Choose those that are firm and heavy for their size, and free of cracks or soft spots. Store, unwashed, in cool, dry location up to 7 days; do not refrigerate.

ASIAN (JAPANESE)
Domestic: *July–May*
Global: *none*

ASIAN (OKINAWA) AND BONIATO (CUBAN)
Domestic: *year-round*
Global: *none*

ORANGE FLESH (BEAUREGARD, JEWEL, GARNET) AND YELLOW FLESH (JERSEY)
Domestic: *year-round; peaks September–January*
Global: *none*

PREP

Scrub just before using under cold running water. If baking with skin on, pat dry thoroughly with paper towels or clean kitchen towel. If peeling or cutting, use stainless-steel knife to prevent discoloration. When cut, if not using immediately, submerge in cold water to prevent discoloration. Sweet potatoes can be diced, sliced, shredded, or cut into long matchsticks.

USE

Bake, boil, sauté, steam, or deep-fry. If baked with skins on, skin can easily be slipped off after baking for mashing or puréeing. To bake, pierce with fork in 3–4 places and place in 400-degree oven on baking sheet for about 45–60 minutes, or until easily pierced with fork (moist-fleshed varieties take a little longer than dry-fleshed varieties). Use shredded in muffins, quick breads, or potato pancakes. Or cook and purée, then add milk, eggs, butter, sugar, spices, and a smidgen of flour, then use as pie filling.

NUTRITIONAL INFO

1 cup is an excellent source of vitamin A; significant source of vitamin B_6 and potassium.

Japanese

Okinawa

Boniato

BEAUREGARD

Light copper skin with moist, bright-orange flesh. ▪ *Sweet. Retains slight firmness when cooked.*

BONIATO

(Cuban, batata, and white) **Russet to burgundy-colored skin with cream-colored flesh.**
▪ *Flakier and less sweet than orange- or yellow-fleshed sweet potatoes.*

GARNET

Dark red to purple skin with deep orange, moist flesh. Often labeled "yam." ▪ *Sweet, damp consistency. Best used mashed in pies, cakes, and breads.*

JAPANESE

Burgundy to russet-colored skin with light-colored flesh similar in appearance to boniato.
▪ *Nutty flavor similar to roasted chestnut. Starchy, dry texture.*

JERSEY

Tan or creamy-yellow skin with yellow flesh. ▪ *Intensely sweet and flaky texture.*

JEWEL

Copper-colored skin with bright yellow-orange flesh. ▪ *Very sweet with moist flesh.*

OKINAWA

Light, almost white skin with dark purple flesh. Ends are rounded, not pointed. ▪ *Full-bodied flavor, with deep sweetness. Starchy, dry texture.*

SERVING SUGGESTIONS

Baked and spiked: Bake skin-on until fork tender (see Use). Slit lengthwise down one side and cautiously squeeze from either end to expose flesh. Season to taste with salt and pepper and a gentle squeeze of fresh lime juice. Top with plain yogurt or sour cream and either chopped chives or thinly sliced green onion.

Chili: Add chunks of sweet potatoes to pot of chili; simmer until just tender.

Spicy coconut soup: Cook 2 medium sweet onions (roughly chopped) in 1 tablespoon vegetable oil in Dutch oven on medium heat until softened. Add 2 medium sweet potatoes (peeled, cut into ¾-inch dice), 1 serrano chili (seeded, minced), 2 cloves garlic (minced), and ½-inch slice fresh ginger (minced); cook 2 minutes, stirring frequently. Add 1 (14-ounce) can coconut milk, 2½ cups water, salt to taste, pinch ground

turmeric, and ½ teaspoon ground coriander. Bring to boil on high heat. Reduce heat to medium and simmer 20–25 minutes, or until sweet potato is tender. Place a scoop of cooked rice in each of 6 shallow soup bowls, then ladle soup over rice. Garnish with chopped cilantro and accompany with wedges of fresh limes.

Crisp oven-baked wedges: Cut each washed and dried sweet potato into 6 lengthwise wedges. Toss with enough canola oil to coat. Place on lightly oiled, rimmed baking sheets, leaving plenty of space between wedges. Season with coarse salt. Bake on bottom rack in preheated 400-degree oven until lightly browned on bottom, about 15 minutes. Using spatula, turn sweet potatoes. Return to oven and bake until crisp and nicely browned on outside and tender on inside, about 10 minutes. Serve with fresh lime wedges for optional squeezing.

Jersey

Jewel

Garnet

gratin of green apples and sweet potatoes

Baked until the apples and sweet potatoes are fork-tender, this flavorful gratin makes a delicious side dish with holiday turkey or ham. If desired, you can substitute baking potatoes (such as russets) or butternut squash for half of the sweet potatoes. This dish can be made ahead through Step 3 and refrigerated. Reheat until hot in a 325-degree oven and add bread crumb mixture; broil until nicely browned.

Butter for greasing pan

3 medium green apples, such as Granny Smiths

2 tablespoons butter or margarine

OPTIONAL: *2 tablespoons Calvados or other apple brandy*

2 sweet potatoes

Salt and white pepper to taste

3/4 teaspoon ground cinnamon

1 1/2 cups heavy whipping cream

1/2 cup fresh bread crumbs (see Cook's Notes)

1/4 cup chopped pecans

3 tablespoons melted butter

OPTIONAL GARNISH: sprigs of fresh mint

COOK'S NOTES: Fresh bread crumbs can be made quickly in food processor fitted with metal blade. Tear bread into quarters and process, using pulsing technique.

1. Using butter, grease 9- or 10-inch-long gratin (oval) baking dish or 9–10-inch quiche pan (round baking dish about 1 3/4 inches deep, often fluted). Preheat oven to 375 degrees.

2. Peel, core, and slice apples. In large, deep skillet, melt 2 tablespoons butter on medium-high heat. Add apple slices (and Calvados, if using). Cook until softened about 6–8 minutes, stirring frequently. Remove from heat and set aside.

3. Peel sweet potatoes and thinly slice. Layer half sweet potatoes, overlapping, in prepared pan. Season with salt and white pepper. Place apples on top. Sprinkle on ground cinnamon. Top with remaining sweet potatoes, overlapping the slices. Season to taste with salt and white pepper. Drizzle whipping cream over potatoes and cover with aluminum foil. Bake in a preheated 375-degree oven 1 hour or until potatoes are tender.

4. Remove potatoes from oven and position oven rack 7–8 inches below broiler element. Preheat broiler. Remove foil from potatoes. In small bowl, stir bread crumbs and pecans; sprinkle on top of potatoes. Drizzle with melted butter and season lightly with salt. Place under broiler until crumbs are nicely browned. Watch carefully to prevent burning.

5. If desired, garnish with sprigs of fresh mint and serve immediately.

YIELD: 6–7 SIDE-DISH SERVINGS

NUTRITIONAL INFORMATION (PER SERVING):
Calories 460; fat calories 324; total fat 36 grams; sat fat 20 grams; cholesterol 105 milligrams; sodium 250 milligrams; total carbohydrates 34 grams; fiber 5 grams; sugars 15 grams; protein 4 grams; vitamin A IUs 350%; vitamin C 35%; calcium 8%; iron 6%.

taro root, also dasheen, eddo

LARGE

SMALL

PERHAPS THIS TROPICAL TUBER'S most well-known use is in *poi*, that gooey paste that's enjoyed in Polynesian cuisine. But if you don't like poi, don't give up on taro root. It can be deliciously nutty and subtly sweet, especially when sautéed or deep-fried.

There are more than 100 varieties of this starchy tuber. Generally two varieties of taro roots are available in the marketplace, large and small. Both are covered with barklike brown skin. The larger ones (about 4 inches in diameter and 12 inches long) are generally shaped like plump cylinders; they're usually sold cut into manageable pieces about 6 inches long. The small variety (about 1 inch in diameter and 3 inches long) has a bigger-in-the-middle barrel shape that tapers toward both ends. Small taro roots have flesh that is softer and creamier than the large.

The flesh is creamy white or pale pink, sometimes tinged with purple or dotted with purple specks. Used like potatoes, once cooked they have a nutty-sweet taste.

Large Taro Root

Baby Taro Root

BUYING AND STORING

When choosing small variety, look for skin that isn't cracked or split. When choosing large variety, examine cut ends; they should be free of mold. Either variety should be free of soft spots or shriveling. Store at room temperature in a cool, dark location, or refrigerate loose in crisper drawer up to 1 week.

Domestic: *year round*
Global: *year round*

PREP

Some find taro irritating to their skin, so wear plastic gloves if necessary and do not touch face or eyes. Trim ends and remove thick skin with sharp paring knife, cutting from end to end (some like to do this under running water). Discard skin and store trimmed taro in bowl of cold water. Or, if using small taro root, scrub, then steam or boil with skin intact until tender. When cool enough to handle, skin easily slips off.

If removing skin before cooking, boil, steam, or simmer, cut into 1-inch chunks. For baking, cut in half lengthwise. If frying for chips, cut into very thin slices, preferably with a mandoline. Taro root can also be shredded and added to soup.

USE

Not eaten raw. Use like potatoes, boiled, steamed, simmered, fried, or baked. If baking, first blanch until tender-crisp; during baking, baste with pan juices (if roasting with meat) or butter. For all except deep-fried taro, serve piping hot, as consistency changes as it cools.

NUTRITIONAL INFO

1 cup is a significant source of vitamin B_6 and potassium.

SERVING SUGGESTIONS

Taro "tostada" appetizers: Cut large peeled taro root into 1/4-inch slices. Deep-fry in 360-degree vegetable or peanut oil until crisp and lightly browned. Drain on paper towels and season with coarse salt. Mash cooked black beans with puréed canned chipotle chile in adobo sauce (to taste). Place spoonful of warm bean mixture on top of each fried taro disk. Top with fruit salsa of choice, such as Mango salsa (see page 62).

A beautiful mash: Cut ³/₄ pound peeled taro root, 1 large peeled sweet potato, and ½ pound peeled and seeded butternut squash into 1-inch chunks. Bring 1 quart water to boil in large pot on high heat. Add taro chunks and boil until starting to soften, about 10 minutes. Add sweet potato and squash; boil until soft, about 12–15 minutes. Drain and mash with enough heavy whipping cream and butter to achieve a creamy consistency. Season with salt and white pepper. Serve immediately.

Shredded into soup: Finely shred a small amount of taro into Southeast Asian–style hot-and-sour soup about 5 minutes before the end of cooking time. Taro will thicken soup (see Chicken noodle hot and sour soup with galangal, page 192).

Pan-Fried: Boil 1-inch chunks of 1½ pounds peeled taro until just barely tender, about 10 minutes. Drain and cut chunks in halves. Heat 3 tablespoons vegetable oil in large, deep skillet on medium-high heat. Add 1 large onion (roughly chopped) and cook until starting to soften. Add taro and sauté, stirring frequently, until taro starts to brown. Remove from heat. Stir in 2 tablespoons minced fresh Italian parsley or cilantro. Season to taste with salt and pepper. Serve immediately.

tindora, also tendora

SHAPED LIKE TINY CUCUMBERS, these diminutive wonders are about 2–3 inches long and ½ inch wide at the thickest, middle portion. They have a thick, smooth skin that is most often apple-green variegated with wiggly, lengthwise pale green stripes. Inside the pale green flesh is dotted with almost transparent angular seeds, crunchy-soft and juicy.

Because tindora have a greater skin-to-flesh ratio, they are crunchier than cucumbers and have more pronounced sweetness. Most often they are used fresh or pickled in Indian cuisine.

BUYING AND STORING

Look for crisp, firm tindora; they should snap when broken in half. Avoid those that are shriveled or have soft spots. Refrigerate, unwashed, in plastic bag in crisper drawer 5–6 days.

Domestic: *May–October*
Global: *September–April*

PREP

Wash thoroughly in cold water and pat dry. Do not peel. Serve whole or slice lengthwise in half or quarters; or cut into 3/8-inch-wide slices.

USE

Eat raw out of hand, use in salads or as garnish. Pickle or sauté. Or use in soups or curries.

NUTRITIONAL INFO

1 cup is a significant source of vitamin K.

SERVING SUGGESTIONS

Crunch with cocktails: Cut several tindoras in half lenthwise. Sprinkle with coarse sea salt, such as *fleur de sel* or smoked Danish sea salt. Serve with cocktails.

Tindora salad: Cut tindoras in half lengthwise or into 3/8-inch-wide slices. Place in bowl with slivers of red onion and chopped fresh Italian parsley or fresh dill. Toss with Simple Vinaigrette (page 310). Place sliced tomatoes on platter. Top with tindora salad and serve.

Sautéed and lightly browned: Cut tindoras in half lengthwise. Heat 1/4-inch vegetable oil or canola oil in deep skillet on high heat. Add tindora and sauté until browned on all sides. Drain on paper towel and season with coarse salt. Serve as side dish.

Fire and ice freezer pickles: Trim ends of 2 pounds of tindora. Cut in half lengthwise and place in glass or ceramic bowl. Add 3 tablespoons kosher salt and toss. Leave at room temperature for 2 hours; drain in colander (do not rinse). In large ceramic or glass bowl, stir 2 cups sugar and 2 cups distilled white vinegar until sugar dissolves. Add 1/2 large sweet onion (sliced), 1 red bell peper and 1 yellow bell pepper (both cored, seeded, and cut into 1/4-by-1-inch strips), 3 cloves garlic (minced), 1/3 cup fresh chopped mint, and, if desired, 1/2 fresh serrano chile (thinly sliced). Add drained tindora and toss. Cover and refrigerate overnight. Pack in freezer containers and freeze. Defrost 8 hours in refrigerator before serving.

Tindora

tomatillo, also
mexican husk tomato

AT FIRST GLANCE, tomatillos might look like festive paper lanterns, ready to be strung with lights for an outdoor gala. But beneath the party dress—that almost-sheer, brown-green husk that's veined like a congested city road map—lies a fruit packed with seemingly endless culinary potential.

A pale globe that looks like a small green tomato is the prize inside, and in fact, tomatillo is Spanish for small tomato. But it isn't a tomato. A member of the nightshade family, it's related to tomatoes, along with ground cherries and Cape gooseberries. They have a taste that is something like apples drizzled with lemon juice but with a pleasing, herblike edge. Raw tomatillos have the texture of kiwi. Cooked, they're as soft as grilled eggplant.

In mainstream supermarket chains, they range in size from unshelled walnuts to golf balls. Latin American markets sometimes offer other varieties, stocking a smaller, purple-blushed beauty called *morado*. It has an appealing herbal fragrance. There's also the tiny marble-size *miltomate*, with an intense, sweet-tart taste and a gentle spiciness.

BUYING AND STORING

They fill their husks when they are mature, so look for those with dry, tight-fitting husks. Should be crisp and free of mold. Refrigerate loose in crisper drawer up to 14 days.

Domestic: *year-round*
Global: *year-round*

PREP

Peel off the husks and rinse off the sticky coating, wiping (if necessary) with paper towels.

USE

Can be eaten raw but generally cooked. Use raw cut into thin wedges and added to salad, or dice and use in *salsa cruda*. To cook, grill, roast, or blanch. Most often used cooked to make Salsa Verde (see page 290), a delicious addition to everything from salad dressing to scrambled eggs.

NUTRITIONAL INFO

1 cup is a good source of vitamin C.

SERVING SUGGESTIONS

Tomatillo salad dressing: In a blender, combine ½ cup sour cream (regular, low-fat, or nonfat), ¼ cup Salsa Verde (see recipe), and a dash of seasoned salt. Whirl about 10 seconds or until blended. Toss with mixed lettuce and cherry tomatoes, adding enough dressing to lightly coat leaves. If desired, top salad with crumbled queso fresco (often labeled "ranchero") or shredded Jack cheese. Season with freshly ground black pepper.

Spicy soup: Add Salsa Verde (see page 290) to taste to your favorite chicken soup (either homemade or store-bought), such as chicken vegetable or chicken with rice. Top servings with a dollop of sour cream, and little chopped cilantro (if desired).

Green and glorious rice: In a bowl or glass measuring cup, combine ½ cup Salsa Verde (see page 290), 1½ cups water or chicken broth, pinch salt, and 3 green onions (sliced, including some of the dark-green stalks); set aside. Heat 1 teaspoon of canola oil and 1 teaspoon of butter in a medium saucepan on medium-high heat. Add 2 cloves garlic (minced) and cook 30 seconds. Add 1 cup long-grained rice; cook and stir occasionally, until rice is lightly browned. Add Salsa Verde mixture and bring to a boil; immediately reduce heat to low, cover and cook 18 minutes or until all liquid is absorbed. If desired, stir in ¼ cup chopped cilantro.

Tomatillo

salsa verde

This sauce made with grilled or roasted tomatillos; adds a refreshing citrusy taste to whatever it accompanies. Used alone, it's a delectable dip for tortilla chips. Add it to mayonnaise, and it makes a delicious cold sauce for tuna or salmon salad. Or add diced mango, and it's an irresistible topping for grilled seafood or poultry. If you want a spicier version, substitute serrano chile for jalapeño.

7 medium tomatillos, husked, rinsed, washed, and wiped

1 fresh jalapeño chile, stem removed (see Cook's Notes)

5–6 sprigs fresh cilantro, chopped

¼ cup water

¼ cup finely chopped onion

Salt to taste

COOK'S NOTES: Use caution when handling fresh chiles, taking care not to touch face or eyes and washing carefully afterward.

1. Adjust oven rack to 4–5 inches below broiler element. Preheat broiler. Place tomatillos and chile in single layer on rimmed baking sheet with sides. Broil until blackened in spots and blistered, about 5 minutes. Turn over and roast other side, 3–4 minutes more, or until blistered and soft.

2. Cool on baking sheet. Place in blender, including juices. Add cilantro and 1/4 cup water; blend to coarse purée.

3. Place puréed mixture in nonreactive bowl. Add onion and season with salt to taste.

YIELD: ABOUT 1 CUP

NUTRITIONAL INFORMATION (PER TABLESPOON): Calories 5; fat calories 0; total fat 0 grams; sat fat 0 grams, cholesterol 0 milligrams; sodium 75 milligrams; total carbohydrates 1 grams; fiber 0 grams; sugars 1 gram; protein 0 grams; vitamin A IUs 0%; vitamin C 4%; calcium 0%; iron 0%.

tomato

BEEFSTEAK

CHERRY (ORANGE, RED, AND YELLOW)

COMMON, "ON THE VINE" OR HOTHOUSE (ORANGE, RED, AND YELLOW)

GRAPE

GREEN

HEIRLOOM

ROMA, PLUM

TEARDROP, PEAR (ORANGE, RED, AND YELLOW)

WITH THOUSANDS OF VARIETIES, tomatoes come in a wide range of striking shapes, sizes, and colors. Flavor varies, but at their ripened best, tomatoes pack an alluring wallop of sweetness tinged with moderate acidity. The flavor is further enhanced with an appealing melt-in-your-mouth texture. How could anyone label these delectable gems as poisonous?

Indigenous to the Western Hemisphere, when they were first introduced to Europeans by Spanish explorers in the sixteenth century, they weren't considered edible. It wasn't until the nineteenth century that tomatoes were widely appreciated as a culinary prize.

Beefsteak

Green

Orange Teardrop

Red Teardrop

BUYING AND STORING

Look for plump tomatoes that feel heavy for their size. Avoid refrigerated tomatoes or those with bruises, discoloration, or mold. Fully ripe, they yield to gentle pressure. Generally, red tomatoes have a richer tomato flavor than orange or yellow tomatoes. Store in single layer at room temperature out of direct sunlight. Or use Brown-Bag Ripening approach (see page 309). Do not refrigerate.

ALL VARIETIES EXCEPT HEIRLOOM
Domestic: *year-round*
Global: *year-round*

HEIRLOOM
Domestic: *year-round*
Global: *June–March*

PREP

Wash thoroughly in cold water. To core, use a paring knife with pointed end. Insert tip of knife next to tough core (where stem makes inedible tough circular patch at top of medium or large tomatoes). Holding knife at an angle pointing toward core's center, use sawing motion to cut around and remove core.

If peeling, cut shallow X at bottom. Submerge in simmering water about 20–50 seconds (length of time depends on ripeness). Rinse with cold water. Grab skin at X and pull away from flesh.

To remove seeds and juice, cut in half crosswise (at "waistline") to expose seeds. Gently squeeze.

USE

Use raw out of hand or in salad, salsa, sauce, or sandwiches. Or cook: sauté, roast, simmer, or broil.

NUTRITIONAL INFO (GREEN TOMATOES)

1 cup is an excellent source of vitamin C; significant source of vitamins A and K and potassium.

NUTRITIONAL INFO (ORANGE TOMATOES)

1 cup is an excellent source of vitamins A and C; significant source of folate and potassium.

NUTRITIONAL INFO (RED TOMATOES)

1 cup is a good source of vitamin C; significant source of vitamin A.

NUTRITIONAL INFO (YELLOW TOMATOES)

1 cup is a significant source of vitamin C, folate, and potassium.

SERVING SUGGESTIONS

Cherry tomato stir-fry: Cut 3 cups cherry tomatoes in half lengthwise. Heat 1 tablespoon olive oil in large, deep skillet on medium-high heat. Add tomatoes; fry and gently toss for 1–2 minutes. Add 1 clove garlic (minced); cook 30 seconds, tossing as needed. Remove from heat and toss with 1 tablespoon minced fresh tarragon. Serve as side dish to grilled fish, chicken, or pork. Or toss with cooked orzo.

Roasted plum tomatoes: Heat oven to 325 degrees. Core 3 pounds plum tomatoes; cut in half lengthwise. Place in shallow roasting pan

BEEFSTEAK
Large red fleshy tomatoes that can have 6-inch diameters. Small pulp cavities make them ideal slicing tomatoes.
■ *Rich, deep tomato flavor with pronounced sweetness.*

CHERRY
(orange, red, and yellow)
Almost spherical with tender, thin skin. Varies from large grape to ping-pong ball size.
■ *Juicy with tiny seeds. Rich, sweet flavor profile.*

COMMON—"ON THE VINE" OR HOTHOUSE
(orange, red, and yellow)
Medium-sized with brightly colored skin and flesh. Generally attached to vine. ■ *Sweet tomato flavor. Medium-sized pulp cavities and seeds.*

GRAPE
Elongated, bantam-sized, usually under 1 inch in length. Grown in clusters like grapes. Red, shiny skin. ■ *Juicy, with concentrated sweetness.*

GREEN
Unripe tomatoes, generally medium to large varieties.
■ *Tart and mildly acidic, these tomatoes require cooking. Most often they are dredged in cornmeal and pan-fried.*

HEIRLOOM
(most common include Black Krim, Brandywine, Cherokee, and Marvel Striped)
Odd shapes, some deeply fluted. Intriguing colors, some variegated in two or more colors. Although differing definitions exist, heirlooms are generally described as those in existence for at least 3 generations.
■ *Rich, sweet homegrown tomato taste with relatively low acidity and abundant juice.*

ROMA, PLUM
Elongated shape with meaty, thick flesh and few seeds. Generally red, but yellow varieties exist. ■ *Less acidity and sweetness. Great for sauces or drying.*

TEARDROP, PEAR
(orange, red, and yellow)
Small, teardrop-shaped, usually under 1 inch long. ■ *Juicy texture of cherry tomato but milder flavor profile.*

Grape

Roma

Red Cherry

cut side up. Drizzle with olive oil and season with coarse salt, freshly ground pepper, minced garlic, and smidgen of dried red pepper flakes. Gently toss to coat tomatoes well and return to cut side up position. Roast 1 hour. If desired, cool and peel. Use in recipes calling for canned tomatoes or process in several batches in blender and use as pasta sauce. Or chop and combine with chopped onion, minced chiles, and cilantro to make salsa.

Slumgullion salad: Cut beefsteak tomatoes into ¼-inch-thick slices and place in single layer on platter. Top with thin slivers of red onion and sliced (peeled) cucumber. Drizzle with extra-virgin olive oil and a little vinegar—either sherry vinegar (for light acidity) or cider vinegar (for greater acidity). Season with coarse salt and freshly ground black pepper. If desired, top with fresh basil cut crosswise into narrow strips or sprinkle with crumbled blue cheese.

Scrambled with tomatoes: Dice 1 medium onion (sweet, red, or yellow) and 3 medium tomatoes. In a large bowl, whisk 10 eggs with 1 tablespoon water, ½ teaspoon seasoned salt, and 3 tablespoons minced fresh basil or parsley. Heat 1 tablespoon butter and 1 tablespoon olive oil in large nonstick skillet on medium-high heat. Add onion and cook until softened, about 5 minutes. Add tomatoes and cook 1–2 minutes, or until tomato juices disappear. Reduce heat to low. Add eggs and cook, stirring frequently, until creamy and set. Sprinkle with ¼ cup grated Parmesan cheese or crumbled feta.

baked tomatoes stuffed with couscous

These incredible stuffed tomatoes can be served hot or warm as a side dish or first course, or warm or cold at a picnic or tailgate party. Of course, the more flavorful the tomatoes, the more flavorful the dish. If tomatoes lack sweetness, if desired, sprinkle a tiny bit of sugar inside the hollowed out shells (see Step 2). For a quick variation, 3 cups of cooked rice may be substituted for couscous (skip first two procedures in Step 3).

Either olive oil or parchment paper for preparing roasting pan

10 medium tomatoes

Garlic salt to taste

Freshly ground black pepper to taste

1 cup couscous

1½ cups boiling water

¾ teaspoon salt

½ red onion, finely chopped

1 yellow bell pepper, cored and seeded, finely chopped

½ cup golden raisins, roughly chopped

2 teaspoons Dijon-style mustard

¼ cup white-wine vinegar

½ cup olive oil

½ cup chopped fresh basil

½ cup chopped fresh parsley

OPTIONAL: *½ cup toasted pine nuts*

GARNISH: sprigs of watercress

OPTIONAL GARNISH: 3 ounces prosciutto fried in 4 tablespoons olive oil

COOK'S NOTES: The couscous mixture can be prepared up to 2 days ahead and stored in an airtight container in the refrigerator. The tomatoes can be hollowed out up to 2 hours before baking.

1. Line roasting pan with parchment paper or grease pan lightly with olive oil. Preheat oven to 375 degrees.

2. Cut tops off tomatoes; save tops. Scoop out and discard seeds and core. Season with garlic salt and pepper. Place tomatoes, cut side down, on paper towels for at least 10 minutes.

3. In a large bowl, combine couscous and boiling water. Cover and let rest for about 5 minutes or until water is absorbed. Add salt, red onion, bell pepper, and golden raisins; stir to combine.

4. In a small bowl, prepare vinaigrette: whisk mustard and vinegar. Add olive oil in a thin stream, whisking constantly. Season to taste with garlic salt and pepper. Stir in basil and parsley. If using, add pine nuts and stir.

5. Stir vinaigrette into couscous. Fill tomatoes with couscous, place tomato tops on top of tomato, and bake 25 minutes. Line platter with watercress. Arrange tomatoes on top.

6. For added crunch and flavor, fry prosciutto and crumble on top of tomatoes. Heat olive oil in small, deep skillet on medium-high heat. When hot, separate thin layers of prosciutto. Add just enough prosciutto to make a single layer in oil. As it heats, prosciutto will shrivel and darken; when crisp, remove and drain on paper towels. Repeat until all prosciutto is fried. When cool enough to handle, crumble over tomatoes.

YIELD: 10 SERVINGS

NUTRITIONAL INFORMATION (PER SERVING WITHOUT PROSCIUTTO): Calories 220; fat calories 100; total fat 11 grams; sat fat 1.5 grams, cholesterol 0 milligrams; sodium 340 milligrams; total carbohydrates 27 grams; fiber 3 grams; sugars 9 grams; protein 4 grams; vitamin A IUs 20%; vitamin C 70%; calcium 4%; iron 8%.

tung ho, also tung hoa, chrysanthemum leaf

THESE EDIBLE CHRYSANTHEMUM LEAVES spring from sturdy stems and can have different shapes; some are softly rounded, others sharply ragged and feathery. All have a distinct, chrysanthemumlike aroma that is floral, yet piney.

Quickly cooked, they have a spinachlike flavor and texture. Overcooking causes increased bitterness. Sometimes small amounts are included raw in packaged baby lettuce mixtures.

Tung Ho

BUYING AND STORING

Look for fresh-looking stalks and leaves without discoloration or sliminess (leaves may be droopy, but that is normal). Use as soon as possible. Untie bundle and refrigerate, unwashed, wrapped in slightly damp paper towel in plastic bag for up to 4 days.

Domestic: *year-round*
Global: *November–May*

PREP

Trim and discard small portion at root end. Submerge in cold water; shake dry. Pat dry. For salads, cut or tear into individual leaves and discard stems (or use stems in soup). For stir-fries or to add to soup, cut into 1- or 2-inch pieces.

USE

Include small amount of leaves with other milder lettuces in salads. Or add to soup or stir-fries during last minute or two of cooking.

NUTRITIONAL INFO

1 cup is a significant source of vitamin A; good source of folate.

SERVING SUGGESTIONS

Chrysanthemum soup: Combine 4 cups chicken broth with a little minced fresh ginger and thinly sliced green onion (including $1/2$ of dark green stalks) in large saucepan. Simmer 15 minutes. Taste and add salt or pepper as needed. Add 1 cup tung ho leaves and stems (cut into 1-inch lengths). Simmer 1 minute. If desired, add a cooked pot sticker to each serving.

Salad with Asian flare: Combine butter lettuce or iceberg lettuce (torn into bite-sized pieces) with small amount of tung ho leaves. Prepare dressing by combining ¼ cup rice vinegar with ¼ cup soy sauce and 1 teaspoon Asian sesame oil; whisk in 1 teaspoon sugar and salt to taste. Add enough dressing to lightly coat leaves and toss. Top with toasted sesame seeds. Tung ho leaves can also be added to coleslaw (see Spicy 3-Cabbage Slaw, page 144).

Rice with tung ho: Prepare Asian-style dressing (see salad suggestion above), adding a gentle squeeze of Asian hot sauce and 3 tablespoons roughly chopped tung ho. Spoon sauce over steamed rice.

asian-style steamed whole fish

A good sprinkling of chopped tung ho leaves is a delectable addition to Asian-style steamed fish. It enhances both flavor and appearance. Any nonoily white-fleshed fish, such as red snapper, can be substituted for the striped sea bass in this recipe.

1 (about 2-pound) fresh whole striped sea bass, cleaned, scaled, gills and fins removed

½ teaspoon coarse salt, such as kosher

1 (about 1-inch-long) knob fresh ginger, peeled and thinly sliced

2 large cloves garlic, peeled and thinly sliced

⅔ cup reduced-sodium chicken broth

3 tablespoons reduced-sodium soy sauce

OPTIONAL: 2 tablespoons minced lemon grass

6 green onions, sliced; include most of the dark green stalks, divided use

¼ cup chopped tung ho

1 tablespoon Asian sesame oil

1 tablespoon vegetable oil

2 large shallots, finely chopped

FOR SERVING: cooked rice

1. Thoroughly rinse fish with cold water, removing any trace of blood or membranes in cavity. Pat dry with paper towels. Sprinkle inside fish with salt.

2. Using sharp knife, make crosswise diagonal slices at 30-degree angle (to top of fish) at 1-inch intervals, starting below head and ending above tail, and cutting to bone. Usually there is enough room to make 4–5 cuts on each side of fish. Place 1 slice ginger and 1 slice garlic in each slit. Place fish in steamer above water. (If using bamboo steamer, fish should be in glass pie pan. If using a fish steamer, fish should be in double layer of heavy-duty aluminum foil, formed into pan shape a little bigger than fish. If using larger deep skillet or Dutch oven, fish should be elevated in glass pie pan or heatproof platter.)

3. Pour broth and soy sauce around fish. Add lemon grass (if using) and half green onions to broth mixture. If you have garlic or ginger left over, mince it and add to broth mixture.

Cover pot or steamer and bring water beneath fish to boil.

4. Steam 15–20 minutes, or until fish is opaque (check at bottom of score marks). Add tung ho and cover, steam 1–2 minutes. Remove from heat. Using oven mitts, remove pan (or aluminum foil) containing fish. Using large spatula, lift fish and place on serving platter, reserving juices around fish.

5. Heat Asian sesame oil and vegetable oil in small saucepan on medium-high heat. Add shallots and cook until softened. Remove from heat. Add soy mixture (reserved juices) to shallots and stir to combine. Add remaining green onions.

6. Pour shallot mixture over fish. Serve immediately with rice.

YIELD: 2–3 SERVINGS

NUTRITIONAL INFORMATION (PER SERVING):
Calories 260; fat calories 108; total fat 12 grams; sat fat 2.5 grams; cholesterol 60 milligrams; sodium 1080 milligrams; total carbohydrates 5 grams; fiber less than 1 gram; sugars 1 grams; protein 31 grams; vitamin A IUs 10%; vitamin C 6%; calcium 4%; iron 8%.

water chestnut

FRESH OR CANNED, water chestnuts combine a crunchy, applelike texture with a mildly sweet taste. But the taste is more complex and appealing in fresh water chestnuts. They are juicy and buttery, creamy with a subtle, coconutlike flavor that makes them well worth the effort it takes to clean and peel them.

About 1 inch in diameter, fresh water chestnuts are corms (the enlarged fleshy tip of an underwater stem) shaped like bulbs that are flattened at top and bottom. The off-white flesh is covered in a mahogany-brown skin; often, small dry leaves point toward center of stem end.

BUYING AND STORING

They should be very firm and free of soft spots. Because they grow in mud, they may have dirt on them, which is not a bad condition, because when washed they start to deteriorate. Refrigerate, unwashed, in paper bag up to 7 days.
Domestic: *none*
Global: *yea-round*

PREP

Wash thoroughly. Using small paring knife, cut off top and bottom ends to expose white flesh. Cut in spiral around edge of water chestnut to remove brown skin. Rinse. Leave whole or slice. To prevent discoloration, immerse in acidulated water (cold water with small amount of lemon juice).

USE

Eat raw or cooked. Fresh water chestnuts are so sweet and delicious, they make a wonderful snack eaten out of hand. Or add them to salads or salsas. To cook: stir-fry, braise, or steam.

NUTRITIONAL INFO

$\frac{1}{2}$ cup is a significant source of vitamin B_6 and potassium.

SERVING SUGGESTIONS

Midcentury hip: Water chestnuts wrapped in bacon are a classic appetizer. Combine $\frac{1}{4}$ cup soy sauce and 2 tablespoons sugar in bowl. Add water chestnuts and toss; marinate 30 minutes, tossing occasionally. Cut bacon in half crosswise. Twist each half-strip of bacon around water chestnut and secure with wooden toothpick. Place in single layer on rimmed baking sheet. Bake in 400-degree oven for 15 minutes or until bacon is crisp. Drain on paper towels and serve warm.

Fresh vegetable salad with Asian dressing: In small bowl, combine 3 tablespoons rice vinegar mixed with 2 tablespoons soy sauce, $\frac{1}{2}$ teaspoon sugar, $\frac{1}{4}$ teaspoon cayenne, 1 teaspoon Asian sesame oil, 1 small carrot (finely diced), and salt to taste. Blanch baby bok choy, sno peas, and sugar snap peas in boiling water until tender-crisp. Drain and refresh with cold running water. Drain again and gently pat dry. Place in bowl with fresh water chestnuts (peeled and sliced). Add dressing and toss.

Crunchy burgers: Add finely diced water chestnuts to ground beef or ground turkey. If desired, add minced fresh ginger and chopped green onion and cilantro. For a spicier version, add a smidgen of Asian hot sauce. Form into patties. Grill or fry, then, if desired, serve topped with broiled pineapple (see No-toil broil, page 92).

Fillings and flavorings: Add finely diced water chestnuts to fillings for pot stickers, won tons, and spring rolls. Add to chicken salad, shrimp salad, fried rice, or chow mein.

Water Chestnut

winter squash

ACORN (GREEN, GOLD, AND WHITE)	HUBBARD (BLUE AND ORANGE)
BANANA	KABOCHA
BUTTERCUP	ORANGETTI
BUTTERNUT	RED KURI
CARNIVAL	SPAGHETTI
DELICATA	SWEET DUMPLING
GOLD NUGGET	TURBAN

WINTER SQUASH COME IN A DIZZYING ARRAY OF COLORS, from cool greens to warm yellows and bright oranges. Some are rounded, others fluted. Some are smooth, others bumpy. Most share flesh that has a mellow, slightly sweet flavor, but few varieties are exactly the same in taste or texture.

Hard skin and inedible seeds distinguish them from their soft-skinned cousins, the summer squash (such as zucchini). Winter squash are harvested when fully mature, when their seeds have become woody and large, and their skin has toughened.

Blue Hubbard

Banana

Buttercup

Green Acorn

Kabocha

BUYING AND STORING

Rind should be intact with no signs of decay or soft spots. Avoid squash with cracks or watery areas. Choose squash that seem heavy for their size; a heavier squash contains more edible flesh. Banana squash and Hubbard squash are sold in cut pieces. In this case, look for brightly colored and fresh-looking flesh; avoid discolored pieces; refrigerate in plastic bags up to 5 days.

For storage, generally their thick, hard rinds form a protective barrier around flesh so they can be kept in cool, dark, well-ventilated location for 30–180 days. Do not refrigerate uncooked, uncut winter squash. If cut, refrigerate. Cooked, puréed squash freezes well up to 3 months.

GREEN ACORN, BANANA, BUTTERNUT, KABOCHA, SPAGHETTI

Domestic: *year-round*
Global: *November—September*

ALL OTHER VARIETIES

Domestic: *August–December*
Global: *none*

PREP

All winter squash must be cooked. Can be steamed, baked, microwaved, or boiled, but boiling can make it watery and diminish flavor. When cutting tougher varieties, use a cleaver or hefty chef's knife.

Most winter squash, except butternut, delicata, and spaghetti, have rinds that are so hard it is almost impossible to peel them. It's easier to cut them in half, remove seeds, and bake them. To bake, brush flesh side with oil or butter. Place flesh side down on rimmed baking sheet. Bake in 375-degree oven until tender, about 30–40 minutes.

ACORN

(green, gold, and white)
Acorn-shaped, deeply fluted lengthwise, diameter about 6–8 inches. Mild, fine-textured, pale orange-yellow flesh. Weight: 1–3 pounds. ■ *Cut in half with sturdy knife, either through "equator" or top to bottom. Scoop out seeds.* ■ Makes a natural bowl, so it can be stuffed with things such as cornbread stuffing, cooked sausage mixtures, spinach soufflé, or applesauce. Bake until almost tender; fill with desired mixture and bake until tender and filling is hot.

BANANA

Large and cylindrical with tapered ends, its pinkish-tan or gray or pale blue skin protects bright yellow flesh. Weight: 10–25 pounds. ■ *Often sold cut in chunks. If whole, cut off stem end. Carefully insert cleaver lengthwise into rind, using rubber mallet or rolling pin if necessary to gently hammer where blade meets handle until squash splits. Or pierce in 2–4 places and microwave 1–2 minutes if having trouble splitting (and squash is a manageable size for microwave oven). When split, scoop out seeds.* ■ Bake 25 minutes (see Prep). Meanwhile, in saucepan on medium heat, melt 1/4 cup butter. Stir in 1/4 cup honey and 1 tablespoon minced orange zest (colored part of peel). Turn squash skin down. Spoon mixture over banana squash. Bake 10 minutes or until tender. Season with salt and pepper.

BUTTERCUP

Pumpkin-shaped, medium-sized with dark green or orange rind and light blue-gray turban at stem. Sometimes flecked with gray. Flesh is orange with sweet potato-like taste. Weight: 1^1/$_2$–6 pounds. ■ *Cut in half and bake (see Prep). Or if rind is tender enough, cut in half, remove seeds and cut into rind-on chunks; steam until tender.* ■ Remove cooked squash from rind and purée, or mash with a little butter, plain yogurt, tangerine or orange juice, salt, and pepper.

BUTTERNUT

Cylindrical top rests on bulblike bottom. Smooth, thin, pinkish-tan rind covers sweet, orange flesh. Weight: 2–5 pounds. ■ *Pound per pound yields more flesh than most winter squash. Remove bulb from cylindrical neck by cutting with sturdy knife. Place cylindrical neck cut side down and, starting at top, cut off skin in strips from top to bottom. Remove seeds from bulb. Peel bulb. Cut into cubes.* ■ Steam, bake, or boil. Delectable in soups, pasta, and rice dishes. See Roasted Butternut Squash Risotto recipe, page 304.

CARNIVAL

Cross between acorn and sweet dumpling. Round, flattened at top and bottom, with deep fluting. Yellow, deep green, and cream colors with green speckling. Flesh is deep yellow and sweet. Weight: 8 ounces to 2 pounds. ■ *See Acorn for how to prep.* ■ See Buttercup for how to use.

DELICATA

Cylindrical with shallow, lengthwise fluting. Pale yellow rind with green seams in crease of each flute. Flesh is deep yellow to orange and tastes like cross between butternut and sweet potatoes. Weight: 1–3 pounds. ■ *Peel with vegetable peeler when raw. Cut in half lengthwise and scoop out seeds.* ■ Steaming is best, but can be baked.

GOLD NUGGET

Shaped like small pumpkin with thick, hard-to-cut bright-orange rind. Flesh is orange-yellow and sweet. Weight: 8 ounces to 2 pounds. ■ *Place in microwave 1–1^1/$_2$ minutes. Cut in half with sturdy knife; scoop out seeds.* ■ See Acorn for how to use.

HUBBARD

(blue and orange)

Shaped like an enormous top that is rounder at the bottom and narrows toward stem; they can have orange, blue or green skin that is thick and bumpy. Flesh is yellow-orange. Weight: 5–15 pounds. ■ *Often sold cut into chunks. See Acorn.* ■ Bake or microwave until tender. Mash or purée with a little butter, salt, and pepper. Cook sliced sweet onion in small amount of olive oil until lightly caramelized and season with a pinch of ground cinnamon and sugar. Spoon onions over squash. Or use purée as filling for ravioli.

KABOCHA

Round, flattened at top and bottom. Deep green rind mottled with pale uneven stripes and random markings. Flesh is deep yellow-orange and sweet. Weight: 1^1/$_2$–6 pounds. ■ *See Acorn for how to prep.* ■ See Acorn for how to use.

ORANGETTI, SPAGHETTI

Watermelon-shaped with yellow or orange (Orangetti) skin that is fairly tender. Once cooked, flesh separates into cream-colored spaghetti-like strands. Weight: 1–10 pounds. ■ *Cut in half lengthwise with sturdy knife.* ■ Place cut side down in baking pan with ^{1}/$_4$ inch water. Bake at 375 degrees about 35 minutes. When cool enough to handle scrape out interior and separate into strands. Serve like pasta or cold as salad ingredient.

SWEET DUMPLING

Small, about the size of a grapefruit, with cream-colored rind with deep green lengthwise bands in creases of flutes. Flesh is yellow-orange and very sweet. Weight: 8 ounces to 2 pounds. ■ *See Acorn for how to prep.* ■ See Acorn for how to use.

RED KURI

Bright red-orange rind, sometimes with greenish highlights. Flesh is orange with sweet, nutty flavor. Weight: 3–8 pounds. ■ *See Acorn for how to prep.* ■ See Acorn for how to use.

TURBAN

Unusual shape that looks like a flattened pumpkin wearing a crown. Mostly bright orange with splashes of cream and green, usually in lengthwise stripes. Flesh is orange and ranges from mild to sweet. Weight: 2–10 pounds. ■ *See Gold Nugget for how to prep.* ■ See Hubbard for how to use.

Spaghetti

Butternut

Red Kuri

Carnival

Gold Nugget

Sweet Dumpling

Orange Hubbard

Delicata

Turban

White Acorn

NUTRITIONAL INFO

1 cup cubed is a good source of vitamins A and C; significant source of potassium.

roasted butternut squash risotto

Naturally sweet chunks of butternut squash meld into this creamy risotto, giving it a beautiful orange color and delectable taste. It can be served as a first course or the main event.

1 (3-pound) butternut squash

Salt to taste

About 6 cups reduced-sodium chicken broth, low fat preferred

1 tablespoon unsalted butter

1 medium onion, chopped

1½ cups Arborio rice

1 teaspoon minced garlic

½ teaspoon ground cumin

½ cup dry white wine

1 cup grated Parmesan cheese

1½ teaspoon chopped fresh sage

4 ounces (6 cups loosely packed) clean baby spinach

COOK'S NOTES: If you have leftover risotto, make risotto cakes. Chill leftovers. Form into 3-inch-wide patties. Dip into beaten egg and coat with mixture of fresh bread crumbs and grated Parmesan cheese. Heat 2–3 teaspoons olive oil in nonstick skillet on medium-high heat. Add cakes and cook until browned on each side and heated through.

1. Preheat oven to 450 degrees. Cut squash in half lengthwise and scoop out and discard seeds. Season with salt. Place cut side down on rimmed baking sheet. Roast until tender, about 40–50 minutes. Scoop out flesh and cut into ½-inch chunks.

2. Place broth in medium saucepan and place on low heat.

3. In large, deep skillet, melt butter on medium-high heat. Add onion and cook until softened, about 4–5 minutes. Add rice, garlic, and cumin; cook, stirring frequently, about 3 minutes. Add wine; stir. Cook until wine is absorbed. Reduce heat to medium.

4. Add enough broth to barely cover rice mixture. Cook, stirring frequently, until broth is absorbed. Add ½ cup broth; stir constantly, simmering until broth absorbs. Continue in same manner, adding broth ½ cup at a time, and letting it absorb before adding more. Repeat until rice is very creamy and cooked al dente. (There may be broth leftover.) Stir in squash, cheese, salt, sage, and spinach. Simmer 1 minute. If necessary, add more broth to maintain creaminess. Taste and adjust seasoning as needed. Serve in shallow individual bowls.

YIELD: 6 SERVINGS

NUTRITIONAL INFORMATION (PER SERVING): Calories 260; fat calories 31.5; total fat 3.5 grams; sat fat 2 grams; cholesterol 10 milligrams; sodium 670 milligrams; total carbohydrates 44 grams; fiber 4 grams; sugars 6 grams; protein 12 grams; vitamin A lus 400%; vitamin C 70%; calcium 20%; iron 25%.

yuca root,
also cassava, manioc

SHAPED LIKE A LARGE, ELONGATED SWEET POTATO, yuca root is generally 6–15 inches long. Because this tuber is susceptible to mold, its dark brown, barklike skin is often covered with a layer of wax.

The flesh is usually creamy white, but occasionally has a soft pink blush. Never eaten raw, it has a pleasant chewy texture and starchy sweetness when cooked. Ground into flour and formed into spheres, it becomes tapioca.

BUYING AND STORING

Avoid those with soft spots or mold. They should have a fresh, clean scent. Store in cool, dark location for up to 1 week, or refrigerate (keeping it dry) up to 2 weeks.

Domestic: *none*
Global: *year-round*

PREP

Cut into 4-inch-long pieces. Place cut side down on work surface; remove skin by cutting from top to bottom. Discard skin. Halve lengthwise and remove any inedible fibrous center (or remove after cooking).

USE

Do not eat raw (eaten raw it contains harmful acid). Generally boiled, but it can be roasted, simmered, or thinly sliced and fried for chips. To boil, cook in boiling salted water until fork tender (but still intact). Cooking times vary from 20 to 60 minutes. It's best to stand "over the pot" and remove chunks as they become tender.

NUTRITIONAL INFO

1 cup is an excellent source of vitamin C and significant source of potassium.

Yuca Root

SERVING SUGGESTIONS

Taco filling: Cut yuca into ¼-inch dice (see Prep). Boil until tender; drain and place on platter. Top with tomatillo salsa, Salsa Verde (see page 290), crumbled queso fresco or feta cheese, and chopped cilantro. Serve with warm corn tortillas.

Yuca crisps: Peel 1 pound yuca (see Prep) and cut into ½-inch-wide slices. Boil until tender; drain and pat dry on paper towels. Heat 2 inches of vegetable oil in deep skillet. Fry in batches in 360-degree oil, turning once, until lightly browned, about 5 minutes. Drain on paper towels. Season with coarse salt, and if desired, ground chile powder. Accompany with lime wedges.

Fritters: Peel and cut 2 pounds yuca into 1-inch cubes. Boil until tender and drain. While still warm, add 2 tablespoons butter, 1 teaspoon salt, and 1 teaspoon ground black pepper. Mash. Shape into 3-inch patties. Coat lightly with all-purpose flour and dip in beaten egg. Heat ½ inch vegetable oil or peanut oil in large, deep skillet on medium-high heat. Sauté until browned on both sides. Serve with tomato-based salsa.

sautéed yuca with avocado salad

This tempting side dish is delicious served with grilled meat, such as spicy barbecued pork.

1½ pounds yuca root, peeled, cut into 1-inch cubes

6 tablespoons vegetable oil or canola oil

2 large cloves garlic, minced

5 tablespoons freshly squeezed lemon juice, divided use

Salt and pepper to taste

2 ripe avocados, peeled and diced

½ red onion, finely diced

½ jalapeño chile, seeded and minced

2 tablespoons finely chopped cilantro

1. Cook yuca root until tender (see Use). Gently pat dry with paper towel.

2. Heat oil in large, deep skillet on medium-high heat. Add yuca root and cook for about 10 minutes or until lightly browned, tossing occasionally. Remove from heat. Add garlic; toss. Carefully add 3 tablespoons lemon juice (it may splatter), salt, and pepper. Place in center of platter.

3. Gently toss avocado, red onion, chile, and 2 tablespoons lemon juice. Season to taste with salt and pepper. Spoon mixture around edge of yuca. Sprinkle entire dish with chopped cilantro. Serve.

YIELD: 6 SERVINGS

NUTRITIONAL INFORMATION (PER SERVING): Calories 410; fat calories 207; total fat 23 grams; sat fat 2.5 grams; cholesterol 0 milligrams; sodium 15 milligrams; total carbohydrates 51 grams; fiber 7 grams; sugars 1 gram; protein 3 grams; vitamin A IUs 0%; vitamin C 45%; calcium 2%; iron 2%.

yu choy sum, also gai ngot

ALTHOUGH THIS "CHOY" HAS CURVED LEAVES, yu choy sum's structure and flavor profile is so different from the other "choys," it warranted a separate listing. Unlike bulblike bok choy, choy sum, and gai choy, this vegetable most often has a very sturdy stalk that supports sporadically arranged (large and small) curved stems. The yellow-green stems are topped with dark green, almost oval leaves.

The flavor profile is decidedly sweeter. The fibrous stalks taste like very mild celery, while leaves taste much like spinach.

Yu Choy Sum

BUYING AND STORING

Look for crisp stalks and leaves. Leaves should be bright green. Stalks should snap when broken and appear juicy. Avoid those with brown spots and limpness. Refrigerate unwashed in perforated bag in crisper drawer up to 5 days.
Domestic: *year-round*
Global: *November–March*

PREP

Trim and discard ¼ inch at base. Separate stalks and rinse thoroughly in cold running water. Shake dry. Cut stems into 1-inch lengths and roughly chop leaves.

USE

Stir-fry, braise, steam, microwave, or boil. Use in soups or rice dishes, or use leaves as a spinachlike layer in lasagna.

NUTRITIONAL INFO

1 cup is a good source of vitamins A and C.

SERVING SUGGESTIONS

Spinachlike side dish: Tear 1 pound clean yu choy sum leaves into bite-sized pieces. Cut 3 large peeled shallots into thin slices. In small dish, combine 1 tablespoon dry white wine, 2 tablespoons soy sauce, 1 tablespoon rice vinegar, ½ teaspoon salt, and pinch of sugar. Heat wok or large, deep skillet on high heat. Heat 2 tablespoons vegetable oil. Add shallots and cook 1 minute, stirring occasionally. Add yu choy sum and cook 1 minute, stirring occasionally. Add soy mixture and toss. Cook until liquid evaporates and yu choy sum is tender.

Yu choy sum dip: Prepare yu choy sum as in Spinachlike side dish, above. Cool in colander. When cool, squeeze out liquid and place in food processor fitted with metal blade. Add 6 ounces garlic-and-herb soft cheese (such as Boursin) and 3 tablespoons grated Parmesan cheese. Pulse to purée. Serve with raw vegetables or crackers.

Stir-fry: Substitute leaves and stems of yu choy sum for ong choy (water spinach) in quick stir-fry dish (see Stir-Fried Water Spinach, page 232).

Yu choy sum, proscuitto, cheese, and chicken: Yu choy sum's mild flavor profile pairs beautifully with Italian flavorings. Flatten 4 boneless chicken breasts between pieces of plastic wrap. Season with salt and pepper. Heat 1 tablespoon butter and 1 tablespoon vegetable oil in large, deep skillet on medium-high heat. Add chicken and brown nicely, about 5 minutes on each side. Remove from heat and top each with a little thinly shredded yu choy sum leaves, thin slice of prosciutto, and thin slice of mozzarella cheese. Reduce heat to low. Cover and cook until cheese melts and chicken is thoroughly cooked, about 3 minutes, adding a little dry white wine if pan seems too dry.

glossary and prep help

Gizmos That Help to Prep Produce: Peelers, Pitters, Strippers, and Zesters

A small, sharp paring knife can be an efficient tool for trimming and peeling, but a wide variety of specialty peelers are also available.

SWIVEL-BLADED VEGETABLE PEELERS can make quick work of peeling everything from asparagus to yams. Some have serrated blades that are razor-sharp and can be used to peel soft, delicate produce, such as peaches or tomatoes.

PITTERS are designed to remove a single pit from fruit, such as cherries, olives, or lychees. The most common scissors-style pitter has two handles that activate a solid cylindrical plunger when the handles are drawn together.

STRIPPERS cut long ribbons of citrus peel that are used as garnish, most often in cocktails. Generally they have a short handle topped with a flat metal bar, with a "v-curved" portion set either vertically or horizontally. Pressed firmly against the peel, the stripper is drawn either lengthwise down the peel or, for longer strips, around the circumference.

ZESTERS are designed to remove outer colored portion of citrus peel (called zest). Some zesters have a curved metal bar attached to a handle; the bar has several tiny holes. When drawn lengthwise down the peel, thin ribbons of zest erupt. Another style called a Microplane is a long, stainless steel rasp; some have rubber handles, others don't. To use, swipe citrus down the length of the rasp. Tiny, lacelike shards fall from the blade.

Zest can also be removed with a box grater or swivel-bladed vegetable peeler. Before removing zest, wash and dry fruit thoroughly. For best results, remove zest before cutting or juicing fruit. Also, remove only the outer part of peel; do not include the bitter white pith.

ACIDULATED WATER: Cold water augmented with either lemon juice, lime juice, or white distilled vinegar is used to prevent discoloration of some cut fruits and vegetables (such as apples and artichokes). Generally the cut produce is soaked in the acidulated water, but it can also be used as a cooking medium.

BROWN-BAG RIPENING: To ripen some firm fruit, place in paper bag (check storing information in specific fruit to see if its appropriate). Loosely close top of bag and store at room temperature out of direct sunlight. The paper bag traps ethylene while allowing exchange of air into and out of the bag. Check fruit daily; once it gives to gentle pressure, refrigerate.

CALYX: The leaves attached to the fruit at the stem end.

FREEZING: For freezing, package food in containers that are completely airtight. Freezer burn, a change in color and texture as well as flavor is a result of air coming in contact with frozen food; the air removes moisture and dries food out. Cool food completely before freezing. Label everything, including name of item and date. A permanent ink marker is helpful. Thaw frozen food in refrigerator. For best flavor and texture limit freezing time to no more than 3 months.

CUTTING CITRUS INTO SEGMENTS: Cut top and bottom off citrus, making those two cuts parallel to each other and cutting just below white pith. Place cut-side down on work surface. Cut off peel and pith in strips about 1-inch wide, starting at the top of the fruit and cutting down (following contour of shape). Working over bowl to collect juice, use a sharp, small knife to cut parallel to 1 section's membrane, cut to center; turn knife and cut along the membrane on the other side of that section to remove it. Repeat until all sections are removed and cut from their membranes.

PRODUCE NUTRITIONAL INFORMATION: Terms "excellent," "good," and "significant" relate to percentages of U.S. RDA (recommended daily allowance). If the fruit or vegetable meets 40% to 99% of U.S. RDA, it is rated "excellent." If it meets 25% to 39%, it is rated "good." If it meets 10% to 24%, it is rated "significant."

To prepare simple vinaigrette: Combine 2 tablespoons red-wine vinegar with 2 tablespoons sherry vinegar and ½ teaspoon kosher salt (or fine sea salt) in medium bowl. Whisk to dissolve salt. Whisk in ¾ cup extra-virgin olive oil. Taste and add more salt if needed. If desired, freshly-squeezed lemon juice may be substituted for all or part of vinegar. If a mustardy taste is preferred, add a teaspoon of Dijon Mustard when salt is added. Proportion of acid to oil can be adjusted to suit individual tastes. Vinegars or lemon juice can be doubled, if desired.

availability guide

APRIUM: Domestic (May to June), Global (none)

ARTICHOKE: Domestic (year-round, but peaks March to May and September to November), Global (none)

ASIAN PEAR

Korean: Domestic (none), Global (October to March)

Yali: Domestic (September to December), Global (September to December)

Other Varieties: Domestic (June to January), Global (February to May)

AVOCADO: Domestic (year-round), Global (year-round)

BANANA AND BANANA LEAF

Baby (Finger), Burro, Common, Manzano, Red, Common Plantain, Hawaiian Plantain, Banana Leaf: Domestic (none), Global (year-round)

BEAN

Chinese: Domestic (June to November), Global (November to June)

Dragon Tongue, French (Haricot Vert), Green, Purple Wax, Yellow Wax: Domestic (year-round), Global (December to April)

Fava: Domestic (March to September), Global (October to March)

Soybean (Edamame): Domestic (none), Global (year-round)

BEET: Domestic (year-round), Global (none)

BERRIES

Blackberry: Domestic (March to October), Global (October to March)

Blueberry: Domestic (April to October), Global (year-round)

Boysenberry: Domestic (May to June), Global (none)

Cape Gooseberry: Domestic (September to November, Global (year-round)

Cranberry: Domestic (October to November), Global (none)

Currant: Domestic (March to July), Global (none)

Gooseberry: Domestic (March to May), Global (none)

Loganberry: Domestic (March to April), Global (none)

Raspberry: Domestic (year-round), Global (October to April)

Strawberry: Domestic (year-round), Global (January to March)

Wild Strawberry (Fraise des Bois): Domestic (April to June), Global (none)

BITTER MELON: Domestic (year-round), Global (year-round)

BROCCOLINI: Domestic (year-round), Global (year-round)

BUDDHA'S HAND CITRON (FINGERED CITRON): Domestic (October to January), Global (none)

CABBAGE: Domestic (year-round), Global (year-round)

CACTUS LEAF (NOPAL): Domestic (year-round), Global (year-round)

CACTUS PEAR: Domestic (April to August), Global (June to September)

CARDONI: Domestic (October to April), Global (none)

CELERY: Domestic (year-round), Global (year-round)

CELERY ROOT: Domestic (August to June), Global (none)

CHARD: Domestic (year-round), Global (none)

CHERIMOYA: Domestic (December to June), Global (July to November)

CHILE

All chiles except Hatch: Domestic (June to October), Global (year-round)

Hatch chile: Domestic (June to September), Global (none)

CHINESE OKRA (LOOFAH): Domestic (May to October), Global (November to May)

CHOY (WITH CURVED STALKS)

Baby Bok Choy, Bok Choy, Choy Sum: Domestic (year-round), Global (year-round)

Gai Choy: Domestic (year-round), Global (none)

COCONUT: Domestic (none), Global (year-round)

CORN

Baby, Bicolor, White, Yellow: Domestic (May to September), Global (November to April)

Red: Domestic (July to September), Global (none)

CUCUMBER

Armenian: Domestic (July to August), Global (none)

Baby (Persian), Common, Hot House: Domestic (year-round), Global (year-round)

Japanese: Domestic (year-round), Global (November to April)

Lemon: Domestic (sporadically in spring), Global (none)

Pickling: Domestic (May to August), Global (November to May)

DRAGON FRUIT (PITAYA): Domestic (August to November), Global (none)

EGGPLANT

Baby Purple (Indian), Baby White: Domestic (April to September), Global (November to January)

Chinese, Japanese, Thai: Domestic (April to November), Global: November to March

Common (Purple): Domestic (March to November), Global (November to April)

Graffiti: Domestic (none), Global (September to December)

White: Domestic (March to June), Global (none)

ENDIVE: Domestic (year-round), Global (none)

FEIJOA: Domestic (October to January), Global (April to January)

FENNEL: Domestic (year-round), Global (none)

FIDDLEHEAD FERN: Domestic (March to June), Global (none)

FIG

Black Mission: Domestic (July to October), Global (none)

Brown Turkey: Domestic (June to September), Global (March to May)

Calimyrna (Royal Mediterranean): Domestic (July to October), Global (none)

Kadota: Domestic (July to September), Global (none)

GAI LAN (CHINESE BROCCOLI): Domestic (year-round), Global (none)

GALANGAL: Domestic (year-round), Global (year-round)

GARLIC

Common (Purple, White): Domestic (year-round), Global (year-round)

Elephant: Domestic (year-round), Global (none)

Green (Spring): Domestic (February to June), Global (none)

Rocambole: Domestic (September to March), Global (none)

GINGER: Domestic (November to June), Global (year-round)

GOBO ROOT (BURDOCK): Domestic (June to October), Global (November to May)

GRAPE

Champagne: Domestic (June to September), Global (none)

Common Black: Domestic (August to January), Global (December to June)

Common Green, Common Red: Domestic (May to December), Global (December to June)

Concord: Domestic (August to September), Global (none)

Globe: Domestic (August to January), Global (January to June)

Muscat: Domestic (none), Global (March to May)

Muscato: Domestic (June to October), Global (none)

GRAPEFRUIT

Cocktail: Domestic (January to March), Global (none)

Melogold: Domestic (October to April), Global (none)

Oro Blanco: Domestic (November to March), Global (none)

Pummelo: Domestic (November to March), Global (none)

Pink, Red, Ruby: Domestic (year-round), Global (none)

GREENS: Domestic (year-round), Global (year-round)

GUAVA: Domestic (September to March), Global: (April to June and October to January)

HEARTS OF PALM: Domestic (year-round), Global (year-round)

HORNED MELON: Domestic (July to April), Global (February to June)

HORSERADISH: Domestic (year-round), Global (none)

JACKFRUIT: Domestic (none), Global (May to July)

JICAMA: Domestic (none), Global (year-round)

JUJUBE: Domestic (July to October), Global (none)

KAFFIR LEAF: Domestic (year-round), Global (none)

KIWI

Baby Kiwi: Domestic (September to October)

Green Kiwi: Domestic (October to March), Global (March to October)

Gold Kiwi: Domestic (none), Global (June to September)

KOHLRABI: Domestic (year-round), Global (none)

KUMQUAT: Domestic (November to July), Global (none)

LEEK

Chinese: Domestic (November to April), Global (none)

Baby Leek, Leek: Domestic (year-round), Global (December to February)

Ramps: Domestic (March to June), Global (none)

LEMON

Eureka, Lisbon: Domestic (year-round), Global (none)

Meyer: Domestic (October to May), Global (none)

LEMON GRASS: Domestic (year-round), Global (December to May)

LIME: Domestic (October to March), Global (year-round)

LIMEQUAT: Domestic (July to November), Global (none)

LONGAN: Domestic (October to May), Global (none)

LOQUAT: Domestic (April to June), Global (November to December)

LOTUS ROOT: Domestic (none), Global (year-round)

LYCHEE: Domestic (May to June), Global (May to September)

MALANGA: Domestic (none), Global (year-round)

MANGO

Altaulfo, Haden, Kent, Tommy Atkins: Domestic (none), Global (year-round)

Keitt: Domestic (July to October), Global (year-round)

MELON

Canary, Casaba, Crenshaw, Galia, Persian: Domestic (May to September), Global (November to December)

Cantaloupe, Common Green Honeydew: Domestic (year-round), Global (year-round)

Charentais: Domestic (May to September), Global (January to May)

Sharlyn: Domestic (May to September), Global (none)

Gold Honeydew, Orange Honeydew: Domestic (May to July), Global (none)

Piel de Sapo, Santa Claus: Domestic (May to September), Global (March to April)

Hami: Domestic (May to July), Global (none)

Gaya: Domestic (none), Global (May to June)

Korean: Domestic (May to September), Global (October to April)

Sprite: Domestic (June to September), Global (May to June)

MICROGREENS: Domestic (year-round), Global (none)

MUSHROOM

Common White (Button), Cremini, Enoki, Oyster, Portobello, Portobella, Portobellini, Shiitake, Wood Ear: Domestic (year-round), Global (none)

Chanterelle: Domestic (July to January), Global (February to June)

Lobster: Domestic (July to October), Global (none)

Morel: Domestic (April to June), Global (sporadically July to December)

Porcini: Domestic (June to October), Global (sporadically November to April)

NECTARINE

Honeydew, Saturn: Domestic (July to August), Global (none)

Mango: Domestic (June to August), Global (none)

White-Fleshed and Yellow-Fleshed : Domestic (May to October), Global (December to May)

NIRA GRASS: Domestic (year-round), Global (November to May)

OKRA: Domestic (April to September), Global (November to May)

ONG CHOY (WATER SPINACH): Domestic (year-round), Global (none)

ONION

Spring Onions (Green Onions/Scallions, Mexican BBQ): Domestic (year-round), Global (year-round)

Storage Onions (Boiler, Cipolline, Cipolla, Pearl): Domestic (year-round), Global (none)

Sweet Onions

Maui: Domestic (year-round), Global (none)

Texas Sweets/Oso Sweets: Domestic (January to September), Global (none)

Vidalia (Georgia): Domestic (April to June), Global (none)

Walla Walla: Domestic (June to August), Global (none)

ORANGE

Blood (Moro): Domestic (December to May), Global (year-round)

Cara Cara: Domestic (December to April), Global (year-round)

Navel: Domestic (October to May), Global (year-round)

Seville (Sour): Domestic (January to February), Global (year-round)

Valencia: Domestic (June to September), Global (year-round)

PAPAYA

Green: Domestic (none), Global (year-round)

Maradol: Domestic (none), Global (year-round)

Strawberry, Yellow-Flesh: Domestic (year-round), Global (year-round)

PARSLEY ROOT: Domestic (year-round), Global (none)

PARSNIP: Domestic (year-round), Global (none)

PASSION FRUIT

Common: Domestic (July to February), Global (March to June)

Vanilla: Domestic (none), Global (March to June)

PEA

Black-Eyed (shelled, partially cooked): Domestic (year-round), Global (none)

English: Domestic (May to July), Global (September to April)

Sno (Snow) and Sugar Snap: Domestic (April to November), Global (September to May)

PEA SHOOTS: Domestic (year-round with occasional interruptions due to rain), Global (none)

PEACH

Indian: Domestic (August to September), Global (none)

Saturn: Domestic (June to August), Global (none)

White-Fleshed, Yellow-Fleshed : Domestic (May to October), Global (November to May)

PEAR (all pear varieties are available globally December to April)

Bartlett, Bosc, Red Bartlett: Domestic (June to March)

Comice: Domestic (September to March)

D'Anjou, Red D'Anjou: Domestic (September to July)

Forrelle: Domestic (September to March)

Seckel: Domestic (September to February)

PEPINO MELON: Domestic (none), Global (year-round)

PERSIMMON

Cinnamon: Domestic (October to December), Global (none)

Fuyu, Hachiya: Domestic (October to December), Global (May to June)

Sharon Fruit: Domestic (none), Global December to February

PINEAPPLE: Domestic (year-round), Global (year-round)

PLUMCOT: Domestic (May to July), Global (none)

PLUOT: Domestic (May to September), Global (January to March)

POMEGRANATE: Domestic (August to December), Global (none)

POTATO

Creamers and Regular: Domestic (year-round), Global (none)

Fingerling: Domestic (September to March), Global (none)

PUMPKIN

All varieties except Fairytale: Domestic (September to November), Global (none)

Fairytale: Domestic (October), Global (none)

QUINCE: Domestic (September to December), Global (May to July)

RADICCHIO: Domestic (May to January), Global (February to April)

RADISH: Domestic (year-round), Global (none)

RAMBUTAN: Domestic (October to May), Global (August to October)

RAPINI: Domestic (year-round), Global (none)

RHUBARB: Domestic Hothouse (December to March), Domestic Field-Grown (March to October), Global (none)

RUTABAGA: Domestic (year-round), Global (year-round)

SALICORNIA: Domestic (none), Global (year-round)

SALSIFY: Domestic (none), Global (year-round, with potential gaps in September)

SAPOTE

Mamey: Domestic (July to October), Global (none)

White: Domestic (year-round), Global (none)

SHALLOT: Domestic (year-round), Global (year-round)

SQUASH BLOSSOMS: Domestic (June to July), Global (February to August)

STAR FRUIT (CARAMBOLA): Domestic (year-round), Global (year-round)

SUMMER SQUASH

Those with edible skin:

Crookneck, Goldbar, Summer Green, Summer Yellow, Zucchini: Domestic (May to December), Global (December to May)

Baby Crookneck, Baby Goldbar, Baby Summer Green (Pattypan), Baby Zucchini: Domestic (April to July), Global (year-round, peak in spring and summer)

Baby Scallopini, Scallopini: Domestic (March to April), Global (none)

Eight Ball: Domestic (April to May), Global (January to May)

Tatuma: Domestic (none), Global (year-round)

Those with nonedible skin:

Chayote: Domestic (May to October), Global (October to May)

Cucuzza: Domestic (June to October), Global (none)

Mo Qua: Domestic (May to November), Global (November to May)

Pul Qua (Opo): Domestic (May to December), Global (November to May)

Winter Melon: Domestic (May to October), Global (November to May)

SUNFLOWER CHOKE (JERUSALEM ARTICHOKE): Domestic (October to July), Global (none)

SWEET POTATO

Cuban (Boniato), Okinawa: Domestic (year-round), Global (none)

Japanese: Domestic (July to May), Global (none)

Orange Flesh (Beauregard, Jewel, Garnet and Yellow Flesh (Jersey): Domestic (year-round, peak September to January), Global (none)

TAMARILLO: Domestic (none), Global (April to September)

TAMARINDO (TAMARIND): Domestic (none), Global (year-round)

TANGARINE

All varieties except Pixie and Clementines: Domestic (December to February), Global (none)

Clementine: Domestic (November to March), Global (June to August)

Pixie: Domestic (December to June), Global (none)

TARO ROOT: Domestic (year-round), Global (year-round)

TINDORA: Domestic (May to October), Global (September to April)

TOMATILLO: Domestic (year-round), Global (year-round)

TOMATO

All varieties except Heirloom: Domestic (year-round), Global (year-round)

Heirloom: Domestic (year-round), Global (June to March)

TUNG HO (CHRYSANTHEMUM LEAF): Domestic (year-round), Global (November to May)

TURMERIC: Domestic (year-round), Global (year-round)

UNIQ FRUIT: Domestic (none), Global (November to June)

WASABI: Domestic (year-round, but very rare), Global (year-round but very rare)

WATER CHESTNUT: Domestic (none), Global (year-round)

WATERMELON: Domestic (April to October), Global (October to May)

WINTER SQUASH

Green Acorn, Banana, Butternut, Spaghetti, Kaboca: Domestic (year-round), Global (November to September)

All other varieties: Domestic (August to December), Global (none)

YUCA ROOT (CASSAVA): Domestic (none), Global (year-round)

YU CHOY SUM: Domestic (year-round), Global (November to March)

YUZU: Domestic (September to November), Global (none)

index